THE ROADS TO MODERNITY

Gertrude Himmelfarb has taught at the Graduate School of the City University of New York, where she was named Distinguished Professor of History in 1978 and is now Professor Emeritus. She has received the two highest honours bestowed by the United States for distinguished achievement in the humanities: the Jefferson Lectureship in the Humanities in 1991, and the National Humanities Medal in 2004. She is a Fellow of the British Academy, the American Academy of Arts and Sciences, and the American Philosophical Society, and is a member of the Council of Scholars of the Library of Congress. She lives in Washington, D.C.

ALSO BY GERTRUDE HIMMELFARB

The Moral Imagination: From Edmund Burke to Lionel Trilling

One Nation, Two Cultures

The De-Moralization of Society: From Victorian Virtues to Modern Values

On Looking into the Abyss: Untimely Thoughts on Culture and Society

Poverty and Compassion: The Moral Imagination of the Late Victorians

The New History and the Old

Marriage and Morals Among the Victorians

The Idea of Poverty: England in the Early Industrial Age

On Liberty and Liberalism: The Case of John Stuart Mill

Victorian Minds

Darwin and the Darwinian Revolution

Lord Acton: A Study in Conscience and Politics

Editor

The Spirit of the Age: Victorian Essays

Milton Himmelfarb, *Jews and Gentiles*

Alexis de Tocqueville, *Memoir on Pauperism*

John Stuart Mill, *On Liberty*

John Stuart Mill, *Essays on Politics and Culture*

T. R. Malthus, *On Population*

Lord Acton, *Essays on Freedom and Power*

GERTRUDE HIMMELFARB

The Roads to Modernity

The British, French and American
Enlightenments

WITH AN INTRODUCTION BY
Gordon Brown

VINTAGE BOOKS
London

Published by Vintage 2008

1 3 5 7 9 10 8 6 4 2

Copyright © Gertrude Himmelfarb 2004

Gertrude Himmelfarb has asserted her right under the Copyright,
Designs and Patents Act 1988 to be identified as the author of this work

First published in Great Britain in 2008 by
Vintage
Random House, 20 Vauxhall Bridge Road,
London SW1V 2SA

www.vintage-books.co.uk

Addresses for companies within The Random House Group Limited
can be found at: www.randomhouse.co.uk/offices.htm

The Random House Group Limited Reg. No. 954009

A CIP catalogue record for this book
is available from the British Library

ISBN 9781845951412

The Random House Group Limited supports The Forest Stewardship
Council (FSC), the leading international forest certification
organisation. All our titles that are printed on Greenpeace approved
FSC certified paper carry the FSC logo. Our paper procurement
policy can be found at: www.rbooks.co.uk/environment

Printed in the UK by CPI Bookmarque, Croydon, CR0 4TD

To my husband,
once more and evermore

CONTENTS

INTRODUCTION

I have long admired Gertrude Himmelfarb's historical work, in particular her love of the history of ideas, and her work has stayed with me ever since I was a history student at Edinburgh University.

In a long and distinguished career, Gertrude Himmelfarb has won the most renown for her insight into the ideas and mindset of Victorian Britain – ranging from her brilliant studies of the thoughts of Lord Acton, John Stuart Mill and Darwin, to her analyses of ideas and culture in nineteeth century Britain such as *The Idea of Poverty*, *Victorian Minds*, and *Poverty and Compassion*.

In *The Roads to Modernity*, Professor Himmelfarb steps back into the eighteenth century and offers a unique comparison between the ideas and morals of the British, French and American Enlightenments. This book, reviewed with enthusiasm in America, is now rightly being published in Britain.

Her first task is to reclaim the Enlightenment from those who deny or disparage it as an intellectual movement. As she points out, Enlightenment thinking has moulded the moral universe that we inhabit in the West, as well as being a social and political movement of its time. But the main contribution of this book is to correct a widespread misunderstanding about the Enlightenment.

Historians have generally seen the Enlightenment as a creation of the European continent, in particular France. Yet Professor Himmelfarb shows in this book that the contribution of British thinkers to Enlightenment thinking has been consistently underestimated. In many ways it is the British Enlightenment – the ideas of Hume, Smith, Paine, Gibbon, Addison and others – that has provided the more durable ideas and liberal democratic institutions for the modern world. What this book does, in the author's own words, is to 'bring the British Enlightenment onto the stage of history'.

What was distinctive about the British Enlightenment? Himmelfarb argues persuasively that whereas the essence of the French Enlightenment was 'reason', the British Enlightenment is defined by the idea of 'social virtues' that 'naturally, instinctively, habitually bound people to each other' – virtues such as 'respectability, responsibility, decency, industriousness, prudence and temperance'. The British Enlightenment movement was motivated not by a thirst for revolutionary change, but by a desire to bring about a more decent, humane and compassionate society. Its temper was progressive and reformist; its proponents were social reformers and religious dissenters as well as academics and public intellectuals; and it celebrated the virtues and affections of ordinary people.

'Enlightenment' in the British sense was truly accessible to all, and not just the province of intellectuals or the privileged. Himmelfarb argues that this contrasts with the views of philosophers such as Diderot, according to whom 'the general mass of mankind can neither follow nor comprehend this march of the human spirit'. In this sense, the British Enlightenment was distinctive in placing its faith in the common sense and common humanity of the people.

As a movement, the British Enlightenment was also less oriented towards the establishment of a new political order than its French and American counterparts. In France, the *philosophes*, inspired by the goal of a society based on reason, turned their intellectual fire on the Catholic Church and the aristocratic rule of the *ancien regime*. While in America, the Founding Fathers, inspired in part by British thinkers such as John Locke and Thomas Paine, sought to build a new society through a new constitutional order based on political liberty.

The British Enlightenment, in contrast, did not seek the overthrow of anything. It was not secularist, revolutionary, nor republican. Instead, it both extolled and harnessed the benevolence, sympathy and public-spiritedness of its people, and argued for social improvement in the interests of all. Himmelfarb calls this ethos 'the sociology of virtue', the translation of a private duty into a public responsibility. And while not responsible for such political tumult as witnessed in eighteenth century America and France, it was in its way as profound and radical an approach to bringing about real social progress.

One of the things that makes this book so important is that the 'social virtues' identified as at the heart of British Enlightenment thinking have remained a dominant theme of Britishness ever since. It is a theme that finds its best expression in the British tradition of strong voluntary associations and faith groups, such as the charity schools and friendly societies of the eighteenth century that expressed what Himmelfarb calls 'an ethos that combined a communal spirit with that of self-help'. And it is a theme that the British continue to hold dear. We have consistently regarded a strong civic society as fundamental to our sense of ourselves, defending the idea of a public realm in which duty combines with and balances the pursuit of self-interest.

No one exemplifies this characteristically British approach better than the much misunderstood Adam Smith. 'All for ourselves and nothing for other people' is 'a vile maxim,' wrote Smith. Coming from Kirkcaldy as Adam Smith did, I have come to understand that his *Wealth of Nations* was underpinned by his *Theory of Moral Sentiments*, his invisible hand in the economy supported by the helping hand in civic society.

Of course Smith wanted people freed from the shackles of obedience to kings and vested interests, as he argues in *The Wealth of Nations*. But while he argued passionately for greater individual liberty, he certainly never envisaged a society free of civic bonds and civic duties. For Smith the moral system encompassed the economic system, generating the responsible virtues of industry, honesty, and reliability, and the stable associations in which we accept our responsibilities each to the other – habits of co-operation and trust, the moral sense upon which the market depended.

The British way, expressed most clearly in the works of the British Enlightenment, has always been more substantial than self-interested individualism. For Britain, the passion for liberty has always been coupled with a strong ethos of social responsibility. And at the core of British thinking and British history, as Gertrude Himmelfarb shows in this book, lie the ideas of active citizenship, 'fellow-feeling', 'good neighbourliness' and civic pride.

I strongly believe that there is a golden thread that runs through British history – from the individual standing firm against tyranny, to the individual bound by 'social virtues' to others and actively participating in society. It is a thread that runs from that day in Runnymede in 1215 and on to the Bill of Rights in 1689, to the four great Reform Acts within less than a hundred years. And the strength of that golden thread comes from countless strands of common endeavour in our villages, towns and cities, the efforts and achievements of ordinary men and women, united by a strong sense of social responsibility. It is a Britain where liberty never descended into licence and where freedom has always been exercised with responsibility.

So the two ideologies that have dominated the histories of many other countries have never taken root here – neither dominant state power, which chokes individual liberty; nor crude individualism, which has no resonance for the Britain of thousands of voluntary associations, the Britain of mutual societies, craft unions, insurance and friendly societies and co-operatives, the Britain of churches and faith groups, the Britain of municipal provision from libraries to parks, and the Britain of public service.

So for me Gertrude Himmelfarb has done more in this compelling and important book than restore British Enlightenment thinking to the prominence it deserves. She has also brought out one of the defining features of Britishness – a 'politics of compassion' that has been the inspiration for many of the great reforming movements of British history, from Wilberforce's campaign to abolish slavery to the social reforms of late Victorian Britain, to the founding of the welfare state under Lloyd George and Clement Attlee. It is an approach to progressive change resting on a deep moral sense that continues to characterise our country's view of itself, and its distinctive history of individual liberty moving hand in hand with social responsibility and active citizenship.

The Right Honourable Gordon Brown, November 2007

PREFACE

One of my early collections of essays, *Victorian Minds,* had a section entitled "Proto-Victorians." Not, I am pleased to say, "Pre-Victorians"—"proto," according to my dictionary, suggesting not only first in time but also first in rank or importance. "Proto," on that occasion, was meant to include Edmund Burke, Jeremy Bentham, and Thomas Malthus. Other of my books extended that category to admit Adam Smith, John Wesley, Thomas Paine, and the American Founders. I am happy now to bring into the foreground what was once in the background, to pay proper tribute to thinkers and movements of the eighteenth century without whom the nineteenth—and, indeed, the twentieth and twenty-first centuries—would have been unthinkable.

After these many years, I am also returning to the scene of my youth. My first book, on Lord Acton, brought me into the heart of Victorian England. But I came to Acton by way of the French Enlightenment and Revolution. It was that subject I was studying with one of America's leading scholars of the period, Louis Gottschalk; my master's thesis was on Rousseau and Robespierre. And it was Acton's work on the French Revolution which first introduced me to the most learned and profound historian of the time and thus to the riches of Victorian England. I have now returned to the French Enlightenment, humbled by the wealth of scholarship that has very nearly transformed this subject in the past half century, but that has not obscured the problems which intrigued me then and are still a challenge to historians today.

I was moved to return to the Enlightenment by two invitations: the first, in August 1996, to participate in a colloquium at Castel Gandolfo presided over by the Pope; the second, in May 2001, to deliver the Elie Kedourie Lecture at the British Academy in London. The subject of the colloquium in Rome was "Enlightenment Today," and the paper I was asked to deliver was on poverty and the Enlightenment.[1] This aspect of the Enlightenment had not previously engaged me—nor had it most historians of the Enlightenment—and in researching it I found the dichotomy between the British and French Enlightenments even larger than I had suspected. In my later lecture at the British Academy, I developed the theme of the two Enlightenments beyond the narrow focus of poverty to the larger social and philosophical issues that separated the two countries. In the present book, I have expanded the theme further to embrace the American Enlightenment as well, introducing a third political dimension to the Enlightenment—or Enlightenments, as I now thought of them.

This short book is an interpretive essay rather than a comprehensive scholarly narrative. But it is based, I hope, on the best scholarly evidence. I have quoted extensively from the sources (from primary sources especially), in part because some of my theses controvert the received wisdom and therefore need confirmation and justification, but also because the contemporary writers were so remarkably articulate and thoughtful. It would be sinful to try to paraphrase Smith, Burke, Tocqueville, the American Founders, and others who expressed so trenchantly and elegantly what could only be trivialized and vulgarized by summary or restatement.

My respect for these eminent thinkers also makes me respectful of their vocabulary. Thus, I have retained "America" where one might now say "the United States"; Tocqueville's *Democracy in America* signifies something quite different from *Democracy in the United States.* (As late as 1893, James Bryce published his monumental work under the title *The American Commonwealth.*) So, too, the masculine noun and pronoun, as used at the time, had generic, not gender, connotations that would be violated if they were rendered in the currently correct fashions.

Because the American and French Enlightenments have brought me into what had become relatively unfamiliar terrain, I am grateful to Alan Kors, of the University of Pennsylvania, for reading the first draft of the chapter on France, and to Wilfred McClay, of the University of Tennessee, for reading that on America. Both provided the critical reading I asked for and made helpful suggestions and bibliographical references. And to both I extend the usual absolution, that they not be held responsible either for my views or my faults.

I am also grateful to the Library of Congress for extending to me not only the resources of the library but also the assistance and counsel of some of their staff, including Carol Ambruster of the European division and Prosser Gifford and Lester Fogel of the Office of Scholarly Programs. The American Enterprise Institute facilitated the borrowing of books from the Library of Congress, and lent me the services of their interns, Hans Allhoff and Erin Conroy, who, in successive years, fetched books, Xeroxed articles, and hunted up the occasional elusive note reference.

It gives me great pleasure to work once again with Ashbel Green at Knopf. This is the ninth book of mine that he has seen through the press in the past thirty-five years—something of a record, I suspect, in this age of volatile publisher–author relationships. It is particularly fitting that Ash should be presiding over this book, for one of his ancestors has a cameo role here: an Ashbel Green served in the Revolutionary War, was the chaplain of Congress, later the president of The College of New Jersey (now Princeton), and later still the biographer of an earlier president of the college, John Witherspoon, who helped bring the British Enlightenment to America.

Finally, I thank my husband, Irving Kristol, who has read and commented on the whole of this manuscript, as he has all of my previous books. Many other writers have paid tribute to him as an editor and mentor, but no one has profited more from his wise counsel, his good nature, and his unfailing devotion.

THE ROADS TO MODERNITY

Prologue

This book is an ambitious attempt (more ambitious than its length warrants) to reclaim the Enlightenment—from critics who decry it and defenders who acclaim it uncritically, from postmodernists who deny its existence and historians who belittle or disparage it, above all, from the French who have dominated and usurped it.[1] In reclaiming the Enlightenment, I propose to restore it, in good part, to the British who helped create it—who created, indeed, a very different Enlightenment from that of the French.

The study of the Enlightenment has traditionally focused on France, on the ideas generated by the *philosophes* and the exportation of those ideas to the world at large. These ideas have always been the subject of contention but never more so than today, for it is not this or that idea that is now in dispute but ideas in general. The Enlightenment, which was preeminently a movement of ideas, is especially vulnerable to this kind of intellectual skepticism. The "Enlightenment project," as is sometimes said invidiously, is thought to be obsolete, an illusion, or delusion, of modernity. It recalls a time when such terms as "reason," "nature," "rights," "truth," "morality," "liberty," "progress" could be used without benefit of quotation marks, and without the sense of irony befitting these "privileged" concepts. It supposes, one writer says (in a book fittingly entitled *Enlightenment's Wake*), a "universal

3

emancipation and a universal civilization" that is nothing more than an embodiment of "Western cultural imperialism."[2] "Enlightenment," another explains, "is to postmodernism what 'Old Regime' was to the French Revolution. . . . [It] symbolizes the modern that postmodernism revolts against."[3] Where the *philosophes* believed it liberating to exalt reason over religion, the postmodernist finds reason as tyrannical and "totalizing" as religion itself.

Other historians take exception not to the ideas themselves but rather to a conception of the Enlightenment that is unduly focused upon ideas. For them, the Enlightenment was a social movement as well as (or more than) an intellectual one, and can be best understood by examining the dynamics of classes and institutions, social relations and material forces, which in France conspired together to subvert the Old Regime and prepare the way for the Revolution.[4] Robert Darnton has applied this analysis to the *Encyclopédie,* the organ of the *philosophes,* treating it as an economic and social phenomenon by analyzing its mode of production and distribution, the kinds of authors it attracted, and the censorship it invited and evaded. More recently, Darnton has turned away from the "high Enlightenment," as he puts it, to the "underside" or "low-life" of the Enlightenment, the literature of pornography, sensationalism, and scandal that permeated the popular culture at the time.[5]*

This book, by contrast, is an exercise in the history of ideas. It is unapologetic, and unironic, in dealing with those

---

* There is another "underside" of the Enlightenment: the writings of Denis Diderot, for example, which were published only posthumously and which reveal a very different persona and thinker from the familiar *philosophe.* Today, the author of *Rameau's Nephew* may be a more interesting, complicated, and perhaps congenial figure than the editor of the *Encyclopédie.* The latter, however, is the public and historic Diderot, the Diderot of the Enlightenment.

ideas about reason and religion, liberty and virtue, nature and society, which, in different forms and degrees, shaped the distinctive Enlightenments of the three countries that were so dramatically affected by them: France, Britain, and America.[6] Those ideas spilled over from philosophers and men of letters to politicians and men of affairs, penetrating into what recent historians call the *mentalités* of the people and what Alexis de Tocqueville meant by *moeurs*: the "habits of the mind" and "habits of the heart" that make up "the whole moral and intellectual state of a people."[7] At a critical moment in history, these three Enlightenments represented alternative approaches to modernity, alternative habits of mind and heart, of consciousness and sensibility.

It is in this sense that I conceive of the phenomenon known as "the Enlightenment," and in this sense that I propose to restore it to its progenitor, the British. The French themselves credited that venerable English trinity, Bacon, Locke, and Newton, with the ideas that inspired their own Enlightenment. I go beyond that in directing attention not to these forerunners of the Enlightenment, as I see them, but to the eighteenth century itself, thus challenging the French on their terrain, the time and space that they have taken for their own. It was then, early in the eighteenth century, that the British Enlightenment originated and took a form very different from that of its counterpart on the continent (or from that of its own offspring overseas).[8] The point is not merely to establish the chronological priority of the British Enlightenment but also to establish its unique character and historic importance.

To bring the British Enlightenment onto the stage of history, indeed, the center stage, is to redefine the very idea of Enlightenment. In the usual litany of traits associated with the Enlightenment—reason, rights, nature, liberty, equality, tolerance, science, progress—reason invariably heads the list. What is conspicuously absent is virtue. Yet it was virtue, rather than reason, that took precedence for the British, not personal virtue but the "social virtues"—compassion, benevolence, sympathy—which, the British philosophers believed, naturally, instinctively, habitually bound people to each other. They did not deny reason; they were by no means irrationalists. But they gave reason a secondary, instrumental role, rather than the primary, determinant one that the *philosophes* gave it. To restore the British to prominence, therefore, is to direct attention to a subject not usually associated with the Enlightenment, that is, the social ethic explicit or implicit in each of these Enlightenments.

To redefine the Enlightenment in this fashion is also to redefine, in a sense, the British Enlightenment itself, expanding it to include thinkers and actors not normally identified with it, some of whom, indeed, are more often assigned to the "counter-Enlightenment"—Edmund Burke, most notably, but also, more audaciously, John Wesley, as well as a score of lesser-known (in our time, although not in theirs) philanthropists and reformers who gave practical meaning to that social ethic. Thus, I am engaged in a doubly revisionist exercise, making the Enlightenment more British and making the British Enlightenment more inclusive.

To speak of "the Enlightenment," as I have done, is a concession to popular usage. Not many scholars today share Peter Gay's confidence in *the* Enlightenment, a single Enlightenment, although that is still the popular conception of it. "There was only one Enlightenment," Gay announces in the opening sentence of his trilogy. In various places he represents that Enlightenment as a family, a chorus, an army, a party, containing different individuals in different countries of different opinions, but all united in a common goal, a "single style of thinking." Even more telling is his deliberate use of the word philosophes—not italicized—to describe all these individuals, on the grounds that the French word signifies "an international type."[9] That word, which was not then, and never has

6

been, acclimatized in the English language, suggests what Gay's volumes amply demonstrate, that *the* Enlightenment, as he conceives it, was essentially Gallican in origin and spirit.

In spite of more recent demonstrations by historians that the Enlightenment was so varied, among countries as well as individuals, as to belie the singular term,[10] the Enlightenment is still almost invariably associated with the French, and the terms of discourse are still those made familiar by the *philosophes*. It is something of a puzzle why this is so. The most obvious reason is the existential realization or fulfillment of the French Enlightenment (or so it seemed to contemporaries at the time and to many historians since) in one of the most dramatic events of modernity, the French Revolution, which has been widely regarded (again, at the time and since) as the inauguration of the modern world. "It has been said," Hegel remarked, "that the French Revolution resulted from Philosophy." For once he agreed with the conventional wisdom. "Never since the sun had stood in the firmament and the planets revolved round him had it been perceived that man's existence centers in his head, i.e., in Thought, inspired by which he builds up the world of reality."[11]

It could be said, however, that the American republic was also the product of "thought," albeit a different kind of thought. In promulgating a "new science of politics," the Americans succeeded in creating—in "founding," the word itself is remarkable—the first viable republic in modern times. Hegel himself paid tribute to America as a "world-historical" phenomenon: "America is therefore the land of the future, where, in the ages that lie before us, the burden of the World's History shall reveal itself."[12] That "land of the future," he recognized, owed nothing to the French and much to the English, whose constitution had permitted it to stand its ground "amid the general convulsion."[13]

America may have been the land of the future. But it was not the American Revolution that inspired future revolutions. For the past two centuries, the paradigm of popular revolution, like the paradigm of Enlightenment, has been that of France. "The sad truth of the matter," Hannah Arendt has said, "is that the French Revolution, which ended in disaster, has made world history, while the American Revolution, so triumphantly successful, has remained an event of little more than local importance."[14]

It was not only its association with the French Revolution that gave the French Enlightenment the primacy it now has, but also the deliberate, self-conscious, indeed, self-dramatizing character of its proponents—an acute awareness of their own identity and (long before Hegel) their place in world history. In 1751, in the "Preliminary Discourse" that preceded the appearance of the first volume of the *Encyclopédie,* the editor spoke of the "centuries of enlightenment" that culminated in the present "century of enlightenment," and explained that the *Encyclopédie* would provide a conspectus of knowledge appropriate to this most advanced stage of enlightenment.[15] It was surely the most ambitious such enterprise that had ever been undertaken: twenty-eight volumes (including plates) issued between 1751 and 1772, with an additional seven volumes by 1780—this compared with the English two-volume Chambers's *Cyclopaedia* (which had just been translated into French) and the three-volume *Encyclopaedia Britannica* (not translated) published between 1768 and 1771. (The latter, inspired, or goaded, by the example of the *Encyclopédie,* expanded to ten volumes by 1784 and twenty by the end of the century, the last volume being sharply critical of the *Encyclopédie.*) The titles of these works are themselves significant, the French lacking the national adjective identifying the British (it did not present itself as the *Encyclopédie française*), thus establishing its universal credentials. The subtitles are similarly suggestive: the British, *A Dictionary of Arts and Sciences;*

the French, omitting the modest indefinite article and adding a portentous adjective, *Dictionnaire raisonné des sciences, des arts et des métiers.*

The *Encyclopédie* also had an impressive authorship: *"Une Société de Gens de Lettres."* That attribution suggests yet another reason why the French Enlightenment enjoys the preeminence it does, for it envisions a cohesive group, a "society" of men of letters, or *philosophes,* with a coherent character and purpose. This society, the vanguard, as it were, of the French Enlightenment, presided not only over the *Encyclopédie* but also the salons of Paris, making that city the intellectual capital of Europe. The distinguished historian Franco Venturi denies that there was such a thing as an English Enlightenment, on the grounds that the English thinkers, unlike their French confreres, never thought of themselves as a distinctive class or group. "They did not have an organization or a rhythm of their own. So they did not operate as a new and autonomous political force, which tended to question or replace organisms inherited from the past." Only in Scotland, he said, could be found the essential elements of an Enlightenment, "a new intelligentsia, conscious of its own function and strength" as against the traditional ruling classes. Venturi grants Gibbon the status of the "English giant of the Enlightenment," but goes on to say that he was an "isolated figure in his own country, a solitary figure," because there was no Enlightenment in England.[16]*

---

* Venturi considers the possibility that the eighteenth-century Commonwealthmen—the republicans and deists (or pantheists) who were the heirs of John Toland, John Trenchard, and their colleagues in the preceding century—constituted something like an organized group comparable to the *philosophes.* But according to Caroline Robbins, the great specialist on the subject, they were not an "organized opposition," not a "coherent party," and certainly not revolutionary. Thus, they would not qualify as an English Enlightenment by Venturi's standards.[17]

If the English did not have an "intelligentsia" in Venturi's sense—an organized, dissident, potentially revolutionary class of intellectuals—they did have thinkers, writers, preachers, and reformers who operated under a "rhythm" of their own, and who made London, as well as Glasgow and Edinburgh, a vibrant intellectual center. London may not have had the salons that were the pride of Paris, or the universities that gave distinction to Glasgow and Edinburgh, but it did have coffeehouses and clubs that performed something of the same social function and catered to far more people.

London also had popular journals that provided outlets for writers who could reach a much larger audience than was available to the *philosophes*. Joseph Addison and Richard Steele, the intellectual entrepreneurs responsible for the *Tatler* and *Spectator,* were fully conscious of the purpose of their enterprises. "It was said of Socrates," Addison wrote in the *Spectator,* "that he brought philosophy down from heaven to inhabit among men; and I shall be ambitious to have it said of me, that I have brought philosophy out of closets and libraries, schools and colleges, to dwell in clubs and assemblies, at tea-tables and in coffee houses."[18] As it turned out, the *Spectator* proved to be popular in France as well. It was translated into French in 1714, only five years after its first appearance in London; the *Tatler* was translated twenty years later. In his *Confessions,* Jean-Jacques Rousseau recalled reading those journals while a young man living with his patroness Mme de Warens in the south of France; the *Spectator,* he said, was "particularly pleasing and serviceable to me."[19] In his novel *Emile,* he recommended an exchange of books between Emile and Sophie; she would give him *Telemachus,* and he would give her the *Spectator.*[20]

So, too, the Americans had thinkers, writers, preachers, and, above all, statesmen who constituted a distinctive intellectual class—a class, moreover, that became a political and revolutionary force, as the *philosophes* themselves never quite did.

They also managed to produce works, *The Federalist* most notably, which were far less voluminous than the *Encyclopédie* but more influential and enduring. A century later, John Morley concluded his sympathetic account of the *Encyclopédie* by reflecting, as he replaced those dusty and huge volumes on his shelves, that they would probably never be read again, that they were now a "monumental ruin."[21] That cannot be said of *The Federalist,* which has never gone out of print, has been widely translated (most recently, into Hebrew), and whose principles and arguments continue to be cited, not only in the United States but also by democracies and aspiring democracies abroad. (The *Encyclopédie* has never been reprinted and only selected articles have been translated.)

The decisive advantage of France over Britain and America may have been the term "enlightenment" itself. Here the postmodernist has a point: language often is the reality, or what passes for it. "*Siècle des lumières*" was used as early as 1733 by the abbé Dubos, by Rousseau in the *First Discourse* in 1750, by the co-editor of the *Encyclopédie* Jean le Rond d'Alembert the following year in his *Preliminary Discourse* to the *Encyclopédie,* and by others throughout the century. In Germany, where the language and the culture lent itself to such abstractions, the term *Aufklärung* was formally initiated in 1784 in a debate on the question, "What is Enlightenment [*Aufklärung*]?" "Do we live at present in an enlightened age?" Immanuel Kant asked. "The answer is: No, but in an age of enlightenment."[22]

In Britain, which had the reality of enlightenment but not the appropriate language (where, one might say, the reality discouraged the abstraction), the noun did not come into use until much later. The first English translation of Kant's essay, in 1798, avoided the noun by using the words "enlightening" or "enlightened" in place of "enlightenment."[23] Although the noun did not exist in Britain, the adjective was familiar. In his *Reflections on the Revolution in France* (1790), Burke spoke, ironically, of "the patriotic crimes of an enlightened age," the "refinement in injustice belonging to the philosophy of this enlightened age," the "'enlightened' usurers" ("enlightened," here, in quotation marks) who confiscated church properties, the "solid darkness of this enlightened age."[24]

It took more than a century for the noun to make its appearance in English. In 1837, Thomas Carlyle, in his *History of the French Revolution,* coined the word "Philosophism" to describe the system espoused by the *philosophes.*[25] Four decades later, John Morley, who helped bring the *philosophes* to the attention of the British public in his biographies of Diderot, Voltaire, and Rousseau, used the term "Illumination."[26] As late as 1899, the English translator of Hegel's *Philosophy of History* said that he had to use the French word *Eclaircissement* because "there is no current term in English denoting that great intellectual movement."[27] One historian records "a watershed of sorts" in 1910 with the publication of a book called *The Philosophy of the Enlightenment,* written, significantly, by an American Hegelian.[28] Yet the very next year the famous eleventh edition of the *Encyclopaedia Britannica* appeared, with no article on the Enlightenment. The first such article was in the fourteenth edition in 1929, where the term was applied primarily to the Germans as a translation of *Aufklärung,* and only incidentally to the English (Locke and Newton) and the French.[29]

Even Scotland, which had some of the characteristics Venturi requires of an Enlightenment—a distinctive, self-conscious school—did not earn the title "Enlightenment" until very late. The term "Scottish Enlightenment," so familiar today, was first coined in 1900 to describe the Scottish philosophers known as "moral philosophers" (who literally bore that title, as professors).[30] Adam Smith was the professor of moral philosophy at the University of Glasgow, as Francis

Hutcheson had been before him and Thomas Reid was to be after him; and Dugald Stewart succeeded Adam Ferguson in the chair of moral philosophy at the University of Edinburgh. David Hume did not hold any professorial title or position, but he had been born and raised in Edinburgh, attended the university there (without getting a degree), lived most of his life there, and was indubitably of that school. Many of these philosophers, however, chose to identify themselves as North Britons rather than as Scots, and some tried to avoid any hint of Scottish parochialism. Smith, during his six years at Oxford, made a conscious and successful effort to rid himself of a Scottish accent. Like the others, he published his work in London and wrote much of the *Wealth of Nations* while living there. Hume, who changed his name from the Scottish "Home" to the Anglicized "Hume," was less successful than Smith in camouflaging his accent, but he did take care to remove Scottish idioms from his works.

The Scottish Enlightenment, therefore, was not as parochially or exclusively Scottish as might be thought; nor was the Enlightenment confined to Scotland. John Locke and Isaac Newton are often designated as the fathers of the British Enlightenment. I myself would give that distinction to the third Earl of Shaftesbury, who was also the father of the Scottish Enlightenment although he was neither Scottish nor a professor. But all three of them were indubitably English, as were such other Enlightenment worthies as Bishop Joseph Butler, William Paley, Joseph Addison, Joseph Priestley, Thomas Paine, William Godwin, and Edward Gibbon. Those who were Welsh or Irish by birth—Richard Steele, Richard Price, Edmund Burke—lived and worked in England.*

---

* Gibbon presents a special problem for those historians who do not recognize the English component of the British Enlightenment. As Franco

Until very recently, however, there has been no recognition of a British Enlightenment because the English were conspicuously left out of the fold. This has been the considered judgment not only of Venturi but also of such eminent historians as Alfred Cobban, who wrote in 1960, "The term 'Enlightenment' is hardly naturalized in England";[32] or Robert R. Palmer in 1976, "The term 'English Enlightenment' would be jarring and incongruous if it were ever heard";[33] or Henry S. Commager the following year, who declared England "a bit outside the Enlightenment."[34] Not until the 1980s was England initiated into that select company by John Pocock and Roy Porter, who finally legitimized the idea of a British, as distinct from a Scottish, Enlightenment.[35]

The exclusion of the British from the Enlightenment, by contemporaries as well as historians, is all the more strange because there was so much interaction between French and British thinkers at the time. They read each other, translated and reviewed each other, and visited each other. Voltaire, having lived in England from 1726 to 1728, professed to be guilty of "Anglomania." His *Letters Concerning the English Nation* was first published in London, in English, in 1733, and only the following year in Paris under the title *Lettres philosophiques*. (Although fluent in English, Voltaire wrote the book in French.) In a later book, the *Philosophical Dictio-*

Venturi, in denying to the English any part in the Enlightenment, had to make an exception for Gibbon, an "isolated" and "solitary" figure in his country (this of the best-selling author and celebrity), so a more recent historian, Arthur Herman, making the largest claims for the Scots who "invented the modern world," insists that Gibbon modelled his work on the Scottish historical school and was, "for all intents and purposes . . . intellectually a Scot."[31]

nary, he referred to his meeting with George Berkeley and quoted Locke, Shaftesbury, and, with special reverence, Isaac Newton.

Montesquieu, who was more truly an Anglophile than Voltaire (and who, it might be argued, was more representative of the British Enlightenment than of the French), lived in England from 1729 to 1731 for the deliberate purpose of studying English political institutions. As the celebrated author of the *Persian Letters,* he met the leading Whigs, attended the House of Commons, and received the highest accolade of the British by being elected a member of the Royal Society. Burke's eulogy of Montesquieu, appearing toward the end of his "Appeal from the New to the Old Whigs" (a vigorous critique of the French Revolution), was unmatched in its enthusiasm by any delivered in France by Montesquieu's own compatriots.[36] On the other hand, another *philosophe,* the Baron d'Holbach, visiting England in 1765, was reenforced in his unfavorable view of that country. Rousseau, who was even less an admirer of England, took refuge there in 1766 after he was ordered arrested in France because of the impious views expressed in *Emile;* it was in England that he wrote much of his *Confessions.**

---

* This is one of the more bizarre episodes of the Enlightenment. Hume, who had little in common with Rousseau intellectually or temperamentally, but who sympathized with his plight, arranged for him to take refuge in England, accompanying him on the trip and finding accommodations for him and his mistress. (She came separately, accompanied by James Boswell.) Hume even offered to solicit a pension for him from George III, a proposal Rousseau initially rejected but then agreed to reluctantly. It was not long, however, before Rousseau turned against Hume, accusing him of circulating a satirical letter about him written by Horace Walpole and of conspiring to ruin his reputation. The whole affair became public, to the great distress of Hume, who was obliged to defend himself by publishing their correspondence.

Crossing the Channel in the other direction were such British celebrities as David Hume, Adam Smith, Edward Gibbon, Laurence Sterne, Horace Walpole, Thomas Paine, and Joseph Priestley. Hume, who wrote his masterpiece, *A Treatise of Human Nature,* while living in France as a young man in the 1730s, returned thirty years later to serve as secretary to the British Embassy in Paris and to enjoy the fame that came not from the *Treatise* but from his multivolume *History of England.* Smith, who resided in Paris in 1765–66, nominally as tutor to the young Duke of Buccleuch, was well known for his *Theory of Moral Sentiments* and was properly fêted in the salons. Having started to work on the *Wealth of Nations,* he was pleased to meet such leading physiocrats as Anne-Robert-Jacques Turgot and François Quesnay (without, however, being converted to their views). Gibbon was in Paris only briefly, on his way to Lausanne in 1763, but in those few months he made the acquaintance of Claude Helvétius, the Baron d'Holbach, and other eminences of the Enlightenment. (He had met Voltaire in Lausanne several years earlier.) Paine moved to France after publishing *Rights of Man* in 1792 and was made an honorary member of the National Convention. Priestley had an honorary seat in the National Assembly although he chose to live in America.

Books and ideas circulated even more readily than their authors. Diderot never visited England, but his first work, in 1745, was a translation of Shaftesbury's "An Inquiry Concerning Virtue, or Merit." His own book published the following year, *Pensées philosophiques,* has been described by Venturi as "comments on the margins of the English writer." (But Venturi's description of that work, as "a vigorous appeal to the passions to liberate man from everything which oppresses him," is hardly in the spirit of Shaftesbury, who appealed to the passions not to liberate man but to make him moral.)[37] Smith's *The Theory of Moral Sentiments* was translated twice into French (once by Condorcet's wife), as was the *Wealth of Nations* shortly after its publication in 1776. Condorcet himself wrote a summary of the book which was then translated into Spanish.

The *Encyclopédie* had a more checkered career in Britain. The first edition could be found in several university libraries, including that of Glasgow University, which had received it as a gift from Smith. There were even projects for its translation, one to appear in sixpenny parts. (Eight parts—twenty-four sheets—were actually published in 1752.) Another project in 1768 resulted in the publication of only selections of the first volume. The *Encyclopédie* itself received only a few brief reviews, one an anonymous letter by Smith in 1756 in the *Edinburgh Review,* recommending it with some reservations. It was more often plagiarized than cited, by Oliver Goldsmith among others, and by compilers of English dictionaries. Smith borrowed the famous pin-factory illustration in the *Wealth of Nations* from the article *"Epingle"* in the fifth volume of the *Encyclopédie.*[38]

Both Smith and Hume had a lively interest in French intellectual affairs. In 1759, Hume recommended to Smith that he read Helvétius's *De l'esprit* and Voltaire's *Candide,* which had just been published.[39] (Hume did not, however, accede to Helvétius's request that he translate *De l'esprit.*) A few years earlier, in the newly founded *Edinburgh Review,* Smith referred favorably to d'Alembert's *Preliminary Discourse* and reviewed (not uncritically) Rousseau's *Discourses,* including a lengthy extract from that book. In a later essay, Smith quoted the *Dictionnaire de musique* by "an Author, more capable of feeling strongly than of analyzing accurately, Mr. Rousseau of Geneva."[40] In *The Theory of Moral Sentiments* he quoted Voltaire's *Age of Louis XIV,* referred in passing to his literary works, and included him among the gifted men throughout the ages who "too often distinguished themselves by the most improper and even insolent contempt of all the ordinary decorums of life and conversation, and who have thereby set the most pernicious example to those who wish to resemble them."[41]

In spite of their personal familiarity with each other and with each other's works, the British and French differed profoundly in the spirit and substance of their respective Enlightenments. The British might sympathize with the *philosophes'* hostility to a "papist" church and an authoritarian monarchy, both of which they themselves had discarded, and the French could admire the religious and political liberty that they found in England and that they so much coveted. But they each pursued enlightenment, for themselves and their countrymen, in quite different ways. In France, the essence of the Enlightenment—literally, its *raison d'être*—was reason. "Reason is to the *philosophe*," the *Encyclopédie* declared, "what Grace is to the Christian."[42] It was not that, to be sure, to Rousseau or Montesquieu, but it was to Voltaire, Diderot, d'Alembert, and most of the contributors to the *Encyclopédie*. The idea of reason defined and permeated the Enlightenment as no other idea did.[43] In a sense, the French Enlightenment was a belated Reformation, a Reformation fought in the cause not of a higher or purer religion but of a still higher and purer authority, reason. It was in the name of reason that Voltaire issued his famous declaration of war against the church, "*Ecrasez l'infâme*," and that Diderot proposed to "strangle the last king with the entrails of the last priest."

This was not, however, the Enlightenment as it appeared either in Britain or America, where reason did not have that preeminent role, and where religion, whether as dogma or as institution, was not the paramount enemy. The British and

American Enlightenments were latitudinarian, compatible with a large spectrum of belief and disbelief. There was no *Kulturkampf* in those countries to distract and divide the populace, pitting the past against the present, confronting enlightened sentiment with retrograde institutions, and creating an unbridgeable divide between reason and religion. On the contrary, the variety of religious sects were themselves an assurance of liberty and, often, an instrument of social reform as well as of spiritual salvation.

The driving force of the British Enlightenment was not reason but the "social virtues" or "social affections." In America, the driving force was political liberty, the motive for the Revolution and the basis for the republic. For the British moral philosophers, and for the American Founders, reason was an instrument for the attainment of the larger social end, not the end itself. And for both, religion was an ally, not an enemy. A book on the British or American Enlightenment could never bear the subtitle that Peter Gay gave to the first volume of his work on the Enlightenment: *The Rise of Modern Paganism*.

I have encapsulated the three Enlightenments in phrases borrowed from others and adapted for my purposes. Thus, the British Enlightenment represents "the sociology of virtue," the French "the ideology of reason," the American "the politics of liberty."[44] The British moral philosophers were sociologists as much as philosophers; concerned with man in relation to society, they looked to the social virtues for the basis of a healthy and humane society. The French had a more exalted mission: to make reason the governing principle of society as well as mind, to "rationalize," as it were, the world. The Americans, more modestly, sought to create a new "science of politics" that would establish the new republic upon a sound foundation of liberty.

The heart of this book is an explication—and an appreciation—of the British Enlightenment, with the French and American Enlightenments serving as foils for the British. Within each of these Enlightenments there were important variations and differences; strictly speaking each of them should be pluralized. In Britain, Burke and Paine obviously, but also Francis Hutcheson and Hume, would surely have protested against too close an association with each other. (Hutcheson twice forestalled Hume's bid for a professorship.) So, too, in America, Thomas Jefferson and Alexander Hamilton, the Federalists and Anti-Federalists, politely tolerated while vigorously disputing with each other. And in France, Montesquieu and Rousseau were an exceedingly odd couple, and both were odder still in relation to the other *philosophes.* ("Never has so much intelligence," Voltaire once rebuked Rousseau, "been employed in order to render us stupid.")[45] Yet historically and sociologically, these were distinctive Enlightenments, all the more so by comparison with each other. To be sure, all of them shared some common traits: a respect for reason and liberty, science and industry, justice and welfare. But these ideas took significantly different forms and were pursued in different ways in each country.

The three Enlightenments had profoundly different social and political implications and consequences. There has been much debate, dating back almost to those events themselves, about the relation between the French Enlightenment and the French Revolution, but most historians agree that, in some sense and to some degree, what I have called the "ideology of reason" laid the groundwork for the Revolution. The connection between the "politics of liberty" developed in the *Federalist* and in the American Constitution was more immediate and obvious. And so, too, was that between the "sociology of virtue" and the non-revolutionary, reformist temper that characterized Britain in that revolutionary age.

This is not to say that ideas were the determining factors

in each of these countries. The historical situations were obviously, perhaps decisively, different. As Britain had earlier experienced a religious Reformation, so it also had undergone a "Glorious Revolution," which gave promise of being a permanent political settlement. France, having had neither a religious reformation nor a political revolution, was, in a sense, ripe for both. And America, having had both as a legacy from Britain, sought the independence that it claimed as part of that legacy.

Yet ideas surely influenced these experiences and circumstances. Britain could have had (as Paine and Priestley might have liked) a *Kulturkampf* like France's, designed to disestablish the Church of England together with the monarchy. France could have taken the Montesquieu route (which is to say, the British route) to a more reformist, moderate revolution. And the Americans could have injected into their Revolution a larger utopian mission, rather than the pragmatic, cautious temper conspicuous in *The Federalist* and the Constitution. That the countries did not take these paths had a good deal to do with the ideas and attitudes that prevailed among the influential thinkers, polemicists, and political leaders in each of those countries, who helped frame the terms of discourse and thus affect the temper of the time.

One of the unfortunate consequences of the identification of the Enlightenment with France is the tendency to see the aftermath of the other Enlightenments in the light of the French experience—to treat the American Revolution, for example, as a prelude to or a minor version of the French Revolution, or to regard the non-revolution in Britain as a kind of counterrevolution (or some aspects of the British Enlightenment as a species of counter-Enlightenment). To appreciate the distinctiveness of these Enlightenments is to appreciate as well the uniqueness of each historical situation. And to focus, as I have done, on the British Enlightenment is to remind us of those "habits of the mind" and "habits of the heart" that produced a social ethic all too easily ignored in the light of the more dramatic claims of the French Enlightenment.

I do not go so far as to credit the British Enlightenment, as Roy Porter does, with "the creation of the modern world"; still less do I agree, with Arthur Herman, that "the Scots invented the modern world."[46] But I do find that the British (not only the Scots) confronted the modern world with the good sense—the "common sense," as their philosophers put it—that served them well in a tumultuous period and that still has echoes today in a later stage of modernity.

THE BRITISH ENLIGHTENMENT:
THE SOCIOLOGY OF VIRTUE

1. "SOCIAL AFFECTIONS" AND RELIGIOUS DISPOSITIONS

The British did not have *philosophes*. They had moral philosophers, a very different breed. Those historians who belittle or dismiss the idea of a British Enlightenment do so because they do not recognize the features of the *philosophes* in the moral philosophers—and with good reason: the physiognomy is quite different.

It is ironic that the French should have paid tribute to John Locke and Isaac Newton as the guiding spirits of their own Enlightenment, while the British, although respectful of both, had a more ambiguous relationship with them. Newton was eulogized by David Hume as "the greatest and rarest genius that ever rose for the ornament and instruction of the species,"[1] and by Alexander Pope in the much quoted epitaph: "Nature and Nature's laws lay hid in night;/God said, *Let Newton be!* and all was light." But Pope's *An Essay on Man* sent quite a different message: "The proper study of mankind is man" implied that materialism and science could penetrate into the mysteries of nature but not of man. In an earlier essay, the allusion to Newton was more obvious; it was human nature, not astronomy, Pope said, that was "the most useful object of humane reason," and it was "of more consequence to adjust the true nature and measures of right and wrong, than to settle the distance of the planets and compute the times of their circumvolutions."[2] While Newton received the adulation of his countrymen (he was master of the Royal Mint and president of the Royal Society, was knighted, and given a state funeral), and his scientific methodology was much praised, he had little substantive influence on the moral philosophers or on the issues that dominated the British Enlightenment. (His *Opticks,* on the other hand, was an inspiration for poets, who were entranced by the images and metaphors of light.)[3]

John Locke, too, was a formidable presence in eighteenth-century Britain, a best-selling author and a revered figure. But among the moral philosophers he was admired more for his politics than for his metaphysics. Indeed, the basic tenets of their philosophy implied a repudiation of his. What made them moral philosophers rather than philosophers *tout court* was their belief in a "moral sense" that was presumed to be if not innate in the human mind (as Shaftesbury and Francis Hutcheson thought), then so entrenched in the human sensibility, in the form of sympathy or fellow feeling (as Adam Smith and David Hume had it), as to have the same compelling force as innate ideas.

Locke himself could not have been more explicit in rejecting innate ideas, whether moral or metaphysical. The mind, as he understood it, so far from being inhabited by innate ideas, was a tabula rasa, to be filled by sensations and experiences, and by the reflections rising from those sensations and experiences. The title of the first chapter of his *Essay Concerning Human Understanding* was "No Innate Speculative Principles" (that is, epistemological principles); the second, "No Innate Practical Principles" (moral principles). Even the golden rule, that "most unshaken rule of morality and foundation of all social virtue," would have been meaningless to one who had never heard that maxim and who might well ask for a reason justifying it, which "plainly shows it not to be innate." If virtue was generally approved, it was not because it was innate, but because it was "profitable," conducive to one's self-interest and happiness, the promotion of pleasure and the avoidance of pain. Thus, things could be judged good or evil only by reference to pleasure or pain, which were themselves the product of sensation.[4]

Locke's *Essay* was published in 1690. Nine years later, the Earl of Shaftesbury wrote an essay that was, in effect, a refutation of Locke. This, too, had its ironies, for this Shaftesbury, the Third Earl, was brought up in the household of his grandfather, the First Earl, who was a devotee of Locke and had employed him to supervise the education of his grandchildren. It was this experience that had inspired Locke's *Thoughts Concerning Education*—and inspired as well, perhaps, the pupil's rejection of his master's teachings.[5] Shaftesbury's essay, "An Inquiry Concerning Virtue, or Merit," was published (without his permission but to great acclaim) in 1699 and reprinted in 1711 in somewhat revised form in his *Characteristics of Men, Manners, Opinions, Times.* That three-volume work, reissued posthumously three years later and in ten more editions in the course of the century, rivalled Locke's *Second Treatise* (a political, not metaphysical tract) as the most frequently reprinted work of the time. The hundred-page essay on virtue was the centerpiece of those volumes.

Virtue, according to Shaftesbury, derived not from religion, self-interest, sensation, or reason. All of these were instrumental in supporting or hindering virtue, but were not the immediate or primary source of it. What was antecedent to these was the "moral sense," the "sense of right and wrong."[6]* It was this sense that was "predominant . . . inwardly joined to us, and implanted in our nature," "a first principle in our constitu-

---

* Shaftesbury's "moral sense" was very different from John Rawls's recent use of that term. For Shaftesbury it was an innate sense of right and wrong; for Rawls it is an intuitive conviction of the rightness of freedom and equality.

tion and make," as natural as "natural affection itself."[7] This "natural affection," moreover, was "social affection," an affection for society and the people, which, so far from being at odds with one's private interest, or self-affection, actually contributed to one's personal pleasure and happiness.[8] A person whose actions were motivated entirely or even largely by self-affection—by self-love, self-interest, or self-good—was not virtuous. Indeed, he was "in himself still vicious," for the virtuous man was motivated by nothing other than "a natural affection for his kind."[9]

This was not a Rousseauean idealization of human nature, of man before being corrupted by society. Nor was it a Pollyannaish expectation that all or even most men would behave virtuously all or most of the time. The moral sense attested to the sense of right and wrong in all men, the knowledge of right and wrong even when they chose to do wrong. Indeed, a good part of Shaftesbury's essay dealt with the variety of "hateful passions"—envy, malice, cruelty, lust—that beset mankind. Even virtue, Shaftesbury warned, could become vice when it was pursued to excess; an immoderate degree of tenderness, for example, destroyed the "effect of love," and excessive pity rendered a man "incapable of giving succour."[10] The conclusion of the essay was a stirring testament of an ethic that, by its very nature—the "common nature" of man—was a social ethic: "Thus the wisdom of what rules, and is first and chief in nature, has made it to be according to the private interest and good of everyone to work towards the general good; which if a creature ceases to promote, he is actually so far wanting to himself and ceases to promote his own happiness and welfare. . . . And, thus, Virtue is the good, and Vice the ill of everyone."[11]

The contrast, not only with Thomas Hobbes but with Locke as well, could not be more obvious.[12] Neither was explicitly named by Shaftesbury, perhaps out of respect for Locke, who was still alive when the essay was written (although he had died by the time it was reissued). But no knowledgeable reader could have mistaken Shaftesbury's intention. In 1709 he wrote to one of his young protégés that Locke, even more than Hobbes, was the villain of the piece, for Hobbes's character and "base slavish principles" of government "took off the poison of his philosophy," whereas Locke's character and commendable principles of government made his philosophy even more reprehensible.

> 'Twas Mr. Locke that struck at all fundamentals, threw all order and virtue out of the world. . . . Virtue, according to Mr. Locke, has no other measure, law, or rule, than fashion and custom: morality, justice, equity, depend only on law and will. . . . And thus neither right nor wrong, virtue nor vice are any thing in themselves; nor is there any trace or idea of them *naturally imprinted* on human minds. Experience and our catechism teach us all![13]

As Shaftesbury did not mention Locke in the "Inquiry," so Bernard Mandeville did not mention Shaftesbury in *The Fable of the Bees*—at least not in the first edition, published in 1714. But appearing just then, a year after Shaftesbury's death and at the same time as the second edition of the *Characteristics,* Mandeville's readers might well take it as a rebuttal to Shaftesbury's work. The subtitle, *Private Vices, Public Benefits,* reads like a manifesto *contra* Shaftesbury.[14]

The original version of the *Fable,* published in 1705 as a sixpenny pamphlet (and pirated, Mandeville complained, in a halfpenny sheet), consisted of some thirty verses depicting a society, a hive of bees, where everyone was a knave, and where knavery served a valuable purpose. Every vice had its concomitant virtue: avarice contributed to prodigality, luxury to industry, folly to ingenuity. The result was a grumbling but productive hive, where "... every part was full of Vice, / Yet the whole mass a Paradise." A well-intentioned attempt to rid the hive of vice had the effect of ridding it of its virtues as well, resulting in the destruction of the hive itself, as all the bees, "blest with content and honesty," abandoned industry and took refuge in a hollow tree.[15]

Lest the moral escape his readers, Mandeville reissued the poem in 1714 with a prefatory essay, "The Origin of Moral Virtue," and a score of lengthy "Remarks" amplifying lines of the poem; the editions of 1723 and 1724 added still other essays and remarks. In the enlarged version (now a full-length book), Mandeville elaborated upon his thesis. Self-love, which was reducible to pain and pleasure, was the primary motivation of all men, and what was generally called pity or compassion—the "fellow-feeling and condolence for the misfortunes and calamities of others"—was an entirely spurious passion, which unfortunately afflicted the weakest minds the most.[16] Moralists and philosophers, he conceded, generally took the opposite view, agreeing with the "noble writer" Lord Shaftesbury that "as man is made for society, so he ought to be born with a kind affection to the whole of which he is a part, and a propensity to seek the welfare of it."[17] Mandeville's conclusion was sharp and uncompromising:

After this I flatter my self to have demonstrated that neither the friendly qualities and kind affections that are natural to man, nor the real virtues he is capable of acquiring by reason and self-denial are the foundation of society; but that what we call evil in this world, moral as well as natural, is the grand principle that makes us sociable creatures, the solid basis, the life and support of all trades and employments without exception; that there we must look for the true origin of all arts and sciences, and that the moment evil ceases, the society must be spoiled if not totally dissolved.[18]

The Fable of the Bees profoundly shocked contemporaries, provoking a frenzy of attacks culminating in a ruling handed down by the grand jury of Middlesex condemning it as a "public nuisance." Joining in the near-universal condemnation were most of the eighteenth-century greats—Bishop Berkeley, Francis Hutcheson, Edward Gibbon, Adam Smith. Smith expressed the general sentiment in pronouncing Mandeville's theory "licentious" and "wholly pernicious."[19]*

Mandeville's was a spirited but futile attempt to abort the social ethic that was the distinctive feature of the British Enlightenment. That ethic derived neither from self-interest nor from reason (although both were congruent with it) but from a moral sense that inspired sympathy, benevolence, and compassion for others. Thus, where Locke, denying any innate principles, looked to education to inculcate in children the sentiment of "humanity," "benignity," or "compassion,"[20] Shaftesbury rooted that sentiment in nature and instinct rather than education or reason. "To compassionate," he wrote, "i.e., to join with in passion. . . . To commiserate, i.e., to join with in misery. . . . This in one order of life is right and good; nothing more harmonious; and to be without this, or not to feel this, is unnatural, horrid, immane [monstrous]."[21]

Two years after the publication of the expanded version of

---

* Smith was offended not only by Mandeville's amoralism, his refusal to distinguish between vice and virtue, but also by his mercantilist views, which were a by-product of that philosophy. Because there was no natural moral sense and thus no natural harmony among men, Mandeville assumed that the government had to intervene to convert "private vices" into "public benefits." Mandeville is sometimes taken to be an apologist for capitalism, but it was mercantilism that was the logical deduction from his philosophy.

the *Fable,* Francis Hutcheson entered the debate with *An Inquiry Concerning the Original of Our Ideas of Beauty and Virtue,* reissued the following year with *Virtue or Moral Good* replacing *Beauty and Virtue.* The subtitle of the original edition gave its provenance: *In Which the Principles of the Late Earl of Shaftesbury Are Explained and Defended, Against the Author of the Fable of the Bees.* It was here that Hutcheson first enunciated the principle, "The greatest happiness for the greatest numbers."[22] Unlike Helvétius and Jeremy Bentham, who are often credited with this principle and who rooted it in the rational calculations of utility, Hutcheson deduced it from morality itself—the "moral sense, viz. benevolence."[23]★ These words, "moral sense" and "benevolence," appear as a refrain throughout the book. The moral sense, Hutcheson repeatedly explained, was antecedent to interest because it was universal in all men. "Fellow-feeling" could not be a product of self-interest because it involved associating oneself with such painful experiences as the suffering and distress of others. So, too, the "disposition to compassion" was essentially disinterested, a concern with "the interest of others, without any views of private advantage."[25] It was also antecedent to reason or instruction. Like Burke later, Hutcheson warned of the frailty of reason: "Notwithstanding the mighty reason we boast of above other animals, its processes are too slow, too full of doubt and hesitation, to serve us in every exigency, either for our own preservation, without the external senses, or to direct our actions for the good of the whole, without this moral sense."[26] Elsewhere he explained that reason was "only a subservient power," capable of determining the

---

★ Bentham himself variously attributed this principle to Montesquieu, Barrington, Beccaria, and Helvétius, "but most of all Helvétius." Smith mistakenly attributed the origin of the "moral sense" to Hutcheson rather than Shaftesbury.[24]

means of promoting the good but not the end itself, the innate impulse to good.[27]

"Benevolence," compassion," "sympathy," "fellow-feeling," a "natural affection for others"—under one label or another, this moral sense (or sentiment, as Smith preferred) was the basis of the social ethic that informed British philosophical and moral discourse for the whole of the eighteenth century. The generation of philosophers that followed Shaftesbury qualified his teachings in one respect or another, differing among themselves about the precise nature and function of the moral sense. But they all agreed that it (or something very like it) was the natural, necessary, and universal attribute of man, of rich and poor alike, the educated and uneducated, the enlightened and unenlightened. They also agreed that it was a corollary of reason and interest, but prior to and independent of both.

In his two sermons on "Compassion," Bishop Butler explained that reason alone was not "a sufficient motive of virtue in such a creature as man"; it had to be joined with compassion, which was "a call, a demand of nature, to relieve the unhappy, as hunger is a natural call for food" (the "unhappy" including the "indigent and distressed").[28] There was no contradiction, he insisted, between man's benevolence and self-love, between "public and private affections," because both were integral to his nature and essential to his happiness. "There is a natural principle of benevolence in man, which is in some degree to society what self-love is to the individual."[29] For the philosopher Thomas Reid, it was "common sense," not reason, that was the unique quality of the "plain man." If man had been endowed only with reason, the race would soon have been extinct. Fortunately, reason was complemented by the "benevolent affections," which were "no less necessary for the preservation of the human species than the appetites of hunger and thirst."[30] So, too, Adam Ferguson made "fellow-feeling" or "humanity" so much an "appurtenance of human nature" as to be a "characteristic of the species."[31]

Even Hume, who had a notably unsentimental view of human nature, believed in a "sentiment," a "moral sense," a "moral taste" common to all men.[32] Pain and pleasure were related to that moral sense, insofar as vice was conducive to pain and virtue to pleasure. It was a fallacy of philosophy, ancient as well as modern, he observed, to regard reason as the main motive or principle of human behavior, for reason alone could never prevail over the will and passions or provide the incentive for virtue. The final book of *A Treatise of Human Nature* opened with a section entitled "Moral distinctions not derived from reason," followed by another, "Moral distinctions derived from a moral sense."[33]

Hutcheson criticized Hume for rejecting the idea of benevolence as the primary, innate faculty. But Hume did accept the idea of sympathy as the "chief source of moral distinctions," and the source in particular of "the public good," "the good of mankind."[34] And while he did not give it quite the character of an innate sense, he did make it a common trait of all men. "The minds of all men are similar in their feelings and operations; nor can any one be actuated by any affection, of which all others are not, in some degree, susceptible. As in strings equally wound up, the motion of one communicates itself to the rest; so all the affections readily pass from one person to another, and beget correspondent movements in every human creature."[35] As if to appease Hutcheson, in a later book, *An Enquiry Concerning the Principles of Morals,* Hume made much of the idea of benevolence, using the word synonymously with sympathy and criticizing the "selfish system of morals" of Hobbes and Locke, which failed to recognize that "general benevolence" or "disinterested benevolence"— that is, benevolence divorced from personal relations and affections—was an essential quality of human nature. It was evidently so, Hume argued, in animals, the inferior species; how could it not be in man, the superior species?[36] For himself, he found the sentiment of benevolence so well founded in experience that he could assume it "without further proof." It was not, to be sure, an innate quality of human beings, as Hutcheson would have it, but it was a "tendency" that had virtually the same effect. "It appears that a tendency to public good, and to the promoting of peace, harmony, and order in society does, always, by affecting the benevolent principles of our frame, engage us on the side of the social virtues." And again, more eloquently: "There is some benevolence, however small, infused into our bosom; some spark of friendship for human kind; some particle of the dove kneaded into our frame, along with the elements of the wolf and serpent."[37]

The most nuanced statement of this creed, and the most influential, appeared in Adam Smith's *The Theory of Moral Sentiments.* Today (except among scholars) Smith is identified almost entirely with the *Wealth of Nations.* In his own time, he was as well known, at home and abroad, as the author of *The Theory of Moral Sentiments.* Published in 1759, *Moral Sentiments* went through four editions before *Wealth of Nations* appeared in 1776, and another edition a few years later. So far from being superseded by the later work, the earlier one remained in the forefront of Smith's consciousness, as in that of his contemporaries. He devoted the last year of his life to revising and expanding *Moral Sentiments,* not to bring it into accord with the later book but to strengthen the message of the earlier one. The most important change was the addition of the chapter "Of the Corruption of Our Moral Sentiments, Which Is Occasioned by This Disposition to Admire the Rich and the Great, and to Despise or Neglect Persons of Poor and Mean Condition."

The opening sentences of *Moral Sentiments* set its tone and theme:

> How selfish soever man may be supposed, there are evidently some principles in his nature which interest him in the fortune of others and render their happiness necessary to him, though he derives nothing from it except the pleasure of seeing it. Of this kind is pity or compassion, the emotion which we feel for the misery of others when we either see it or are made to conceive it in a very lively manner. . . . By the imagination we place ourselves in his situation . . . we enter, as it were, into his body and become in some measure the same person with him.[38]

"Pity," "compassion," "benevolence," "sympathy"—Smith used the words almost, but not quite, synonymously, to denote those elemental qualities of human nature that constitute our moral sentiments. "Hence it is that to feel much for others and little for ourselves, that to restrain our selfish and to indulge our benevolent affections, constitutes the perfection of human nature."[39] And hence it is, too, that man finds his own satisfaction in indulging those benevolent affections. In being virtuous, man is fulfilling his own nature for his own sake. "Man naturally desires not only to be loved, but to be lovely. . . . He naturally dreads not only to be hated but to be hateful. . . . He desires not only praise but praiseworthiness. . . . He dreads not only blame but blameworthiness."[40] And again: "We desire both to be respectable and to be respected. We dread both to be contemptible and to be contemned."[41]

It is the "positive" virtues elicited by the sense of "fellow-feeling" that Smith elevated over what he called the "negative" virtues of justice. And it is this that distinguishes Smith from the older "civic humanist" tradition.[42] That tradition, deriving from the Renaissance and espoused by the Commonwealthmen in the seventeenth century, regarded public affairs and political integrity as the essence of virtue. For Smith, the public realm, governed by the principle of justice, was of secondary importance compared with the private realm, where the sentiments of sympathy and benevolence prevail.

> Though the mere want of beneficence seems to merit no punishment from equals, the greater exertions of that virtue appear to deserve the highest reward. By being productive of the greatest good, they are the natural and approved objects of the liveliest gratitude. Though the breach of justice, on the contrary, exposes to punishment, the observance of the rules of that virtue seems scarce to deserve any reward. There is, no doubt, a propriety in the practice of justice, and it merits, upon that account, all the approbation which is due to propriety. But as it does no real positive good, it is entitled to very little gratitude. Mere justice is, upon most occasions, but a negative virtue, and only hinders us from hurting our neighbor.[43]

Anticipating a common misinterpretation of his views, Smith refuted yet again the idea that sympathy was rooted in self-love. Sympathy cannot be regarded as a "selfish principle," for it comes not by imagining oneself in another's piteous condition, but imagining the other in it. Thus, a man might sympathize with a woman in childbirth, although he cannot conceive himself suffering her pains in "his own proper person and character."[44] Nor can sympathy be sufficiently accounted for by reason. Reason was, to be sure, the source of the general rules of morality, but it was "altogether absurd and unintelligible to suppose that the first perceptions of right and wrong can be derived from reason." Virtue "necessarily pleases for its own sake," and vice "as certainly displeases," not because of reason and reflection but because of "immediate sense and feeling."[45]

If reason and interest played a secondary role in the moral schema of these philosophers, so did religion. They either found the source of morality outside religion, or, like Shaftesbury, in "natural religion"; or they invoked orthodox religion, as Bishop Butler did, as an ally of morality. In either case, there was a conspicuous absence of the kind of animus to religion—certainly nothing like the warfare between reason and religion—that played so large a part in the French Enlightenment. Newtonianism, which might have been expected to foster an extreme skepticism, did not have that effect. Newton's God did not merely set the universe in motion; He was a living, active agent in it. "He is *always* and *everywhere*. . . . He is all eye, all ear, all brain, all arm, all force of sensing, of understanding, and of acting."[46] And the *Principia*, it was generally agreed, provided ample evidence of God's providential design for the universe. Newton himself, while denying the trinity (as Locke also did), and going to great pains to correct the Bible on the basis of astronomical calculations, was (as Voltaire, his greatest admirer said) a believing Christian, not a deist.★

Shaftesbury set the tone early in the century by calling for a "good humored religion," which would descend from the "higher regions of divinity" to "plain honest morals."[48] That

---

★ Newton was also for many years a zealous alchemist (and perhaps remained a crypto-alchemist for much of his life). His biographer is reminded of Nietzsche's astute observation, two centuries later: "'Do you believe then that the sciences would ever have arisen and become great if there had not beforehand been magicians, alchemists, astrologers and wizards, who thirsted and hungered after abscondite and forbidden powers?'"[47]

good humor was exhibited in the famous account of his conversation with a friend about the multitude of sects in the world. "All wise men are of the same religion," they said. What was that religion? one lady asked. "Madam," Shaftesbury replied, "wise men never tell."[49] (This witticism has since been attributed to many other wise men, including Hume. Winston Churchill, who was fond of quoting it, cited a character in Benjamin Disraeli's novel *Endymion*.)

Hume was the most skeptical of the philosophers. His essay on miracles (prudently deleted from the *Treatise of Human Nature* but printed later in the *Philosophical Essays Concerning Human Understanding*) earned him the common appellation of "atheist." He was not, in fact, an atheist—an agnostic, perhaps, or even a deist. While he was critical of the philosophical basis of natural religion ("natural theology," he called it), he did not discard the creed itself. And although he was fearful of "zealotry," he was remarkably tolerant of "enthusiasm." After the publication of the final volume of the *Treatise,* he published an essay on "Superstition and Enthusiasm," characterizing both as corruptions of true religion but very different in their nature and effects. Whereas superstition was favorable to priestly power, enthusiasm was even more opposed to religious hierarchy than was reason itself. Enthusiasm started, to be sure, by producing the most cruel disorders in society, "but its fury is like that of thunder and tempest, which exhaust themselves in a little time and leave the air more calm and pure than before." Thus, superstititon was "an enemy to civil liberty" and enthusiasm "a friend to it." The Quakers, for example, started as enthusiasts and became "very free reasoners," as did the Jansenists in France, who kept alive in that country "the small sparks of the love of liberty."[50] (Like so many of his contemporaries, however, he was less than tolerant of Catholics.)

It was for good reason that the *philosophes* found Hume insufficiently atheistic, while he found them excessively dogmatic. Edward Gibbon, recalling his visit to Paris in 1763, was disturbed by "the intolerant zeal" of the *philosophes,* who "laughed at the skepticism of Hume, preached the tenets of atheism with the bigotry of dogmatists, and damned all believers with ridicule and contempt."[51] The following year, a friend of Hume's living in Paris reported to an English correspondent that "poor Hume, who on your side of the water was thought to have too little religion, is here thought to have too much."[52] Indeed, Hume had enough religion to support the church establishment, in part as a corrective to zealotry, but also because the belief in God and immortality had a salutary effect on people's lives. Those who tried to disabuse the people of that belief, he conceded, "may, for aught I know, be good reasoners, but I cannot allow them to be good citizens and politicians."[53] In his *History of England* (the most popular of his works in his own time), he went so far as to argue that "there must be an ecclesiastical order and a public establishment of religion in every civilized community."[54] He was especially taken with the Church of Scotland, accepting with pleasure his appointment as patron to that church and using his influence to advance the views and careers of the Moderates—Christian Stoics, as they thought of themselves—who aspired to reconcile faith and secular ethics, Christianity and commerce.[55]

If Hume was the most skeptical of the philosophers of that generation, Bishop Butler was the least skeptical. Yet Hume was respectful of Butler and regarded his *Analogy of Religion* as the most serious theological work of the century.[56] The *Analogy* was a sober critique of deism and a sophisticated defense of theism. Butler's God, "the intelligent Author of nature and natural Governor of the world,"[57] was the God of revelation as well as nature. He was, moreover, the God who not only created the universe—this the deists conceded—but actively intervened in it, which they denied. He was also the

God who provided the final sanction for morality. Butler agreed with the other philosophers that neither reason nor self-love was a sufficient basis for virtue, but he disagreed with them in attributing virtue to an innate moral sense. It was religion that was the source of the "strongest obligation to benevolence" and that brought together reason and self-love in the pursuit of that virtue.[58]

Even Hutcheson, who followed Shaftesbury most closely in asserting the primacy of the moral sense, conceded that man is as he is because God created him so. Hutcheson did not derive the moral sense from God; instead, he derived God, as it were—a benevolent God—from the moral sense. Since the happiness of man consisted in a "universal efficacious benevolence," it followed that God was "benevolent in the most universal impartial manner."[59] A firm believer in religious toleration, Hutcheson did not extend that toleration to the atheist who denied "moral providence" or the citizen who denied the "moral or social virtues"; both were so hurtful to the well-being of the state that they should be restrained by the force of a magistrate.[60]

Whatever disagreements Hutcheson and Hume had about the precise nature of the moral sense, Adam Smith was a great admirer of both. Some commentators have suggested that Smith was at best a deist like Hutcheson, at worst a skeptic like Hume.★ Whether as deist or skeptic, he displayed in his writings a tolerance toward religion and a benign view of it

---

★ A letter written by Smith while Hume was dying is sometimes taken as evidence that he shared Hume's views: "Poor David Hume is dying very fast, but with great cheerfulness and good humor and with more real resignation to the necessary course of things than any whining Christian ever died with pretended resignation to the will of God."[61]

typical of most of his colleagues. If he did not make of religion the source of morality, he did regard it as a natural ally of the morality inherent in man. Reason and religion had equal but separate functions, reason providing the general rules of right and wrong, and religion reinforcing those rules by the commands and laws of the deity. In acting in accord with those rules and giving them the reverence they deserved, the individual cooperated with the deity and advanced the plan of Providence. Indeed, those rules were the "viceregents of God within us," carrying with them the this-worldly sanctions of rewards and punishments—the "contentment" that came with following the rules, and the "inward shame and self-condemnation" that came with violating them.[62]

Even the belief in immortality, Smith said, was inspired not only by our weaknesses, our hopes and fears, but also by our noblest and best motives, "the love of virtue . . . and the abhorrence of vice and injustice." Religion thus enforced the natural sense of duty. This is why great confidence was placed in the probity of religious men—provided that the natural principles of religion were not corrupted by "the factious and party zeal of some worthless cabal," and provided, too, that the religious person recognized as his first duty the fulfillment of all the obligations of morality, putting justice and benevolence above the "frivolous observances" of religion.[63] It might have been Burke explaining why religion was a more certain support of morality than reason or philosophy. "Religion, even in its rudest form," Smith said, "gave a sanction to the rules of morality, long before the age of artificial reasoning and philosophy. That the terrors of religion should thus enforce the natural sense of duty was of too much importance to the happiness of mankind for nature to leave it dependent upon the slowness and uncertainty of philosophical research."[64]

Smith was a prudent man and it may be that these qualified testimonials to religion veil his own skeptical disposition. In the final edition of *Moral Sentiments,* he added a section on prudence, explaining that the prudent man was always "sincere" but not always "frank and open." He always told the truth, but not always the whole truth. Above all, he respected "with an almost religious scrupulosity all the established decorums and ceremonials of society." Among those eminent men throughout the ages who had failed to observe those decorums, and had "thereby set a most pernicious example" to their admirers, Smith included his own contemporaries Swift and Voltaire.[65]

These reflections on prudence may have been prompted by an episode that haunted Smith for many years. Hume, shortly before his death, asked Smith to see to the publication of a book over which he had long labored, and left him a small legacy for that purpose. The book was the *Dialogues Concerning Natural Religion,* which even like-minded friends had urged Hume not to publish because it denied the validity not only of revealed religion but of natural religion as well. Smith felt obliged to tell his best friend on his deathbed that he could not honor his request, giving some feeble reason for his refusal. (To the publisher he explained that he thought the "clamor" provoked by the *Dialogues* would hurt the sale of the new edition of Hume's works.) Perhaps to ease his conscience, Smith appended to Hume's *My Own Life,* published the following year, a tribute concluding with an epitaph adapted from the *Phaedo:* "Upon the whole, I have always considered him, both in his lifetime and since his death, as approaching as nearly to the idea of a perfectly wise and virtuous man, as perhaps the nature of human frailty will permit." That eulogy, Smith later observed, "brought upon me ten times more abuse than the very violent attack I had made upon the whole commercial system of Great Britain."[66] It also brought him a less than panegyric obituary in the *Times,* which recalled his "labored eulogium on the stoical end of David Hume."[67]

Hume died in 1776. That same year, the *Wealth of Nations* was published. Toward the end of that book, in a section on education, Smith made some observations about religion which were both prudent and practical. The state, he explained, had an interest in the education of the young, because the more educated they were, the less liable they were to those "delusions of enthusiasm and superstition" which, in backward countries, were the occasion for dreadful disorders. He quoted a long passage in Hume's *History of England* defending the proposal that the state pay the clergy of Dissenting sects, on the grounds that if clerics were left to their own resources, they would be more vigorous in promoting their own sects and more inclined to infuse their religion with superstition and delusion. Indolence rather than energy was the desideratum, and that could be achieved by paying the clergy a fixed salary. Smith amended Hume's proposal by pointing out that zeal was dangerous only if there were a few sects in society. If there were many sects, no single one would be strong enough to disturb the public order. Each sect, surrounded by so many adversaries, would find it expedient to respect the others and make concessions for their mutual benefit. In time, their doctrines would be largely reduced to a "pure and rational religion, free from every mixture of absurdity, imposture, or fanaticism." This, Smith observed, is what wise men had always sought, and it could be achieved without the intervention of positive law, which itself tended to be influenced by superstition and enthusiasm.[68]*

---

* Smith's argument recalls Voltaire's almost half a century earlier: "If one religion only were allowed in England, the government would very pos-

Religious sects were also valuable in promoting a distinctive ethos.

> In every civilized society, in every society where the distinction of ranks has once been completely established, there have been always two different schemes or systems of morality current at the same time, of which the one may be called the strict or austere; the other the liberal, or if you will, the loose system. The former is generally admired and revered by the common people; the latter is commonly more esteemed and adopted by what are called people of fashion.[70]

The "liberal" or "loose" system, favored by "people of fashion," was prone to the "vices of levity"—"luxury, wanton and even disorderly mirth, the pursuit of pleasure to some degree of intemperance, the breach of chastity. . . ." The "strict or austere" system, generally adhered to by "the common people," regarded such vices, for themselves at any rate, with "the utmost abhorrence and detestation," because they knew—or at least "the wiser and better sort" of them knew—that these vices were almost always ruinous to them; a single week's dissipation could undo a poor workman forever. This is why, Smith explained, religious sects arose and flourished among the common people, for they preached the system of morality conducive to the welfare of the poor.[71]

If Smith's views on religion were dictated, at least in part, by prudence, it was public as well as personal prudence that

sibly become arbitrary. If there were but two, the people would cut one another's throats. But as there are such a multitude, they all live happy and in peace."[69] *The Federalist* later made much the same observation: "A religious sect may degenerate into a political faction in a part of the Confederacy; but the variety of sects dispersed over the entire face of it must secure the national councils against any danger from that source."

he had in mind. He may have been, in public, better disposed to religion than he was privately inclined to be. But he genuinely believed in the moral and social utility of religion. And the utility not only of natural religion, and not even of the religion of the established church, which might be thought to be a valuable instrument of public order and stability, but the religion of those Dissenting sects which, in the name of a purer, more rigorous faith, inspired a stricter, more austere morality. In this respect, Smith was perhaps more appreciative of religion than even those of his colleagues who had official positions in the established churches—Bishop Butler, most notably, or the Moderates in the Church of Scotland.

The year 1776 was truly an *annus mirabilis,* in the history of the British Enlightenment no less than in the history of the American republic. It saw the publication of two works recognized as classics in their own time, as in ours: *An Inquiry into the Nature and Causes of the Wealth of Nations* and the first volume of *The Decline and Fall of the Roman Empire.* Edward Gibbon was not a moral philosopher, but he was a moral historian, and his great work was a notable contribution to the British Enlightenment. His friend Hume wrote to him shortly after the first volume appeared (and only a few months before his own death) warning him that he might be tainted by the same charges that had been levelled against himself. Commending Gibbon for having displayed a "very prudent temperament," Hume feared that the last two chapters of the book would create a "clamor" against him. "The prevalence of superstition in England," he predicted, "prognosticates the fall of philosophy and decay of taste; and though nobody be more capable than you to revive them, you will probably find a struggle in your first advances."[72]

In fact, the book defied Hume's prediction and was successful far beyond the expectations of Gibbon or his publisher. The first edition of one thousand copies was exhausted in a few days, as were two other printings that quickly followed, in spite of the fact that those chapters proved to be every bit as provocative as Hume had said. While some reviewers and readers hailed the work as a masterpiece, others vilified the author as an atheist. The chapter introducing the subject of Christianity was deceptively entitled "The Progress of the Christian Religion, and the Sentiments, Manners, Numbers, and Condition of the Primitive Christians." But the progress of Christianity, as Gibbon described it, was synonymous with the progress of superstition, in evidence of which he adduced the belief in miracles, the doctrine of immortality, the afterlife that consigned unbelievers to eternal hell, and the suspension of the laws of nature for the benefit of the church. Paying tribute to the primitive Christians whose faith was buttressed by personal virtues, Gibbon observed that their lives were purer and more austere than those not only of their pagan contemporaries but also of their "degenerate successors." He spoke ironically of a church that became more outwardly splendid even as it lost its internal purity; and of the poor who had cheerfully to contemplate the promise of future happiness in the kingdom of heaven, while the rich were content with their possessions in this world.[73] Recounting the persecution endured by the early Christians on the part of the Romans, he concluded the following chapter with the "melancholy truth which obtrudes itself on the reluctant mind": that the Christians, in the course of their own dissensions, had "inflicted far greater severities on each other than they had experienced from the zeal of infidels."[74]

In his *Memoirs* written many years later, reflecting upon the enormous success of his work—"my book was on every table and almost on every toilette"—Gibbon bitterly recalled the accusations of impiety: "Had I believed that the majority of

English readers were so fondly attached even to the name and shadow of Christianity; had I foreseen that the pious, the timid, and the prudent would feel, or affect to feel, with such exquisite sensibility, I might, perhaps, have softened the two invidious chapters, which would create many enemies and conciliate few friends." Fortunately, he added, those clamorous voices were not persuasive.[75] And there were other voices to salve his wounded ego, not only Hume but Smith, who assured him, after the publication of the final volumes: "I cannot express to you the pleasure it gives me to find that by the universal assent of every man of taste and learning, whom I either know or correspond with, it sets you at the very head of the whole literary tribe at present existing in Europe."[76]

It is difficult to characterize Gibbon's variety of unbelief, if it was that. It has been said that his skepticism was that of a historian rather than a theologian.[77] In the first of the "invidious" chapters, Gibbon himself suggested this: "The theologian may indulge the pleasing task of describing Religion as she descended from Heaven, arrayed in her native purity. A more melancholy duty is imposed on the historian. He must discover the inevitable mixture of error and corruption which she contracted in a long residence upon earth, among a weak and degenerate race of beings."[78] The historian and the theologian, however, were not so neatly distinguished, the skepticism of the one inevitably informing the other. Moreover, Gibbon's skepticism was not the familiar defense of primitive Christianity in contrast to the later, corrupt church; it was the miracles and superstitions of Christianity at its very inception that he took to be the source of the evil. Nor was it only the Catholic Church, or, indeed, any church, that he objected to; he was equally critical of the natural religion of modern deists and Dissenters, who hoped to preserve the form of religion without its substance, faith without revelation. This was one of his criticisms of Joseph Priestley, who, in turn, rebuked Gibbon for mocking the idea of the afterlife.

Gibbon, then, was a thoroughgoing skeptic—a skeptic, however, not an atheist. Atheism was too dogmatic, too enthusiastic, to satisfy either the historian or the citizen. Like Shaftesbury, he had no use for the breed of "enthusiasti-cal atheists."[79] Gibbon's comment on the *philosophes,* who "preached the tenets of atheism with the bigotry of dogma-tists,"[80] has been attributed to the elderly Gibbon rather than the young author of the *Decline and Fall.* Yet even in his ear-lier days he had little sympathy with them. On the rare occa-sions when he cited the *Encyclopédie,* he did so disapprovingly, and he did not think it important enough to buy the work for his own library.[81] It has been suggested that he was misrepre-sented by later Victorian commentators who tried to appro-priate him for their own secular rationalism.[82] If he did not quite have the "quasi-religious sensibility" that this historian attributes to him, he did have a spirit of skeptical tolerance that made the latitudinarianism of the Church of England much more congenial to him than atheism. So far from want-ing to disestablish the church, he came to distrust the fanati-cism of the rebels against the church more than that of the religious believers.

That Gibbon was an eminent member of the British Enlightenment is not now in doubt. But he himself felt the need to reassure his readers of his confidence in that Enlight-enment. He realized that his theme, the decline and fall of the Roman Empire, could well be taken as an object lesson for his own time. Would not the high civilization of modernity fall prey to the same forces of darkness that had overtaken the high civilization of antiquity? His answer was unequivocal: the achievements of civilization would not be lost. "We may therefore acquiesce," he closed the third volume, "in the pleas-ing conclusion that every age of the world has increased and still increases the real wealth, the happiness, the knowledge, and perhaps the virtue of the human race."[83]

It is interesting, especially by contrast to the situation in France, to see how far some of the representatives of the British Enlightenment could go in "naturalizing" religion without repudiating religion itself, and how far others could go in rejecting even that natural religion without rejecting the church itself—indeed, how far even the clerics among them could go without jeopardizing their standing in the church. Many years ago, the historian H. R. Trevor-Roper traced this tolerant attitude back to the seventeenth century with the emergence of Arminianism and Socinianism, the first celebrating free will, religious toleration, and the lay control of the church; the second applying secular, critical reason to religious texts and problems. Both were heresies of the right, Trevor-Roper said (disputing the conventional view of Socinianism as a heresy of the left), and both contributed to an Enlightenment forged in an atmosphere not of "ideological revolution and civil war" but "ideological peace and *rapprochement.*"[84]

More recent historians have endorsed this view. J. G. A. Pocock explains that there was no hue and cry in England about "*Ecrasez l'infâme*" because there was "no *infâme* to be crushed." The Anglican Church, turned Erastian in the seventeenth century in response to Puritanism, regarded rational religion as supportive rather than subversive of clerical authority, and the church was sufficiently latitudinarian to accommodate the likes of Gibbon. Thus, there was no "Enlightenment project" in England, as there was in France, designed to discredit religion, to disestablish the church, or to create a civil religion in its stead.[85] Similarly, Roy Porter, refuting "the rise of modern paganism" theory of Peter Gay,

finds that the Enlightenment in England throve *"within* piety."
"There was no need to overthrow religion itself, because
there was no pope, no inquisition, no Jesuits, no monopolis-
tic priesthood."[86] J. C. D. Clark has gone further in extending
this latitudinarianism to Methodists and Evangelicals as well
as to mainstream Anglicans, all of whom subscribed to a
"political theology" that was supportive of both church and
state.[87]

But something more than latitudinarianism and tolerance
were responsible for the very different intellectual climate in
Britain. There was no oppressive church or dogmatic theology to rebel against, to be sure, but neither was there a new
authority or ideology to incite rebellion. In France, reason
was that authority and ideology, a reason so paramount as to
challenge not only religion and the church but all the institutions dependent upon them. Reason was inherently subversive, looking to an ideal future and contemptuous of the
deficiencies of the present, to say nothing of the past—and
disdainful also of the beliefs and practices of the uneducated
and lowborn.

The British moral philosophy, on the other hand, was
reformist rather than subversive, respectful of the past and
present even while looking forward to a more enlightened
future. It was also optimistic and, in this respect at least, egali-
tarian, the moral sense and common sense being shared by all
men, not merely the educated and wellborn. And it had no
quarrel with religion itself—with a benighted or antisocial
religion, to be sure, but not religion per se. It could even
tolerate, as Shaftesbury and Hume did, enthusiastic religion,
thus opening the door to the most enthusiastic religion of the
time, Methodism.

This was the England that Montesquieu encountered early
in the eighteenth century. The English, he said, "know better
than any other people upon earth how to value, at the same

time, these three great advantages—religion, commerce, and liberty."[88] And it was the England that Tocqueville rediscovered more than a century later: "I enjoyed, too, in England what I have long been deprived of—a union between the religious and the political world, between public and private virtue, between Christianity and liberty."[89]

2. POLITICAL ECONOMY AND MORAL SENTIMENTS

Adam Smith had a double role in the British Enlightenment, as moral philosopher and as political economist. It used to be thought that the two Smiths were incongruent—"*Das Adam Smith Problem,*" the Germans called it. Much recent scholarship has been devoted to solving that problem.[1] Yet it was not a problem for contemporaries, who saw nothing anomalous or contradictory in his two great works, *The Theory of Moral Sentiments* published in 1759 and *An Inquiry into the Nature and Causes of the Wealth of Nations* in 1776.

The *Wealth of Nations* was not, in fact, as late a book as the publication date suggests. Some of the leading ideas of both books were the subjects of Smith's lectures as professor of logic and then of moral philosophy at the University of Glasgow in the early 1750s. In 1755, Smith delivered a short paper to a local society outlining some of the leading ideas of the *Wealth of Nations;* as if to stake out his claim of priority, he pointed out that he had expressed them in lectures at Edinburgh even before taking up his position at Glasgow.[2] He worked on the actual text of the book for many years, to the despair of some of his friends, who regretted the delay and feared that its bulk would discourage readers. When it was finally published, David Hume consoled Smith that while it required too close a reading to become quickly popular, it would, by its "depth and solidity and acuteness" as well as its "curious facts," eventually capture the public attention.[3] The publisher was no more optimistic. The first edition, in two volumes and over a thousand pages, consisted of five hundred copies selling for the standard price of £1 16s., for which Smith received the grand sum of £300—this for the author of the well-known and highly regarded *Theory of Moral Sentiments,* which had appeared in a new edition only two years earlier. Those five hundred copies sold out in six months, a second edition was published two years later, and three others followed in the dozen years before Smith's death in 1790. The book was translated during his lifetime into French, German, Italian, Danish, and Spanish, and received the imprimatur of success in the form of a lengthy abridgement. Some of the most eminent men of the time, across the political spectrum, declared themselves his disciple: Edmund Burke and Thomas Paine, Edward Gibbon and Richard Price, William Pitt and Lord North.

The success of the *Wealth of Nations* did not at all detract from the importance or the message of *Moral Sentiments.* Having reviewed the first glowingly when it appeared, Burke was as admiring of the second a quarter of a century later. The appreciative memoir of Smith by Dugald Stewart, written three years after his death, devoted twenty-six pages to the early book and only seventeen to the later one.* Later

---

* In a note appended to the memoir, Stewart explained that Smith's posthumous reputation was somewhat under a cloud at the time. While England was at war with France, there was a tendency, "even among men of some talents and information" (the memoir was delivered before the Royal Society of Edinburgh), to confound the "speculative doctrines of political economy" with the "first principles of government." Thus, the doctrine of free trade was seen to have a "revolutionary tendency." Some people who had prided themselves on their intimacy with Smith and their admiration for his economics began to question the expediency of "subjecting to the disputations of philosophers the arcana of state policy."[4]

commentators on Smith, focusing on the *Wealth of Nations,* often saw little of *Moral Sentiments* in it—or of any moral philosophy. Indeed, some have read the second book as a refutation, in effect, of the first, interpreting the *Wealth of Nations* as an attempt to de-moralize political economy and divorce it from any moral content. John Ruskin was more intemperate than most when he inveighed against that "half-bred and half-witted Scotchman" who deliberately perpetrated the blasphemy, "Thou shalt hate the Lord thy God, damn His laws, and covet thy neighbor's goods."[5] A century later, the historian E. P. Thompson made the point less dramatically when he contrasted the older "moral economy" with Smith's new political economy, which was "disinfested of intrusive moral imperatives"—not, Thompson hastened to add, because Smith was personally immoral or unconcerned with the public good, but because that was the objective consequence of his doctrine.[6]

The economist Joseph Schumpeter, on the other hand, complained not that Smith de-moralized political economy but rather that he failed to do so. Smith, he said, was so steeped in the moral tradition derived from scholasticism and natural law that he could not conceive of economics per se, a discipline divorced from ethics and politics.[7] The point is well taken, although not necessarily in criticism. So far from having its origins in medieval philosophy, Smith's economics reflected the eminently modern philosophy that he and his contemporaries were propounding under the name of "moral philosophy."

Nor was Smith's political-*cum*-moral economy meant to elevate or exalt the business class (not yet named "capitalists") whom some critics have presumed to be its principal beneficiaries. On the contrary, the spirited rhetoric of the *Wealth of Nations* is almost always directed against that class. Of the three "orders" in society—landlords, laborers, and merchant-manufacturers—Smith saw the first two as acting in accord with the interests of the public; only the last tended to be at variance with the public interest.

> The proposal of any new law or regulation of commerce which comes from this order ought always to be listened to with great precaution, and ought never to be adopted till after having been long and carefully examined, not only with the most scrupulous but with the most suspicious attention. It comes from an order of men whose interest is never exactly the same with that of the public, who have generally an interest to deceive and even to oppress the public, and who accordingly have, upon many occasions, both deceived and oppressed it.[8]

> Our merchants and master-manufacturers complain much of the bad effects of high wages. . . . They say nothing concerning the bad effects of high profits. . . . They are silent with regard to the pernicious effects of their own gains. They complain only of those of other people.[9]

Merchants and manufacturers—the phrase appeared repeatedly and often invidiously. To further their own interests at the expense of "the poor and the indigent," they engaged in "clamour and sophistry," "impertinent jealousy," "mean rapacity," "mean and malignant expedients," "sneaking arts," "interested sophistry," and "interested falsehood."[10] There are, surely, enough "intrusive moral imperatives" in the *Wealth of Nations* to satisfy a moralist like Thompson and to distress a non-moralist like Schumpeter.

These invectives may seem to be at odds with Smith's famous dictum: "It is not from the benevolence of the butcher, the brewer, or the baker, that we expect our dinner, but from their regard to their own interest."[11] This principle was based on the assumption that the butcher, brewer, and baker—and laborer as well—operated in a "system of natural liberty,"[12] a free market that allowed for the exchange of goods and services to the mutual benefit of all the partners in that exchange. It was the mercantile system, which sought to direct the economy in the interests of national wealth and power, that encouraged men to "conspire," "deceive," and "oppress" each other. The free market, to be sure, did not entirely eliminate such temptations. "People of the same trade seldom meet together, even for merriment and diversion, but the conversation ends in a conspiracy against the public, or in some contrivance to raise prices." Although it was impossible, Smith added, to prevent such meetings by any law consistent with liberty and justice, the free market made it more difficult to engage in such pernicious activities.

Shortly before that memorable pronouncement about the "benevolence of the butcher, the brewer, or the baker," Smith had observed that in civilized society, "man has almost constant occasion for the help of his brethren." The question was whether to obtain that help from "benevolence only" or from "self-love."[13] It was the "system of natural liberty," and only that system, that made self-love (or self-interest) conducive to the general interest. Self-interest, as Smith understood it, was not as lofty as benevolence, but in the marketplace at least it was more reliable and practical—and moral as well.

Hovering over self-interest was the ubiquitous "invisible hand," which ensured that individual interests worked together for the general good. This metaphor, so often associated with the *Wealth of Nations,* appeared earlier, in almost the same wording and to much the same effect, in *Moral Sentiments.* In both books, it was the good of society, and most notably of the poor, that was advanced by the unintended consequences of individual actions. In the earlier book, it was the distribution of the necessities of life that was facilitated by the invisible hand; in the later one, the maximization of the revenues of society.[14] The metaphor has been criticized for giving too much latitude to the individual, for sanctioning whatever anyone might choose to do, regardless of the consequences for others. But it also had the opposite effect of shifting the weight of the argument from the individual to society by making private interests serve the public good.

The metaphor has also been given a teleological interpretation, as if some benevolent agent was active in bringing about that desirable end. Smith meant it to be a truly invisible hand, indeed, not really a hand at all. This was the genius of the system of natural liberty. Without outside intervention and without his own conscious knowledge, each individual was "led by an invisible hand to promote an end which was no part of his intention." Moreover, by pursuing his own interest in this fashion, "he frequently promotes that of society more effectually than when he really intends to promote it."[15]

Smith's "invisible hand" may be reminiscent of Hegel's "cunning of reason."* Yet it was profoundly different, precisely because Hegel's doctrine was teleological. For Hegel, the ends that were unwittingly furthered by the exercise of individual wills and interests were those of a providential History and a transcendent Reason. Smith's "general interest" was also significantly different from Rousseau's "general will." The latter was something more and other than the sum of

---

* There is no evidence that Hegel was inspired by Smith when he coined that phrase in his *Philosophy of History*. Yet he had read Smith (as well as later political economists such as Say and Ricardo), and there are echoes of Smith in the *Philosophy of Right*, especially in the concept of civil society, the realm intermediate between the individual and the state where individuals pursue their private interests.

individual interests, whereas Smith's general interest was simply the totality of interests of all the people who constituted society.

Perhaps the most novel aspect of the *Wealth of Nations* was the idea of nation itself. The title referred not to the nation as the mercantilist understood it—the nation-state whose wealth was the measure of its strength *vis-à-vis* other states—but to the people comprising the nation. And people not in the then familiar political sense of those who had an active part in the polity, but in the social sense of those living and working in society, the vast majority of whom, Smith pointed out, were in the "lower ranks." It was their well-being, their "wealth," that would be promoted by a "progressive" political economy, for only such a free economy could bring about a "universal opulence which extends itself to the lowest ranks of the people . . . a general plenty [which] diffuses itself through all the different ranks of society."[16] To those who complained that if the poor shared in the "general plenty," they would no longer be content with their lot in life, Smith put the question: "Is this improvement in the circumstances of the lower ranks of the people to be regarded as an advantage or an inconveniency to the society?" His answer was unequivocal:

> Servants, labourers and workmen of different kinds, make up the far greater part of every great political society. But what improves the circumstances of the greater part can never be regarded as an inconveniency to the whole. No society can surely be flourishing and happy, of which the far greater part of the members are poor and miserable. It is but equity, besides, that they who feed, clothe and lodge the whole body of the people should have such a share of the produce of their

own labour as to be themselves tolerably well fed, clothed and lodged.[17]

Smith's opposition to mercantilism is generally read as a criticism of government regulation and a defense of a policy of laissez-faire.* It was that, and much more as well. Mercantilism not only inhibited a progressive economy by interfering with the natural processes of the market. It was also, Smith charged, unjustly biased against workers because it set maximum rather than minimum wages, thus benefiting merchants and manufacturers at the expense of the workers. Mercantilism also promoted the prevailing view that low wages were both natural and necessary: natural because the poor would not work except out of dire need, and necessary in order to maintain a favorable balance of trade. As Arthur Young memorably put it: "Every one but an idiot knows that the lower classes must be kept poor, or they will never be industrious."[18] Young admitted that excessively low wages would be counterproductive. "Two shillings and sixpence a day will undoubtedly tempt some to work, who would not touch a tool for one shilling."[19] But he intended this as an argument for subsistence wages, not high wages.

Smith was not the first to question the desirability of low wages, but he was the first to defy the received wisdom by taking a positive view of high wages and offering a systematic

---

* It is by now generally accepted that Smith was not the rigorous laissez-fairist that some of his disciples (in the twentieth as well as nineteenth century) made him out to be. The whole of the final book of the *Wealth of Nations,* on the duties and functions of government, testifies to that. Moreover, Smith's own life belies that view. As Commissioner of Customs for Scotland (a post he sought and conscientiously fulfilled—it was not a sinecure), he supervised the collection of revenue that was to be used for the proper functions of the state: defense, justice, public works, education.

rationale for them. And he did so because he had confidence that the laboring poor were worthy of such wages and would respond favorably to them.

> The liberal reward of labour, as it encourages the propagation, so it increases the industry of the common people. The wages of labour are the encouragement of industry, which, like every other human quality, improves in proportion to the encouragement it receives. A plentiful subsistence increases the bodily strength of the labourer, and the comfortable hope of bettering his condition and of ending his days perhaps in ease and plenty animates him to exert that strength to the utmost. Where wages are high, we shall always find the workmen more active, diligent, and expeditious, than where they are low.[20]

Smith's benign view of the poor extended to the indigent as well as to the laboring poor. England was the first country—and for a long time the only country—to have a public, secular, national (although locally administered) system of poor relief. Unlike some of his successors—Thomas Malthus, most notably—Smith had no quarrel with poor relief as such. What he did oppose, and vigorously, were the settlement laws establishing residency requirements for the poor, which not only limited their mobility and opportunities for improvement, but also deprived them of the liberty enjoyed by other Englishmen.[21] In the same spirit, he supported proportional taxation and taxes on luxuries rather than necessities, so that "the indolence and vanity of the rich is made to contribute in a very easy manner to the relief of the poor."[22]

All of this was a corollary of Smith's conception of a "progressive economy." Because high wages were the result of increasing wealth and at the same time the cause of increasing population, only in an expanding economy, where the demand for labor kept abreast of the supply, could real wages remain high. The division of labor was crucial for the same reason, because it resulted in greater industrial productivity and a flourishing economy, thus making it possible for wealth to extend to the "lowest ranks of the people."[23] In effect, Smith refuted in advance Malthus's theory that the growth of population inevitably resulted in the "misery and vice" of the lower classes. A free market, Smith argued, combined with the division of labor would permit the economy to expand, absorbing the higher wages and increased population, and bringing with it not misery and vice for the common man but a "plentiful subsistence" and the comfortable hope of "bettering his condition."[24]

Smith's optimism failed him at one point. Toward the end of the *Wealth of Nations,* in what has come to be known as the "alienation" passage, he described the effects of the division of labor on a man who spent his life performing a few simple operations, with no opportunity to "exert his understanding" or "exercise his invention."

He naturally loses, therefore, the habit of such exertions, and generally becomes as stupid and ignorant as it is possible for a human creature to become. The torpor of his mind renders him, not only incapable of relishing or bearing a part in any rational conversation, but of conceiving any general, noble, or tender sentiments, and consequently of forming any just judgment concerning many even of the ordinary duties of private life. Of the great and extensive interests of his country he is altogether incapable of judging; and unless very particular pains have been taken to render him otherwise, he is equally incapable of defending his country in war. The uniformity of his stationary life naturally corrupts the courage of his mind, and makes him regard with abhorrence the irregular, uncertain, and adventurous life of a soldier. It corrupts even the activity of his body, and renders him incapable of exerting his strength with vigor and perseverance, in any other employment than that to which he has been bred. His dexterity at his own particular trade seems, in this manner, to be acquired at the expense of his intellectual, social, and martial virtues.[25]

This was a damning indictment—all the more because these were the laboring poor whom Smith had earlier lauded and for whom he had held out such high promise. It was also in patent contradiction to the central theme of the book. The first three chapters are on the division of labor, and the opening sentence of the first reads: "The greatest improvement in the productive powers of labour, and the greater part of the skill, dexterity, and judgment with which it is any where directed, or applied, seem to have been the effects of the division of labour."[26] Yet toward the end of the book, that skill, dexterity, and judgment—and much else—seem to be belied by that same division of labor.

One explanation for this apparent contradiction may be found in the final sentence of that passage: "But in every improved and civilized society this is the state into which the labouring poor, that is, the great body of the people, must necessarily fall, unless government takes some pains to prevent it."[27] It was to forestall this dire condition that Smith went on to propose a state-administered, state-supported, state-enforced system of education that was remarkable for its time. He called upon the government to establish in every district a school where children, including those "bred to the lowest occupation," would be instructed in reading, writing, and arithmetic. The burden of the cost of this system would be borne by the state, although parents would be charged a fee so modest that even the common laborer could afford it. The schools themselves would not be compulsory (there were already pauper schools and varieties of private schools), but some form of schooling would be, and to ensure a proper level of instruction, Smith suggested that an examination in the three R's be required before anyone could enter a guild or set up in a trade.[28]

Marxists have made much of this "alienation" passage, without attending to Smith's proposal for mitigating that problem. Marx himself, however, in *Capital,* after quoting Smith on the deleterious effects of the division of labor, did refer to that proposal, which "commends education of the people by the state, but prudently, and in homoeopathic doses."[29] Marx's own idea of a proper educational reform might strike a modern reader as not so much prudent or homoeopathic as primitive and regressive. Writing almost a century after Smith, and only a few years before the Forster Act of 1870 established the principle of free, compulsory public education, Marx took as his model for educational reform the Factory Act of 1864, which permitted children under the age of fourteen to work only if they spent part of the day at schools provided by the employer. He criticized that measure as "paltry," but he was taken with the idea of combining education with work. Although factory children received only half the education of regular day students, he accepted the claim of the factory inspectors that they learned "quite as much and often more" as day-school children. He himself proposed an education that was heavily weighted toward work. "When the working class comes into power, as inevitably it must, technical instruction, both theoretical and practical, will take its proper place in the working class schools." Such technical instruction (vocational schooling, we would now call it) would make workers fit for a "variety of labors, ready to face any change of production," thus solving the problems of excessive specialization and redundancy inherent in the division of labor.[30]

This concept of education was no passing thought on Marx's part. Almost twenty years earlier, in *The Communist Manifesto,* he had derided the "bourgeois claptrap" about education, proposing, as an intermediate step on the road to communism, free education with the proviso: "combination of education with industrial production."[31] One is reminded of Hannah Arendt's observation that no thinker ever reduced man to an *animal laborans* as totally as Marx did. Locke, she pointed out, made of labor the source of property; Smith made of labor the source of wealth; Marx made of labor the very essence of man.[32]

If Marx's solution to the problem of alienation was very different from Smith's (Smith did not at all link education with work), his concept of the problem itself was very different. This has been obscured by later Marxists who have interpreted this passage in the *Wealth of Nations* as exposing a fatal flaw in capitalism. For Smith, it was not capitalism that was flawed but the division of labor inherent in modern industry itself. Ironically, this was close to the position of the "early Marx," for whom alienation arose in the earliest stages of society, with the separation of man from physical nature and the division of labor in the family. The "mature Marx," on the other hand, abandoning that metaphysical idea of alienation, located the problem in capitalism—the divorce of workers from the means of production. Communism, however, did not solve that problem because it was as much dependent upon industrialism, hence upon the division of labor, as capitalism itself.

Apart from the belated appearance of this pessimistic theme, the tone of the *Wealth of Nations,* like that of the *Theory of Moral Sentiments,* was notably optimistic.[33] Industrialism and commerce were not only the instruments for material improvement—a "universal opulence" or "general plenty" extending to the "lowest ranks of the people."[34] They were also the means by which men could exercise their natural desire for "betterment." "Prodigality," the "passion for present enjoyment," was sometimes the occasional by-product of industry and commerce; but the more common and constant effect was the desire to save and improve one's condition.

> The principle which prompts to save is the desire of bettering our condition, a desire which, though generally calm and dispassionate, comes with us from the womb, and never leaves us till we go into the grave. . . . The uniform, constant, and uninterrupted effort of every man to better his condition, the principle from which public and national, as well as private opulence is originally derived, is frequently powerful enough to maintain the natural progress of things toward improvement, in spite of both the extravagance of government and of the greatest errors of administration.[35]

"The system of natural liberty," which was the most effective stimulant of commerce, also promoted a spirit of liberty in general. In a seminal work on Smith, Joseph Cropsey has made freedom—not only economic freedom but freedom in all its aspects—the prime principle of Smith's political economy. "Commerce generates freedom and civilization," Cropsey observes, "and at the same time free institutions are indispensable to the preservation of commerce." Most people might be inclined to defend a commercial civilization not out of love of freedom but simply out of love for monetary gain. But for Smith, it was the love of freedom that had priority. He "advocated capitalism for the sake of freedom"—not only economic freedom but civil and religious freedom as well.[36]

Smith himself gave credit to Hume for calling attention to yet another beneficent aspect of commerce. "Commerce and manufactures gradually introduced order and good government, and with them, the liberty and security of individuals, among the inhabitants of the country, who had before lived almost in a continual state of war with their neighbors and of servile dependency upon their superiors." Hume, Smith said, was the only writer to have taken notice of this least observed but by far most important effect of commerce: its civilizing, moderating, and pacifying effect on peoples and societies.[37]

Beyond material improvement, beyond even liberty, security, and tranquility, perhaps the most remarkable aspect of Smith's political economy was its implicitly democratic character—democratic not in a political sense but in a natural, human sense. This emerges again and again in the course of his book, in the passage on commerce, for example, in the almost passing observation on its salutary effect in reducing the "servile dependency" of men upon their superiors, or the argument against the Settlement Laws because they deprived the poor of the liberty of movement enjoyed by the rich. Smith used the conventional words to describe what we would now call the "working classes": "lower ranks," "lower classes," or, simply, "the poor." But it was the functional, rather than the hierarchic, order of classes that concerned him. He defined the classes not by their social rank—upper, middle, and lower—but by the source of their income: rent, wages, and profit. In his scheme, wage earners, or laborers, constituted not the third order, as was customary at the time (and still is in general discourse), but the second order, taking precedence over merchants and manufacturers, who were the third order.[38] The laborer was a full partner in the economic enterprise, indeed, the most important partner, in the sense that labor was the source of value. Moreover, labor, like rent and profit, was a "patrimony," a form of property entitled to the same consideration as any other kind of property.

> The patrimony which every man has in his own labour, as it is the original foundation of all other property, so it is the most sacred and inviolable. The patrimony of a poor man lies in the strength and dexterity of his hand; and to hinder him from employing this strength and dexterity in what manner he thinks proper without injury to his neighbour is a plain violation of this most sacred property.[39]

Democratic, too, was the concept of human nature implicit as much in Smith's political economy as in his theory of moral sentiments. The celebrated passage about the natural "propensity" to trade appears early in the book, where the division of labor is said to depend upon "a certain propensity in human nature . . . the propensity to truck, barter, and exchange one thing for another."[40] Smith refused to speculate about the origin of that propensity—whether it was innate in human nature, or, as he thought more probable, a consequence of the faculties of reason and speech. In either case, this elemental trait, "common to all men," was the lynchpin of a progressive economy, just as the moral sentiments common to all men were the basis for a good and just society. It was these modest attributes that made the laborer a fully moral being, capable and desirous of bettering himself and his family, of exercising his interests, passions, and virtues, and of enjoying the liberty that was his right as a free individual and a responsible member of society. No enlightened despot, not even an enlightened philosopher or legislator, was required to activate these qualities or to harmonize them for the general good.

This idea of a common human nature, of the natural

propensities and sentiments of all men, inspired an even more remarkable testament of democratic faith.

> The difference of natural talents in different men is, in reality, much less than we are aware of; and the very different genius which appears to distinguish men of different professions, when grown up to maturity, is not upon many occasions so much the cause as the effect of the division of labour. The difference between the most dissimilar characters, between a philosopher and a common street porter, for example, seems to arise not so much from nature, as from habit, custom, and education. . . . By nature a philosopher is not in genius and disposition half so different from a street porter, as a mastiff is from a greyhound, or a greyhound from a spaniel, or this last from a shepherd's dog.[41]

Even today this is a bold assertion of the priority of nurture over nature, an affirmation of the natural equality of all people—not, to be sure, political, economic, or social equality, but a basic equality of human nature. A philosopher not so very different from a street porter! This does not have quite the ring of that "self-evident" truth, "All men are created equal." Yet it does seem providential that the *Wealth of Nations* (although written long before) should have been published only months before the American Declaration of Independence. For its time and place, without the provocation of revolution or radical discontent, Smith's statement is memorable, all the more because it came from one of England's most eminent philosophers. It is striking that Britain's other eminent philosopher at the time, and Smith's best friend, had made much the same observation. "How nearly equal," Hume observed, "all men are in their bodily force, and even in their mental power and faculties, till cultivated by education."[42]

It is also striking to find the most distinguished philosopher of the preceding century, who is generally assumed to be the father of the British Enlightenment, taking exactly the opposite position. John Locke did not presume to explain the enormous difference, as he saw it, in men's capacity to understand and reason, but he did not hesitate to "affirm that there is a greater distance between some men and others in this respect than between some men and some beasts."[43] This assertion of the natural inequality of men stands in dramatic contrast to the pronouncements of Smith and Hume, who made a point of minimizing the natural differences, and thus the natural inequality, of men.

By the same token, the British moral philosophers stand in sharp contrast to the French *philosophes*. One cannot imagine Voltaire or Diderot (or even Rousseau) likening himself to a street porter. When Helvétius was bold enough to claim that circumstance, education, and interest accounted for differences in *"l'esprit,"* Diderot rebuked him. "He has not seen the insurmountable barrier that separates a man destined by nature for a given function, from a man who only brings to that function industry, interest and attention."[44] "Destined by nature for a given function"—Diderot might have been rebuking Smith as well.

3. EDMUND BURKE'S ENLIGHTENMENT

E dmund Burke and Thomas Paine—avowed disciples of
Adam Smith. This takes some explaining, not only
because they hardly seem compatible with one another,
but because they oblige us to rethink the British Enlightenment itself. If Smith was unquestionably a member in good
standing in the Enlightenment, surely his disciples must be
brought into that fold as well. This is not a problem for Paine,
who has always been given Enlightenment status, but it is for
Burke, who has been denied it—indeed, who is convention-
ally associated with the reaction to the Enlightenment—the
"Counter-Enlightenment," as Isaiah Berlin put it.[1] It is not
only critics of Burke who have assigned him this role. Some of
his admirers have as well, seeing in him a welcome antidote to
both the Enlightenment and the French Revolution.

There are a few, but only a few, historians who defy the
conventional view and admit Burke into the Enlightenment—
and not only the Burke (the "young Burke," as is often said)
who wrote the treatise on aesthetics, *The Sublime and Beautiful,*
or the Burke who was an enthusiastic follower of Smith and an
eloquent spokesman for the Americans, but the Burke of
Reflections on the Revolution in France, who was an implacable
opponent of the *philosophes* as well as of the French Revolution. Burke, John Pocock maintains, was "an Enlightened figure, who saw himself defending Enlightened Europe against

the *gens de lettres* and their revolutionary successors"; his was "one kind of Enlightenment in conflict with another."[2] Conor Cruise O'Brien agrees. Burke never attacked the Enlightenment as a whole, and he opposed the French Revolution on liberal and pluralist grounds. "He was himself, intellectually, a child of the early Enlightenment, that of Locke and Montesquieu"; what he was hostile to was the anti-Christian Enlightenment of Voltaire and the "ambiguous and emotion-led neo-religiosity" of Rousseau.[3]

Among Burke's contemporaries, Gibbon, an unexceptionable member of the Enlightenment, professed the highest admiration for Burke. He himself, he said, entirely agreed with Burke on the subject of the French Revolution. "I admire his eloquence, I approve his politics, I adore his chivalry, and I can almost excuse his reverence for church establishments." As if echoing Burke, he went on to give his own view of the spirit that animated the Revolution: "I have sometimes thought of writing a dialogue of the dead, in which Lucian, Erasmus, and Voltaire should mutually acknowledge the danger of exposing an old superstition to the contempt of the blind and fanatic multitude."[4]

If Rousseau and Montesquieu can both be contained within the French Enlightenment, as they normally are in spite of their differences with each other and with the other *philosophes,* one might think that the same latitude could be extended to Burke and Paine in the British Enlightenment. And if the *Reflections* weigh so heavily (and unfairly, it might be argued) in consigning Burke to the anti-Enlightenment, surely his other writings and speeches, which were unquestionably in the spirit of the Enlightenment, deserve more serious consideration than they are often given.

Burke's affinity with Smith, when it is recognized at all, is presumed to be confined to economics. An often quoted but possibly apocryphal remark (it originated with Burke himself) has Smith telling Burke, after a discussion of economics, that "he [Burke] was the only man who, without communication, thought on these topics exactly as he [Smith] did."[5] Later in life, Burke boasted of having been a student of political economy from his early youth, while it was still in its infancy in England and before it had been taken up by "speculative men" on the continent.[6] Both of these claims may have been hyperbolic. But there is little doubt that Burke regarded himself, and was regarded by others, as a disciple of Smith, a proponent of free trade and a free market economy.

It may have been his partiality to Ireland that made Burke so ardent a supporter of free trade, which was in the interests of Ireland. But that could not have been his motive in delivering his speech on "Economical Reformation" in 1780, four years after the publication of the *Wealth of Nations*. If he had any political motive then, it was to reduce the influence of the Crown over Parliament by restricting the funds available for patronage, pensions, and other royal favors. But there were also good economic reasons to urge the reduction of public expenditures and the public debt. Above all, there was the classical Smithian principle, reformulated by Burke, that commerce flourishes best when left to itself and that "all regulations are, in their nature, restrictive of some liberty."[7] Fifteen years later, Burke invoked the same principle in arguing against a bill to regulate wages. "Of all things," his pamphlet *Thoughts and Details on Scarcity* opened, "an indiscreet tampering with the trade of provisions is the most dangerous, and it is always worst in the time when men are most disposed to it; that is, in the time of scarcity." At such a time the proper role of government was to do nothing. "Charity to the poor is a direct and obligatory duty upon all Christians," but "meddling with the subsistence of the people" would be a violation of economic laws and an illegitimate intrusion of authority. Echoing Smith's "invisible hand," Burke paid homage to "the benign and wise disposer of all things, who obliges men, whether they will or not, in pursuing their own selfish interests, to connect the general good with their own individual success."[8]

Burke's views on economics suggest that there may be something like an "Edmund Burke Problem"—a "two Burkes" phenomenon comparable to the "Adam Smith Problem." Just as the altruistic principles of the *Theory of Moral Sentiments* have been thought inconsistent with the individualistic ones of the *Wealth of Nations,* so the laissez-fairism of the *Scarcity* pamphlet may be thought inconsistent with the traditionalism—and even, on occasion, the statism—of the *Reflections.*[9] In both cases, however, the inconsistency was superficial. There were not two Burkes any more than there were two Smiths. The pamphlet on scarcity dealt with a specific economic issue in a specific context; the book on the French Revolution with political and social issues in quite a different context and of a quite different nature.★

Nor was there any inconsistency in Burke's pride in being a disciple of Smith while attacking the "economical politicians," the "sophisters, economists, and calculators," in the French Revolution.[10] These economists, he claimed, perverted the true principles of economics by promoting policies that were inimical to the welfare of the country. In the *Reflections,* he dwelt at length upon measures that amounted to a revolution in property comparable to the revolution in politics: the confiscation of church property, the issuing of *assignats,* the irresponsible mode of coping with the public debt, the encouragement of speculation, and in general the partiality for

---

★ Modern liberals and conservatives have been charged with the same inconsistency, liberals for granting a large measure of state intervention in economic affairs but withholding it in the social realm (family, religion . . .); and conservatives, reversing that formula, being largely libertarian in economics and interventionist in social affairs.

the new "monied interest" at the expense of the old landed interest. Beyond these objections was a still more serious charge, the failure of the revolutionaries to recognize that commercial and economic activities had need of those "natural protecting principles"—nobility, religion, honor, manners—which had traditionally sustained them. A people could exist, Burke said, without trade and manufactures but with its ancient institutions and sentiments. The reverse, however, trade and manufactures in the absence of those civilizing conditions, could only lead to barbarity and ferocity.[11]

Economics was not the only, or the chief, point of resemblance between Smith and Burke—still less the only, or chief, claim of Burke to membership in the Enlightenment. That claim goes back to one of his earliest works, *A Philosophical Enquiry into the Origin of Our Ideas of the Sublime and Beautiful.* Almost twenty years before Smith's *Wealth of Nations,* with its memorable pronouncement about the natural kinship of "a philosopher and a common street porter," Burke opened the introduction to *The Sublime and Beautiful* with a similar observation: "On a superficial view, we [individuals] may seem to differ very widely from each other in our reasonings, and no less in our pleasures; but notwithstanding this difference, which I think to be rather apparent than real, it is probable that the standard both of reason and taste is the same in all human creatures."[12] This idea of the commonality of human nature was a feature of his later works as well. In *The Sublime and Beautiful,* it appeared as "our common nature," the "agreement of mankind," the principles "common to all mankind";[13] in *Reflections,* as "common feelings," "natural feelings," the "wisdom of unlettered men."[14]

For Burke as for Smith, this common nature was prior to reason. It is often supposed that Burke's suspicion of reason was a product of his critique of the French Revolution. In fact, it was a very young Burke who, in his first pamphlet, *A Vindication of Natural Society,* protested against the "abuse of reason." "What would become of the world if the practice of all moral duties, and the foundations of society, rested upon having their reasons made clear and demonstrative to every individual?"[15] In his next work, *The Sublime and Beautiful,* he explained that God "did not confide the execution of his design to the languid and precarious operation of our reason"; instead, "the senses and imagination captivate the soul before the understanding is ready either to join with them or to oppose them."[16] Here, two years before Smith's *Moral Sentiments,* Burke also anticipated Smith on the origin of the social virtues. Burke's section on "Sympathy" reads like an excerpt from Smith's work: "It is by the first of these passions [sympathy] that we enter into the concerns of others; that we are moved as they are moved, and are never suffered to be indifferent spectators of almost anything which men can do or suffer."[17] In his review of *Moral Sentiments,* quoting passages very like this, Burke pronounced the book "one of the most beautiful fabrics of moral theory that has perhaps ever appeared."[18]

The Burke who emerged in the Wilkes affair several years later also belies the conventional image of him. John Wilkes had been expelled from the House of Commons in 1764 for libelling the king in the press and had then been convicted for publishing an obscene poem. Reelected three times by his Middlesex constituency, he was each time refused his seat by Parliament. Instead of excoriating this radical, as a reactionary or even a conservative might have done, Burke vigorously defended him, rejecting the charge of obscenity and criticizing Parliament for defying the expressed will of the electors. Wilkes, he said, had been persecuted by the government and had found favor with the populace simply because he had ventured to oppose the "court cabal." He was pursued not for his vices but for his virtues—"for his unconquerable firmness, for his resolute, indefatigable strenuous resistance against oppression."[19]

For Burke, the case of Wilkes was illustrative of a larger problem, the corruption of Parliament. The great cause of discontent in the previous century, he wrote in 1770, had been "the distempers of monarchy"; now it was "the distempers of Parliament." The usual proposals for reform—universal suffrage, annual parliaments, equal electoral districts—would not avail because they were irrelevant to the real problem, which was the cabal in Parliament that toadied to the king rather than serving the interests of the people and the nation. Indeed, such reforms might actually aggravate the real problem. One of the memorable passages in this essay is often quoted as evidence of Burke's Hobbesian view of society and government: "Our constitution stands on a nice equipoise, with steep precipices and deep waters upon all sides of it. In removing it from a dangerous leaning towards one side, there may be a risk of oversetting it on the other."[20]* But if Burke had been a proper Hobbesian, he would not have been so forthright in exposing the "discontents" of the people and the "distempers" of the government. Nor would he have been so eloquent in defense of the people as against the cabal that ruled them.

> I am not one of those who think that the people are never in the wrong. They have been so, frequently and outrageously, both in other countries and in this. But I do say that in all disputes between them and their rulers, the presumption is at least upon a par in favor of the people. When popular discontents have been very prevalent, it may well be affirmed and supported that

---

* Almost exactly the same passage appeared thirty years later as the concluding sentence of *Reflections*—belying yet again the hypothesis of the "two Burkes," an early and late Burke.

there has been generally something found amiss in the constitution or in the conduct of government. The people have no interest in disorder. When they do wrong, it is their error and not their crime. But with the governing part of the state, it is far otherwise. They certainly may act ill by design as well as by mistake.[21]

Burke's position on India also refutes the thesis of an early liberal Burke superseded by a later conservative one. At the very time that he was inveighing against the French Revolution, he was passionately (obsessively, some of his colleagues thought) denouncing British rule in India, in the person of Warren Hastings, the governor-general. Burke had started that campaign long before in a speech in Parliament attacking the royal charter that had bestowed a monopoly on the East India Company. There was a more primary and sacred charter that the East India Company had grievously violated: "the rights of men—that is to say, the natural rights of mankind."[22] After twenty years of English rule, Burke complained, the conditions of the Indian people were worse than ever. The young Englishmen in the service of the company had no more intercourse with the natives than if they had been residing in England, and no other interest in the country than realizing their own fortunes. "England has erected no churches, no hospitals, no palaces, no schools; England has built no bridges, made no highroads, cut no navigations, dug out no reservoirs." All it had bequeathed to India was an "oppressive, irregular, capricious, unsteady, rapacious, and peculating despotism."[23]

This speech, like others by Burke, was not an argument against commercial venture in India. On the contrary, it was an argument against the politicization of commerce, the creation of a monopoly sanctioned by the British government, thus preventing the normal operation of competition that would have served as a brake on avarice and abuse. Nor was

Burke quarrelling with the idea or practice of imperialism. His was a plea for a benevolent imperialism—a liberal imperialism, it would later be called—an empire worthy of an enlightened England that would respect the rights of the Indian people and the traditions of an ancient civilization.

In the period between the American Revolution and the French Revolution, the subject of India occupied Burke more than any other. He took the lead in the impeachment trial of Warren Hastings in 1788, and when the acquittal finally came, seven years later, he said that if he were to deserve a reward, it would be for the many years in which he had displayed the most industry and had had the least success. Yet even then, in that moment of failure, he deemed this one of the most important causes he had ever undertaken and was proud of his perseverance in pursuing it.[24]

If it is curious that Burke's position on India has not earned him an honorable place in the British Enlightenment, it is even more curious that his position on America has failed to do so. There was a time, not so long ago, when Burke's "Speech on Conciliation with the Colonies," written on the eve of the Revolution, was memorized by schoolchildren in the United States, not only as a model of rhetoric but also as a sympathetic account of the American cause. Yet it does not appear in anthologies of the Enlightenment and is rarely or only slightingly mentioned in books on that subject. In Burke's own time, however, that speech (the word itself is misleading; the "speech" occupies over sixty pages in his collected works), as well as his others on the American Revolution (a volume of them comes to over two hundred pages), were important political events both in America and in England, earning him the respect and admiration even of some radicals.[25]

Half a dozen years before that speech, Burke warned his

countrymen that the conflict with America was assuming revolutionary proportions. Although the Stamp Act of 1765 had been repealed, Parliament was levying new if somewhat less onerous taxes on the colonies. Such restraints were intolerable, Burke said, to a people who were, after all, "descendants of Englishmen, and of a high and free spirit." Just as England could not abandon the principle of sovereignty over America without abandoning the empire, so America could not tolerate the arbitrary exercise of that power. The problem was real, to be addressed not by speculation but by wise policies and politics. And politics, Burke reminded his countrymen (as he was later to tell the French), "ought to be adjusted not to human reasonings but to human nature, of which the reason is but a part, and by no means the greatest part."[26]

England did not follow this counsel of prudence, and the situation rapidly deteriorated. In his memorable "Speech on Conciliation," delivered in March 1775, Burke reminded Parliament once again that the issue could be resolved not by abstract ideas of right or theories of government, but by consulting the nature of the people and the circumstances of the time. Almost in passing he introduced the phrase that has since been so tellingly applied to other situations. England, he said, should return to the policy of "a wise and salutary neglect," which had served the country, and the colonies, so well for so long.[27]

It was not this phrase that made the speech memorable at the time but Burke's account of the "temper and character" of Americans, which fostered their love of liberty. As the descendants of Englishmen, Americans were naturally devoted to liberty—not abstract liberty, but "liberty according to English ideas and on English principles." In America, that liberty took on distinctive characteristics. In the northern colonies, it was the particular form of Protestantism that was especially conducive to liberty; in the South, it was the presence of slaves that made freemen cherish their freedom all the more. And everywhere liberty was shaped and promoted by the provincial legislative assemblies that constituted, in effect, a popular, representative government; by the system of education, particularly the study of the law, that made the people anticipate and resist every infringement on liberty; and by geography, the three thousand miles of ocean that separated them from the mother country.[28]

This analysis of the American temper and character, occupying only half a dozen pages, was astute and remarkably sympathetic. It was the portrait of an enlightened America, as Americans might portray themselves. And it was all the more striking by comparison with Smith's attitude toward America, which was less favorable. In the *Wealth of Nations* (written before the outbreak of war and published the following year), Smith considered the situation largely from a fiscal and economic point of view. America, he advised, should be granted the same rights of free trade that Englishmen enjoyed, while being represented in the British Parliament exactly as Englishmen were. The American leaders, unfortunately, were "ambitious and high-spirited men," who, refusing to be taxed by Parliament, chose instead "to draw the sword in defence of their own importance."[29] In a private memorandum in 1778, Smith predicted that the Americans would come to regret their separation from England and would detest the new government they had violently established in its stead.[30]

While Smith was predicting the failure of the Revolution, Burke was urging his own government, which was pursuing its military campaign in America (and, at the same time, suspending habeas corpus at home), to respect the liberties of both Americans and Englishmen. His argument anticipated that which he was to make many years later on the occasion of another revolution.

Civil freedom, gentlemen, is not, as many have endeavored to persuade you, a thing that lies hid in the depth of abstruse science. It is a blessing and a benefit, not an abstract speculation. . . . Far from any resemblance to those propositions in geometry and metaphysics which admit no medium, but must be true or false in all their latitude, social and civil freedom, like all other things in common life, are variously mixed and modified, enjoyed in very different degrees, and shaped into an infinite diversity of forms, according to the temper and circumstances of every community. The *extreme* of liberty (which is its abstract perfection, but its real fault) obtains nowhere, nor ought to obtain anywhere. . . . For liberty is a good to be improved, and not an evil to be lessened. It is not only a private blessing of the first order, but the vital spring and energy of the state itself, which has just so much life and vigor as there is liberty in it.[31]

America prompted Burke to comment on another subject that was to loom large in the *Reflections.* In the "Speech on Conciliation," he made much of religion as a component of liberty in America. "The people are Protestants," he reminded his countrymen, "and of that kind which is the most adverse to all implicit submission of mind and opinion." All Protestantism was a form of dissent, but the kind prevalent in the northern colonies was "a refinement on the principle of resistance; it is the dissidence of dissent, and the Protestantism of the Protestant religion."[32] This went went well beyond the familiar argument for toleration, which merely advocated the toleration of religious dissent. For Burke, religion itself, and religious dissent most notably, was the very basis of liberty—of all liberty, not only religious liberty. This principle was all the more remarkable because it came from an Anglican (of Irish lineage) who was a vigorous defender of the principle of a religious establishment as well as of religious toleration.

Before the outbreak of the war with America, the English Methodists (then still within the Church of England) had opposed a bill to relieve Dissenters from compulsory subscription to the Thirty-nine Articles of the Anglican creed. Burke defended the bill, reminding the Methodists that the Dissenters were opposed not to established religion but only to atheism. He also took the occasion to argue in favor of toleration for Catholics, a position that some people at the time (and some historians and biographers since) attributed to his "crypto-Catholicism."★ It has even been suggested that Burke was for toleration for Dissenters only because he was for toleration for Catholics. In fact, he favored toleration not only for Dissenters and Catholics but for non-Christians as well. He told the author of a book dedicated to him, who had praised him for supporting the Church of England, that his defense of the establishment did not preclude toleration for other religions. On the contrary, it was consistent with the widest toleration. "I would give a full civil protection, in which I include an immunity from all disturbance of their public religious worship, and a power of teaching in schools as well as temples, to Jews, Mohammedans, and even Pagans, especially if they are already possessed of those advantages by long and prescriptive usage, which is as sacred in this exercise of rights, as in any other." All the more would he extend that

---

★ Burke's father, born a Catholic, had been converted to Anglicanism before Burke's birth, and his son was brought up as an Anglican and remained one. Burke's mother and his wife, although both converted to Anglicanism after their marriages, were thought to have been privately practicing Catholics. Burke himself was suspected of being a Catholic and was sometimes caricatured as a Jesuit.

toleration to all Christian sects, at home and abroad, finding nothing amiss in them but their hatred of each other.[33]

The French Revolution raises once again the specter of two Burkes, the pro-American and anti-French Burkes, the first exemplifying the "soft virtues" of the "Speech on Conciliation"—liberty, compromise, religious toleration; the second the "hard virtues" (if they are deemed to be virtues) of the *Reflections*—authority, tradition, religious establishment. In the final sentences of the *Reflections,* Burke implicitly anticipated the charge of inconsistency. Reflecting on his lifelong struggle for liberty (perhaps with India or America in mind), he spoke of himself as one who maintained his consistency by "varying his means to secure the unity of his end." Reverting to the metaphor he had used earlier, of the vessel whose equipoise was endangered by overloading it on one side, he described his own function as bringing "the small weight of his reasons to that which may preserve its equipoise."[34] Those reasons were, in fact, consistent. In his speeches on America, he had said that the issue should be decided not in terms of "abstract speculation" and "metaphysics," but of the particular "circumstances" of the people and the times.[35] Fifteen years later, he repeated that injunction, more passionately than before, because the metaphysical abstraction had become more abstract and the circumstances more dire.

> I cannot stand forward and give praise or blame to any thing which relates to human actions and human concerns, on a simple view of the object, as it stands stripped of every relation, in all the nakedness and solitude of metaphysical abstraction. Circumstances (which with some gentlemen pass for nothing) give in reality to every political principle its distinguishing color and discriminating effect. The circumstances are what ren-

der every civil and political scheme beneficial or nox-ious to mankind.[36]*

Burke did not (to the great regret of historians) explicitly compare the American and French Revolutions. But he did make a large point of contrasting the French Revolution and the English "Glorious Revolution," a century earlier. The English "Declaration of Rights" of 1688, he pointed out, incorporated, in the same sentence, "the rights and liberties of the subject" and the "succession of the crown," making the two "bound indissolubly together." That declaration did not, *contra* Richard Price and his Revolution Society, sanction any permanent right to resistance. On the contrary, the English Revolution was intended to be a "parent of settlement, and not a nursery of future revolutions."[38]

The settlement, moreover, was intended to perpetuate lib-erty as well as the succession, the hereditary monarchy being the warrant not for the rights of men but for the hereditary rights of Englishmen. These rights belonged to the English as "a patrimony derived from their forefathers," a "hereditary title," a "hereditary right," an "entailed inheritance." They were, indeed, a form of property, enjoying all the security of property, as well as the potential for acquiring additional prop-erty—that is, additional liberties. "The people of England well know that the idea of inheritance furnishes a sure principle of conservation and a sure principle of transmission, without at all excluding a principle of improvement. . . . We receive, we

---

* Coleridge, having earlier (like Wordsworth) accused Burke of betraying his principles, later defended him for being faithful to them. The reader of Burke's writings on the two revolutions, Coleridge wrote, "will find the principles exactly the same and the deductions the same; but the practical inferences almost opposite in the one case from those drawn in the other; yet in both equally legitimate and in both equally confirmed by the results."[37]

hold, we transmit our government and our privileges, in the same manner in which we enjoy and transmit our property and our lives."[39]

The French, Burke conceded, did not have that fortunate "pedigree of liberties." They did have, however (changing the metaphor), the dilapidated walls and foundations of an old edifice. Rather than repairing those walls and building upon those foundations, the revolutionaries chose to tear them all down and build anew. Instead of preserving the "variety of parts" of that old constitution, the "opposed and conflicting interests" that were the basis for a "rational and manly freedom," the French regarded that variety as a blemish to be done away with, to be replaced by the metaphysical abstractions of right and the "delusive plausibilities of moral politicians."[40]

Where the revolutionaries spoke of "rights" and "reason," Burke invoked "virtue" and "wisdom." What made his words more provocative was the qualification he attached to them: "actual or presumptive." "You do not imagine," Burke protested, "that I wish to confine power, authority, and distinction to blood, and names, and titles. No, Sir. There is no qualification for government but virtue and wisdom, actual or presumptive." "Actual" virtue and wisdom were "the passport of heaven to human place and honor."[41] "Presumptive" virtue and wisdom, once removed from the actual, were mediated by property, position, title, or whatever society deemed worthy. For Burke, the actual and the presumptive were not diametrically opposed. On the contrary, they existed in a continuum, the presumptive having as its standard and taking its measure from the actual; and the presumptive, in time, aspiring to become the actual.

Even more provocative was Burke's defense of prejudice. "You see, Sir, that in this enlightened age I am bold enough to confess that we are generally men of untaught feelings;

that instead of casting away all our old prejudices, we cherish them to a very considerable degree, and, to take more shame to ourselves, we cherish them because they are prejudices; and the longer they have lasted, and the more generally they have prevailed, the more we cherish them." There was good reason—indeed, reason itself—for the praise of prejudice. As actual virtue and wisdom existed, for Burke, in a continuum with presumptive virtue and wisdom, so prejudice existed in a continuum with reason. Prejudice itself contained a kind of reason, a "latent wisdom," not the kind of reason that would satisfy the radicals in his own country or the *philosophes* abroad but one that a moral philosopher would recognize and respect.

We are afraid to put men to live and trade each on his own private stock of reason, because we suspect that this stock in each man is small, and that the individuals would do better to avail themselves of the general bank and capital of nations and of ages. Many of our men of speculation, instead of exploding general prejudices, employ their sagacity to discover the latent wisdom which prevails in them. If they find what they seek, and they seldom fail, they think it more wise to continue the prejudice, with the reason involved, than to cast away the coat of prejudice and to leave nothing but the naked reason, because prejudice, with its reason, has a motive to give action to that reason, and an affection which will give it permanence. Prejudice is of ready application in the emergency; it previously engages the mind in a steady course of wisdom and virtue, and does not leave the man hesitating in the moment of decision, skeptical, puzzled, and unresolved. Prejudice renders a man's virtue his habit, and not a series of unconnected acts. Through just prejudice, his duty becomes a part of his nature.[42]

So, too, superstition coexisted in a continuum with religion. In excess, Burke granted, superstition was a great evil. But, like all moral subjects, it was a matter of degree, and in moderate forms, superstition, like prejudice, was a virtue. "Superstition is the religion of feeble minds; and they must be tolerated in an intermixture of it, in some trifling or some enthusiastic shape or other, else you will deprive weak minds of a resource found necessary to the strongest."[43] Burke was not advocating, as some have thought, superstition *pour les autres,* for the lower classes, still less religion *pour les autres.* "Man," he pronounced, "is by constitution a religious animal."[44] All men, the strongest as much as the weakest, had need of religion. The strong, in fact, required it even more than the weak, because they were more exposed to temptation, pride, and ambition, therefore more needful of the consolations as well as the instructions of religion.[45] The church establishment itself was part of this continuum; indeed, it was a form of prejudice—"the first of our prejudices, not a prejudice destitute of reason, but involving in it profound and extensive reason."[46]

Burke's vindication of superstition and prejudice, like his contempt for metaphysical abstractions, have opened him to the charge of having no guiding principles, no philosophy beyond prudence and expediency.[47] Yet there is a philosophy here, a serious and respectable one. He did not use the expression "the Great Chain of Being," but this was the vision that brought together those supposedly disparate elements: reason and prejudice, religion and superstition, manners and morals, authority and liberty, the state and the individual. It was as a proponent of religious toleration that Burke also defended the principle of a church establishment: "Every sort of moral, every sort of civil, every sort of politic institution, aiding the rational and natural ties that connect the human understanding and affections to the divine, are not more than necessary in order to build up that wonderful structure, Man."[48] And it was the disciple of Smith who made the memorable rationale for the state:

The state ought not to be considered as nothing better than a partnership agreement in a trade of pepper and coffee, calico or tobacco, or some other such low concern, to be taken up for a little temporary interest, and to be dissolved by the fancy of the parties. It is to be looked on with other reverence, because it is not a partnership in things subservient only to the gross animal existence of a temporary and perishable nature. It is a partnership in all science; a partnership in all art; a partnership in every virtue and in all perfection. As the ends of such a partnership cannot be obtained in many generations, it becomes a partnership not only between those who are living, but between those who are living, those who are dead, and those who are to be born.[49]

Burke was much ridiculed at the time (and has been since) for his paean to Marie Antoinette, "glittering like the morning star, full of life, and splendor, and joy."[50] The thought of the queen, almost naked, fleeing the mob who had broken into her chamber, prompted reflections about the larger cultural and social significance of that event. "The age of chivalry is gone," he lamented, and with it all the sentiments and principles—loyalty, honor, obedience—which kept alive, "even in servitude itself, the spirit of an exalted freedom."[51] And not only the spirit of freedom, but that of equality.

It was this which, without confounding ranks, had produced a noble equality, and handed it down through all the gradations of social life. It was this opinion which mitigated kings into companions, and raised private men to be fellows with kings. Without force or opposition, it subdued the fierceness of pride and power; it obliged sovereigns to submit to the soft collar of social esteem, compelled stern authority to submit to elegance, and gave a domination, vanquisher of laws, to be subdued by manners.[52]

But all that, Burke feared, was now changed. The age of chivalry had given way to an age of reason, with the most unfortunate consequences.

> All the pleasing illusions which made power gentle and obedience liberal, which harmonized the different shades of life . . . are to be dissolved by this new conquering empire of light and reason. All the decent drapery of life is to be rudely torn off. All the superadded ideas, furnished from the wardrobe of a moral imagination, which the heart owns and the understanding ratifies as necessary to cover the defects of our naked shivering nature and to raise it to dignity in our own estimation, are to be exploded as a ridiculous, absurd, and antiquated fashion.[53]★

★ It is generally assumed that Paine's famous charge that Burke "pities the plumage but forgets the dying bird"[54] referred to the poor, whom Burke had forgotten in his zeal for the queen. In fact, Paine was speaking of the prisoners in the Bastille, aristocrats as often as not, who had fallen out of favor with the king. Political tyranny, not economic misery, was the subject of Paine's metaphor.

Burke has also been criticized for calling the populace "the swinish multitude." Conor Cruise O'Brien points out that Burke spoke of "a swinish multitude," a particular mob on a particular occasion, not the people as a whole.[55] Burke himself quoted Richard Price (whose sermon to the Revolutionary Society provoked the *Reflections*), who referred to the few thousand voters paid to vote as "the dregs of the people."[56]

This, finally, was at the heart of Burke's indictment of the French Revolution. Unlike the American Revolution, which was a political revolution, the French Revolution, he insisted, was nothing less than a moral revolution, a total revolution, a revolution of sentiment and sensibility penetrating into every aspect of life. Burke is often accused today (as he was in his time) of being excessive, even hysterical, in his description of that revolution: "a ferocious dissoluteness in manners . . . an insolent irreligion in opinions and practices . . . laws over-turned, tribunals subverted, industry without vigor, commerce expiring . . . a church pillaged . . . civil and military anar-chy . . . national bankruptcy. . . ."[57] All this, it must be remem-bered, was written in 1790, well before the creation of the republic, the execution of the king and queen, the declaration of war, and the institution of the Terror. Yet much had hap-pened by 1790 to alarm Burke: the storming of the Bastille, the march to Versailles and removal of the king to Paris, the abolition of the nobility and feudal privileges, the confiscation of church property, the Civil Constitution of the Clergy, the *jacqueries* in the countryside and riots in towns, prisons liber-ated, runs on the banks, and the devastating effects upon the schools, charities, hospitals, and all the other functions tradi-tionally performed by the church.* What is remarkable is not that Burke reacted so strongly, and adversely, to these events,

---

* Few contemporaries (and not many historians) paid attention, as Burke did, to one of the anti-clerical measures adopted by the Revolution, the act making marriage a civil contract, with divorce permitted at a month's notice and "at the mere pleasure of either party." The result, Burke noted, was a precipitous rise in the divorce rate. In the first three months of 1793, there were 562 divorces in Paris compared with 1,785 marriages, a ratio, he calculated, of almost one to three—"a thing unexampled, I believe, among mankind."[58]

but that many thoughtful people (and not only young poets like Shelley or Wordsworth) took so benign a view of them.

Even more remarkable is Burke's anticipation of the more momentous events that were to come. Regicide, war, and terror are all prefigured in the *Reflections,* as if they had already happened. Burke took the measure of the Revolution at the outset. It was then, when the Paris mob marched to Versailles and seized the king, that "the most important of all revolutions" took place, "a revolution in sentiments, manners, and moral opinions." This moral revolution was later to become the rationale and dynamic of the Terror, an event that Burke dramatically foretold. "Justifying perfidy and murder for public benefit, public benefit would soon become the pretext, and perfidy and murder the end; until rapacity, malice, revenge, and fear more dreadful than revenge could satiate their insatiable appetites."[59]★

It was this powerful moral imagination, rather than any political ideology, that was Burke's distinctive contribution not only to the analysis of the French Revolution but to the British Enlightenment itself. This is why "liberal" and "conservative" do not adequately describe his response to such events as the Wilkes affair and the Hastings impeachment, the American Revolution and the French Revolution. The moral philosophers posited a moral sentiment in man as the basis of the social virtues. Burke took this philosophy a step further, by making the "sentiments, manners, and moral opinions" of men the basis of society itself, and, ultimately, of the polity as well.

★ Pocock goes so far as to say that Burke anticipated not only the Terror but such monstrosities of our own time as Nazism, the Red Guards, and the Khmer Rouge. Burke's *Letters on a Regicide Peace,* describing the "dreadful energy" of the Revolution which liberated the human intellect from all social restraints, was "the *1984* of its generation." In that work, Pocock says, Burke "had discovered the theory of totalitarianism and was enlarging it into prophecy."[60]

4. RADICAL DISSENTERS

While Edmund Burke is rarely admitted into the pantheon of the British Enlightenment, his critics, commonly labelled radicals, are firmly entrenched there. Yet they make strange bedfellows with the moral philosophers who were the charter members, as it were, of the Enlightenment. Richard Price and Joseph Priestley wrote books that were explicitly directed against Francis Hutcheson and the Scottish school of philosophy.[1] And Thomas Paine and William Godwin made reason so preeminent as to leave little or no room for anything like a moral sense. Philosophically and theologically, as well as politically, they were far removed from the Enlightenment of Shaftesbury and Hutcheson, Smith and Hume.*

---

* Jeremy Bentham is usually included among these radicals. But at this time he was neither a radical nor a public figure of note. He opposed parliamentary reform at home, to say nothing of republicanism, and derided such French revolutionary measures as the confiscation of church property and the Declaration of the Rights of Man; indeed, he ridiculed the very idea of "rights." His own writings attracted little attention. He later claimed that his *Fragment on Government,* published anonymously in 1776, created a "sensation." In fact, only five hundred copies were printed, and a large number of these were later found in a warehouse. His *Introduction to the Principles of Morals and Legislation,* in 1789, "passed unnoticed," Elie

It might even be said that these radicals belong more to the history of the French and American Enlightenments than to the British. Paine spent much of his adult life in America and France, and was a member, not of the British Parliament but of the French National Convention. Even after his imprisonment during the Terror and the withdrawal of his French citizenship, he remained in France, returning, finally, not to England but to America, where he died. Priestley was awarded an honorary seat in the National Assembly but chose to live in America rather than France; he, too, died in America. Price and Godwin did live out their lives in England, as ardent sympathizers of the French Revolution. Godwin's great work had more in common with Condorcet than with any of his own compatriots.

One historian refers to Price and his associates as "late Enlightenment luminaries," to distinguish them, presumably, from the other luminaries.[3] Yet this chronological distinction is deceptive. Smith and Price were almost exact contemporaries (both were born in 1723, and Price died a year after Smith, in 1791). Burke was younger than both and survived them both, and was only several years older than Priestley and Paine. Adam Ferguson, born the same year as Smith and Price, outlived them all. Only Godwin was of a distinctively later generation. What differentiated the two groups was not their age but their ideas. The radicals did not represent a late Enlightenment in Britain so much as an alternative Enlightenment—a "dissident" Enlightenment, in the political as well as theological sense of that word.

In the preface to his very first work, Burke made one of his

Halévy remarked. And his book on the Panopticon two years later, printed at his own expense, was generally ignored. It was not until 1808, when he met James Mill, that he came into his own. "Philosophical Radicalism" was Bentham's distinctive contribution—to the early nineteenth century, however, rather than the late eighteenth.[2]

prescient observations: "The same engines which were employed for the destruction of religion might be employed with equal success for the subversion of government."[4] Thirty-odd years later, he had reason to recall that remark, as the French Enlightenment gave way to the French Revolution—the destruction of religion, as he saw it, culminating in the subversion of government. The English radicals had already set out on that path. Unlike Hume, who never translated his religious skepticism into religious radicalism (the disestablishment of the church), still less into political radicalism (republicanism), these radicals—"rational dissenters," as they were known—pursued their religious dissent as vigorously as their political dissent. Indeed, both were part of a single agenda.[5] They sought to illegitimize the political order to the same degree, and for the same reasons, as the religious establishment.

Paine was a deist of a familiar, if extreme form, his deism verging on a rationalism that allowed for the largest claims of reason in religious as well as in political affairs. Price's Unitarianism had a more theological basis. A convert to Arianism, he combined that with a Lockeanism that he took to be the political analogue of Arianism, free will and reason joining together to assure the religious autonomy of the individual and the political liberty of the citizen.[6] Priestley took a different heretical turn, toward Socinianism rather than Arianism and toward materialism rather than rationalism; thus, he rejected both the the divinity of Christ and free will.

The three also differed on their attitude to republicanism. Priestley, often credited with originating the utilitarian principle of the greatest happiness of the greatest number, was less concerned with the participation of the people in government ("political liberty," as he put it) than with their personal liberty ("civil liberty"); political liberty had the secondary role of guarding and guaranteeing civil liberty. Thus, he was less insistent than Paine or Price upon a republican form of government.[7] But the three of them were at one, and

were generally viewed as such, in rejecting the existing political as well as religious order and in welcoming a radical reformation that would subvert both.

The quarrel between Burke and Price has been immortalized
in the *Reflections*. But it had its origins fifteen years earlier at
the time of the American Revolution, when Price published
his *Observations on the Nature of Civil Liberty*, defending the
Americans on the same principles he was later to invoke in
praise of the French—and in disparagement of the English. It
is generally assumed that Burke had this book in mind two
years later (although he did not mention Price by name)
when he criticized those who conceived of free government
in terms of "metaphysical liberty and necessity" rather than
"moral prudence and natural feeling." Because he himself
was so strongly identified with the American cause, he may
have felt it necessary to dissociate himself from writers like
Price, who called any government not willed by the people a
"tyranny and usurpation."[8]

This exchange (so to speak) between Price and Burke on
the subject of America was prophetic, for it was in almost
exactly the same terms that they conducted the great debate
on the French Revolution. Price's sermon in 1789, "The Love
of Our Country," ostensibly commemorating the English Revolution a century earlier but actually eulogizing the French,
might well have gone unnoticed (certainly for posterity, if not
for contemporaries) had it not provoked Burke's *Reflections*.
Price criticized England for violating what he took to be the
basic rights established by its revolution: religious liberty, resistance to the abuse of power, and self-government. The last was
belied, he claimed, by the inequality of representation, a defect
in the constitution so gross and palpable as to vitiate legitimate
government and make of the existing government "nothing
but an usurpation." It was time, he declared, for an "amend-

ment" in human affairs: "the dominion of kings changed for the dominion of laws, and the dominion of priests giving way to the dominion of reason and science." His peroration must have been especially pleasing to the French National Assembly, to whom he sent the sermon together with a congratulatory message. "Tremble all ye oppressors of the world! Take warning all ye supporters of slavish governments and slavish hierarchies! . . . Struggle no longer against increasing light and liberality. Restore to mankind their rights and consent to the correction of abuses, before they and you are destroyed together."[9]

An advocate of free trade and minimal government, Price regarded himself as a disciple of Smith. But Smith did not so regard him. Shortly after Price's sermon, Smith appended to a new edition of *The Theory of Moral Sentiments* two sections implicitly directed against Price, one criticizing the principle of reason as the basis of morality, the other refuting the idea that "the love of our own country" derived from "the love of mankind."[10] Privately, Smith was even more derogatory. "I have always considered him," he wrote to an economist friend, "a factious citizen, a most superficial philosopher, and by no means an able calculator [economist]."[11]

It remains something of an embarrassment to latter-day radicals that Price, Priestley, and Paine all professed to be disciples of Smith. In fact, Priestley was more laissez-fairist than Smith himself. Taking it as the fundamental maxim of political economy that the state not interfere in the economy, Priestley deduced from this principle (as Smith did not) that the Poor Laws should be abolished. A state provision for the poor, he argued, taxed the industrious and rewarded the idle, encouraging the poor to become improvident and spend everything in the most extravagant manner, knowing that the state would provide for them. Lacking all prudence and foresight, they were reduced to the condition of beasts. It would have been better, Priestley concluded, if government had not interfered with the poor at all, the needy being sufficiently taken care of by the charity of the well disposed.[12] Nor should the government interfere (as Smith had proposed) in the education of children; every man should be free to educate his children "in his own way."[13] By the same token, the government should have no part in religion. Again, unlike Smith, for whom religious liberty meant religious toleration and a plurality of sects, Priestley insisted upon nothing less than the disestablishment of the Church of England.

Paine, too, opposed the Poor Laws, and for the same reasons, because they penalized industriousness and caused an unwanted intrusion of the state into the economy. But it was not only the economy that he wanted to protect from the state; it was society itself. *Common Sense,* published in America shortly before its Revolution, and *Rights of Man,* published in England shortly after the French Revolution (in rebuttal to Burke's *Reflections*), were vigorous defenses of both revolutions in the name of reason and rights. They also contained trenchant arguments for a minimal government based upon a sharp distinction between society and state.

> Society is produced by our wants and government by our wickedness; the former promotes our happiness *positively* by uniting our affections, the latter *negatively* by restraining our vices.[14]

> Society is in every state a blessing, but government, even in its best state, is but a necessary evil.[15]

> It is but few general laws that civilized life requires, and those of such common usefulness that whether they are enforced by the forms of government or not, the effect will be nearly the same.[16]

Society performs for itself almost everything which is ascribed to government.[17]

These passages go well beyond Smith in their distrust of government. The *Wealth of Nations,* published only months after *Common Sense,* treated government respectfully, assigning it such important "positive" functions as the military protection of society (the invention of firearms, for example, which might seem to be pernicious, was "certainly favorable both to the permanency and to the extension of civilization"); the administration of justice, upon which depended the liberty as well as security of every individual; and the provision of public works and institutions (such as schools for the poor) which were beyond the resources of individuals or groups.[18] Even on the subject of taxation, Smith was far more moderate than Paine, distinguishing different kinds of taxes in terms of equity and efficiency.

Paine, on the other hand, regarded government itself as little more than an instrument for raising taxes. Monarchy was "a mere court artifice to procure money"; the English constitution was "the most productive machine for taxation that was ever invented"; "taxes were not raised to carry on wars, but . . . wars were raised to carry on taxes."[19] In contrast to Burke's theory of the state as "a partnership not only between those who are living, but between those who are living, those who are dead, and those who are to be born," Paine posited a radical disjunction of past, present, and future. The living, he insisted, owed nothing to the dead. Each "generation" was a new "creation," beholden only to itself.[20] He even went beyond Price, who illegitimized the English constitution because it did not fulfill the promise of the Glorious Revolution. Paine illegitimized it at its birth, so to speak, as the product of conquest rather than reason. William III could not atone for the original sin of William the Conqueror.

The second part of *Rights of Man,* published in 1792, was even more subversive than the first—and more successful, partly because the price had been reduced from three shillings to sixpence, and partly because of the publicity resulting from Paine's flight to Paris following his indictment on the charge of seditious libel. In denouncing the monarchy—any monarchy—as illegitimate and tyrannical, Paine in effect sanctioned revolution, compounding the offense a few months later in a pamphlet calling for a convention to draft a republican constitution—this while England was engaged in war with France.

If Smith would have been appalled by the revolutionary message of *Rights of Man,* he would have been pleased by some of its reflections on commerce and self-interest.

All the great laws of society are laws of nature. Those of trade and commerce, whether with respect to the intercourse of individuals, or of nations, are laws of mutual and reciprocal interest. They are followed and obeyed because it is the interest of the parties to do so, and not on account of any formal laws their governments may impose or interpose.[21]

I have been an advocate for commerce, because I am a friend to its effects. It is a pacific system, operating to unite mankind by rendering nations, as well as individuals, useful to each other. . . . The most effectual process is that of improving the condition of man by means of his own interest; and it is on this ground that I take my stand. If commerce were permitted to act to the universal extent it is capable of, it would extirpate the system of war and produce a revolution in the uncivilized state of government.[22]

A very different Paine, however, emerged in the final pages of the second part of *Rights of Man*. Just as Smith, toward the end of the *Wealth of Nations,* seemed to reverse course by suddenly presenting the image of workers so debilitated by the division of labor as to necessitate a state-supported educational system, so Paine, toward the end of his book, took a turn that appeared to belie the principles he had expounded earlier. After arguing, for two hundred–odd pages, in favor of a society liberated from government by a free economy, a flourishing commerce, and the absence of taxes, Paine introduced an elaborate program of social reform that required the active intervention of government and the imposition of new taxes. In place of the Poor Laws, he proposed a comprehensive welfare system to be subsidized by the government, including a budget worked out in precise bookkeeping detail. The plan was designed for "that class of poor which need support"—one fifth of the population, Paine estimated (which was larger than the current class of paupers). It provided allowances for poor children and the aged, with different sums for those of different ages; education grants for children who did not qualify as poor but who could not afford schooling; birth and marriage stipends for those who applied for them; funeral expenses for people who died away from home; and workhouses to employ and if necessary house and feed the "casual poor." All of this was to be financed partly by excise taxes (which would eventually be phased out), but largely by a system of progressive taxation on estates, ranging from 3d per pound on the first £500 to a confiscatory 20s per pound at the highest level. Thus, the Poor Laws ("those instruments of civil torture") would be replaced by a system that would provide relief not as a charity but as "a right."[23]

Paine must have been aware of the contrast between his proposals and Smith's. Smith, too, had favored a system of progressive taxation (although not a confiscatory one) that would benefit the poor, with taxes on luxuries rather than necessities, a land tax but not a window tax, and taxes on the salaries of higher officials but not on the wages of workers. And the Poor Laws he approved of were intended only for paupers, not, like Paine's plan, for the far larger class of the poor. In one respect, Smith's was the bolder proposal: his education scheme called for government subsidies and supervision, whereas Paine's provided for education allowances to parents who would be responsible for finding teachers for their children. "Distressed clergymen's widows," he suggested, would suit that purpose.[24]

To some historians, Paine's program was a harbinger of the "welfare state," a "state system of social security," even "social democracy."[25] It differed from them, however, in one crucial feature. Where the welfare state and social security, to say nothing of social democracy, are "across the board" programs, designed for the population as a whole, Paine's was intended specifically for the "class of poor." Nor did Paine's later pamphlet, *Agrarian Justice,* bring him, as one historian claims, "to the threshold of socialism."[26] So far from seeking the abolition of private property, Paine was writing in rebuttal to "Gracchus" Babeuf, who favored an "Agrarian Law" that would have done just that. Defending the principle of the private ownership of land, Paine proposed only some measure of redistribution by way of taxation and allowances.

If the economic views of the British radicals do not conform to present-day notions of radicalism, some of their religious views may be still more disconcerting—or would be, were they more widely known—to those who celebrate them as the apostles of reason. Paine was the more familiar type of rational dissenter. "I believe in one God, and no more," he announced in the opening pages of *Age of Reason.* "I do not believe in the creed professed by the Jewish church, by the Roman church, by the Greek church, by the Turkish church, by the Protestant church, nor by any church that I know of. My own mind is my own church."[27] His own mind was so self-sufficient that he boasted he did not own a copy of the Bible. He apparently acquired one, however, before writing the second part of that book, because there he engaged in a systematic refutation of the scriptures, including a denial of the miracles of the Bible, of revelation, and, finally, of Christianity itself (but not, he added, the idea of God).

This was rational dissent in its classic form. But Price and Priestley were decidedly not in this genre, although the term is often applied to them and may even have originated with them. Nor can their religious beliefs be dismissed as the amiable, inconsequential eccentricities of otherwise rational men. Those beliefs were, in fact, at the heart of their radical-ism—their political as well as religious radicalism.[28] Priestley himself wrote a critique of *Age of Reason,* agreeing with Paine in rejecting the Trinity and divinity of Christ, but ardently affirming the Bible as the product of divine revelation. In-deed, both Price and Priestley were obsessed by religion, not in the sense that an aggressively anti-religious thinker may be said to be obsessed by it, making a religion of irreli-gion, but in a truly religious sense. They were as passionate in pursuing scriptural evidence for the millennium—a spiritual and temporal millennium in one—as they were in their opposition to any established church. William Hazlitt called Priestley "the Voltaire of Unitarianism."[29] But Voltaire would have been appalled by Priestley's apocalyptic millenarianism based upon a literal reading of biblical prophecies as revealed truth.

For Price, as for Priestley, the rebellion against a religious establishment was based as much upon religion itself as upon reason. The disestablishment of the church was to be accom-panied by the overthrow of the monarchy and the dissolution of all civil and ecclesiastical authorities, thus preparing the way for the millennium, complete with the resurrection of Christ and of all mankind. Price's account of the American Revolution as portending the final stage of history, when the "old prophecies would be verified" and "the last universal empire" of reason, virtue, and peace would be established,[30] may sound like the "city on a hill" credo of American evangelicals. But it went beyond that in affirming, not symbolically or figuratively but literally, the coming of the millennium, not in the distant future but in the present, and not in an otherworld but on this earth. Sedulously scouring the scriptures for prophecies and catastrophes, Price related them to current events and to the imminent appearance of the Messiah, who would come "in glory to abolish death, to judge mankind, to execute justice on the wicked, and to establish an everlasting kingdom, in which all the virtuous and worthy shall meet, and be completely and unchangeably happy."[31]

Priestley's millenarianism was even more remarkable than Price's, not only because he himself was a respected scientist (a chemist), but also because he combined millenarianism with the rigorously materialistic and deterministic philosophy of his mentor, David Hartley. Now remembered as the father of associational psychology, Hartley was also (this is less well known) a fervent believer in the literal, empirical truth of scriptural prophecy. Like Hartley (but unlike Price), Priestley rejected the dualism of mind and matter and with it the idea of free will. But he believed all the more in the resurrection of Christ, the details of which he disputed at some length with Price. For Price, the soul did not die with the death of the body but only slept, awaiting resurrection; for Priestley, the resurrection was all the more miraculous because the soul, inseparable from the body, had died with the body.

It is ironic that Burke's conventional, latitudinarian idea of religion should have disqualified him (for many historians) from membership in the Enlightenment, whereas the millenarianism of Priestley and Price did not. Their millenarianism, moreover, was not the bland utopianism that infected so many radicals. Nor was it inspired by the heady experiences of the American and French Revolutions, for it long predated those events. "Whatever was the beginning of this world," Priestley had predicted in 1768, "the end will be glorious and paradisiacal, beyond what our imaginations can now conceive." A few years later, he foresaw the downfall of church and state leading to "some very calamitous, but finally glorious, events."[32] At the height of the Terror in France, and from the safety of his home in America, Priestley wrote of himself, in the third person: "The Declaration of Rights in one hand, and the Book of Revelation in the other, Priestley awaited the imminent fall of the Papacy and the Ottoman Empire and the return of Jews to Judea."[33] The Bible also confirmed him in the assurance that all the monarchies in Europe would be destroyed: the ten horns of the great beast in Revelation corresponded to the ten crowned heads of Europe, the first of those horns falling off with the execution of the king of France. Even this scenario—the destruction of the papacy and monarchy and the repatriation of Jews—was relatively restrained compared with his prediction of the return, within twenty years, of Christ to earth.[34] He regretted that he himself might not live to see that glorious event, but he comforted Benjamin Rush (the noted American physician and signer of the Declaration of Independence) with the thought that Rush was probably young enough to witness it.[35]

William Godwin also looked forward to a millennium—a thoroughly secular one, however. He was more truly a rational dissenter than the others because his vision of the future was based upon an idea of reason that left no room for any religion, even natural religion, let alone for the revelations of the Bible. He was also more radical than the others, his commitment to liberty being as absolute as his commitment to reason. His major work, published in 1793—*An Enquiry Concerning Political Justice, and Its Influence on General Virtue and Happiness*—professed to be based upon a universal science of politics and morals, a demonstration of "the one best mode of social existence" for all of mankind, where all individuals would be perfectly free and perfectly rational.[36]

Unlike the other radicals, who subscribed to one or another version of deism, Godwin was an avowed atheist. Where they called themselves disciples of Smith, Godwin abhorred the very idea of political economy, dismissing the interests motivating any political economy as immoral and irrational.[37] Where they recommended, at most, a partial redistribution of property, Godwin proposed the entire abolition of private property. Where they sought to replace monarchical government with republican government, Godwin wanted to do away with government itself. And not only government, but all the institutions created by government: constitutions, laws, juries, courts, contracts, prisons, punishments, schools. And not only the institutions of government, but those of society: religion, marriage, the family. And not only these official and quasi-official institutions, but all collective or cooperative enterprises, whether voluntary or compulsory, having to do with either work or leisure. Concerts and plays, for example, were oppressive because rational men had no desire to "repeat words and ideas not their own," to "execute the compositions of others," or to engage in activities requiring an "absurd and vicious cooperation."[38]

The principle behind all these injunctions and proscriptions was the sovereignty of reason. Only in the absence of all oppressive institutions (and all institutions were, by nature, oppressive) could mankind be thoroughly rational—and, being rational, also virtuous, free, and equal. There would be no passion or prejudice to inhibit the intellect, no error or false-hood to stand in the way of the truth, no self-love or self-interest to interfere with benevolence, no acquisitiveness or competitiveness to undermine equality, no coercion or coop-eration to restrict individuality. Without families to divert them from their higher obligations, individuals would be able to devote themselves to humanity at large. And without mar-riage (that "most odious" of all institutions) or other con-tracts to bind them to a future course of action, they would be rational and free at every moment of their lives.[39]

In a much quoted and criticized passage, Godwin illus-trated his "science of morals" by positing a situation in which the philosopher Fénelon and his chambermaid were trapped in a fire and only one of them could be rescued. Godwin had no doubt that it should be Fénelon, because he was more worthy and important than the maid, just as a man was more worthy and important than a beast. The choice would be the same if the chambermaid happened to be the rescuer's wife or mother. "What magic is there in the pronoun 'my' to overturn the decisions of everlasting truth? My wife or my mother may be a fool or a prostitute, malicious, lying or dis-honest. If they be, of what consequence is it that they are mine?"[40] In the second edition of *Political Justice,* hoping to pacify his critics, Godwin changed the chambermaid to a valet, and the wife or mother who might be a prostitute to a brother or father who might be profligate.

Toward the end of the book, contemplating the inven-tions that would enable one man to do what now required the cooperative effort of many (half an hour a day, he pre-dicted, would suffice to provide all of a person's needs), God-win cited the "conjecture" of Benjamin Franklin that "mind would one day become omnipotent over matter." Carrying out that thought (to a point hardly intended by Franklin), Godwin suggested that just as political and social affairs could be conducted in a purely voluntary manner, so could all bodily functions. "If volition can now do something, why should it not go on to do still more and more?" If it could cure all our social ills, surely it could cure our physical and mental ills as well. The result would be an infinite prolongation of life and the "total extirpation of the infirmities of our nature"—disease, sleep, languor, anguish, melancholy, resentment.[41]

With the extirpation of all those infirmities would come, finally, the extirpation of that other infirmity: sexuality. Godwin opened his book with the self-evident principle that "the happiness of the human species is the most desirable object for human science to promote; and that intellectual and moral happiness or pleasure is extremely to be preferred to those which are precarious and transitory."[42] By the end of the book it appeared that sex was the most "precarious and transitory" of pleasures. "The tendency of a cultivated and virtuous mind is to render us indifferent to the gratification of sense," especially that of a "mere animal function." Thus, an enlightened mankind could look forward to the diminution and eventual elimination of sexuality. Anticipating the obvious objection that this would soon lead to the elimination of mankind itself, Godwin introduced an even bolder proposition: that men might become immortal. He did not commit himself to this as a certainty, only as a real possibility within the lifetime of "the present race of men."

The men therefore who exist when the earth shall refuse itself to a more extended population will cease to propagate, for they will no longer have any motive, either of error or duty, to induce them. In addition to this they will perhaps be immortal. The whole will be a people of men, and not of children. Generation will not succeed generation, nor truth have in a certain degree to recommence her career at the end of every thirty years. . . . There will be no war, no crimes, no administration of justice, as it is called, and no government. Beside this, there will be neither disease, anguish, melancholy, nor resentment. Every man will seek, with ineffable ardor, the good of all.[43]

After this heady vision of perfectibility, it was anticlimactic to be told that this was a matter of "probable conjecture," which did not affect the "grand argument" of the rest of the book.[44] This disclaimer, coming in the final sentence of the chapter, was too belated and tentative to detract from the dramatic image of mankind in a perfect and perpetual state of reason, virtue, and freedom. Moreover, that promise of perfectibility had pervaded the entire book. From the very beginning, Godwin pronounced the distinctive characteristic of man to be his "perfectibility."[45]

In later editions, Godwin qualified some of these pronouncements. In 1796, he reaffirmed the principle of perfectibility, stopping short, however, of predicting the total elimination of sleep, disease, and death. Two years later, he slightly softened the condemnation of feelings, affections, even sensual and sexual pleasures. Marriage, for example, was slightly demoted, from being the "most odious" of all monopolies to being the "worst." He even conceded that marriage could become a "salutary and respectable institution" if it allowed for liberty and "repentance" (presumably divorce).[46]

What intervened between the first and third editions was Godwin's meeting and love affair with the writer Mary Wollstonecraft. She had achieved some celebrity in 1790 with her *Vindication of the Rights of Men,* the first of several replies to Burke's *Reflections,* anticipating Paine's *Rights of Man* and establishing her credentials as an intellectual and a radical. Written in great haste (it appeared within weeks of the *Reflections*), her book was not so much an analysis of the rights of men—"men" in the plural—as a rambling, repetitive, passionate attack on Burke.★ Her *Vindication of the Rights of Woman* two years later ("woman" in the singular, perhaps modelled on Paine's *Rights of Man*) was no more cohesive or systematic. Here Rousseau was the villain, his idea of education being especially objectionable because it consigned women to an inferior, domestic role—a role, Wollstonecraft bitterly reported, that most women accepted all too willingly. Few writers at the time, a recent editor of that work observes, were as critical of women. "She did not like women as they were. Indeed, that is putting it far too mildly. At times she seemed to despise her sex. What she wanted above all was nothing short of a transformation of women into their opposite."[48] Like Professor Higgins in Shaw's *Pygmalion,* she wanted women to become like men, or, rather, like men at their best—rational, independent, well educated; only then would they be good wives, mothers, and citizens. (Education was a prominent theme in her book, and by far the most original and interesting part.)

Godwin was forty and Wollstonecraft thirty-seven when they met. He was a bachelor and almost certainly celibate. She had an illegitimate child from an earlier affair and had something of a reputation for promiscuity. The well-known author of the scientific tome that denigrated emotions and

---

★ Yet four years later, in her history of the French Revolution, she echoed Burke in criticizing the "rabble" who engaged in all manners of "barbarity." She was especially harsh on the women who had marched on Versailles: "the lowest refuse of the streets, women who had thrown off the virtues of one sex without having power to assume more than the vices of the other." And her sympathetic description of the queen, violated by the mob in "the chaste temple of a woman," might almost have been written by Burke.[47]

sexuality as irrational and immoral found himself writing love letters that were almost a parody of the form. The scandal was not their liaison—although that was hardly consistent with his views of sexuality—but their marriage (that "most odious" institution) a year later when she became pregnant. She died giving birth to the child. A few years later Godwin remarried, acquiring, along with a not very congenial wife, a substantial family entailing considerable financial obligations and involving him, in spite of his principled objections to commerce, in several unsuccessful publishing ventures.

The rest of Godwin's life was no less at odds with his great work. He doted on his daughter Mary, and was dismayed when, at the age of sixteen, she ran off with Shelley, who was married and a father. Shelley, a great admirer of Godwin, acting on his mentor's professed principles—the pursuit of freedom and happiness and the contempt for such oppressive conventions as monogamy or marriage—left his pregnant wife and took up residence with Mary, with whom he eventually had three children (while also having affairs with at least one, and possibly two, of her stepsisters). Godwin was unreconciled to this ménage and refused to see his grandson until, two years later, after Shelley's wife had committed suicide, Shelley reluctantly agreed to marry Mary. Relating this happy event to his brother, Godwin boasted of his daughter's marriage to the eldest son of a baronet. "You will wonder, I daresay," he wrote, "how a girl without a penny of fortune should meet with so good a match. . . . For my part I care but little, comparatively, about wealth, so that it should be her destiny in life to be respectable, virtuous, and contented."[49] If these sentiments were inconsistent with his principles, his behavior was even more so. So far from caring little about Shelley's wealth, he cared enough about it to make repeated, and successful, demands for money—this even before the marriage, when they were barely on speaking terms.

Godwin had hoped to realize Benjamin Franklin's dream

of the triumph of mind over matter. Instead, he experienced the triumph of matter (the exigencies of his own life) over the creations of his own mind. This dramatic personal story may distract attention from the true drama of *Political Justice,* which looked forward to a polity that denied the very idea of polity (government, law, property, political economy), and envisaged a reformed humanity that defied the very idea of human nature (fallibility, mortality, sexuality, family). In his last important work, a four-volume history of England, Godwin reluctantly conceded the improbability of his millennial visions. "It is comparatively easy for the philosopher in his closet to invent imaginary schemes of policy, and to show how mankind, if they were without passions and without prejudices, might best be united in the form of a political community." Unfortunately, he added, "men in all ages are the creatures of passion."[50]★

If it is difficult to understand how Godwin could have entertained these illusions, it is even more difficult to understand why so many of his contemporaries were taken in by them. *Political Justice* appeared at a most inauspicious time, in Febru-

---

★ Living to the ripe age of eighty, Godwin had ample time to reconsider his not so youthful fantasies. Condorcet never had that opportunity, having personally fallen victim to them. His *Sketch for a Historical Picture of the Progress of the Human Mind,* written shortly after Godwin's work, was animated by the same vision of perfectibility—moral, intellectual, and physical. Like Godwin, he anticipated a time, in the not distant future, when men would be sufficiently rational to overcome their sensuality and devote themselves to the welfare of mankind rather than "foolishly to encumber the world with useless and wretched beings."[51] Written while he was hiding from the Terror (his enthusiasm for the Revolution stopped short of regicide), the book was published posthumously in 1795 after he died in prison.

ary 1793, after France declared war on Britain and radicalism of any kind smacked of sedition. (Paine had been indicted and had fled to Paris only weeks before.) Yet the book was instantly hailed as a masterpiece and Godwin declared a genius. Three thousand copies of the two large volumes were sold at the considerable price of three guineas—which may have been its salvation, for the prime minister, William Pitt, refrained from proscribing it on the grounds that it could do no harm to those "who had not three shillings to spare."[52] Although it did reach some of the poor in cheap pirated editions and extracts, it had its greatest success among intellectuals. In London and at the universities, it was greeted as a new dispensation, with Wordsworth, Southey, and Coleridge declaring themselves Godwin's disciples. His novel *Adventures of Caleb Williams,* published the following year and expressing some of the same views, was also enthusiastically received. Within a few years, however, the tide turned, partly because of the mockery caused by his private life, but also because events in France and at home created a more sober intellectual and political climate. It was only then that some of his most ardent admirers began to repudiate his views, as he himself, although only partially and regretfully, was eventually to do.

The initial popularity of *Political Justice,* however, takes some explaining. Some of its most audacious precepts seemed all the more plausible because they were familiar, carrying to the logical conclusion principles enunciated by his predecessors. As early as 1757, in his first book, Price announced that "reason alone, did we possess it in a higher degree," was the basis for all human relations. "There would be no need of the parental affection were all parents sufficiently acquainted with the reasons for taking upon them the guidance and support of those whom nature has placed under their care, and were they virtuous enough to be always determined by those reasons."[53] Similarly, Paine's disparagement of government—"society is produced by our wants and government by our wickedness"—

came close to illegitimizing all government, providing the rationale for Godwin's anarchic view of the state.★ So, too, Priestley's vision of a "glorious and paradisiacal" future anticipated by decades Godwin's secularized millennium.

Then there was the French Revolution. One winces now at those all too familiar lines from Wordsworth's *Prelude:* "Bliss was it in that dawn to be alive, / But to be young was very Heaven!" Godwin himself was not young; he was thirty-seven when *Political Justice* was published. But the poets who were enraptured by it were young—Wordsworth was twenty-three, Coleridge twenty-one, Southey nineteen. They were attracted to the French Revolution, as Wordsworth put it, as to "the attraction of a country in romance!"—and to Godwin's philosophy, as to a philosophy in romance. It might have been Godwin, rather than Wordsworth, celebrating Reason as the "prime enchantress," liberating mankind from "the meagre, stale, forbidding ways / Of custom, law and statute." To be sure, by Godwin's time, the Revolution was beginning to lose its glamour. The execution of the king and queen, the declaration of war against Britain, and the establishment of the Terror—all of this was beginning to take the bloom off the revolution. But the romance of reason, of "human nature seeming born again" (Wordsworth again), died hard, and it took a while before the Romantics became reconciled to the death of that idyll.

Finally, over and beyond radicalism and romanticism there

★ In the first edition of *Political Justice,* Godwin accepted the term "anarchy" as connoting "the likeness, a distorted and tremendous likeness, of true liberty." In the revised edition, he distinguished anarchy from "a well conceived form of society without government," but even then he insisted that anarchy was preferable to despotism, the first being transitory and the second permanent. Moreover, anarchy had the salutary effect of awakening thought, whereas under despotism, "mind is trampled into an equality of the most odious sort."[54]

was the long tradition of millenarianism, which derived from a more ancient source. Seeking salvation in *gnosis,* in absolute knowledge or reason, the early Christian Gnostics rejected the institutions and arrangements of this world as profoundly, irremediably defective. Theirs was a consciously esoteric cult confined to those select few who could aspire to absolute reason. Modern millenarians democratized and secularized that ideology, making available to all of mankind what had been the privilege of the elite, and seeking to establish in this world the perfection of reason and virtue that Gnosticism had assigned to another world.

With Godwin, the radical Enlightenment in Britain reached its apogee. And with him, it died. What remained was the other Enlightenment, less dramatic but more practical and durable. Unlike the radicals who aspired to transform and rationalize Britain, the moral philosophers sought to reform and humanize it, to create an age of Enlightenment that was not an age of reason but, as one contemporary put it, "an age of benevolence."[55]

5. Methodism: "A Social Religion"

Just as Burke is generally excluded from the Enlightenment, so is Methodism, on the grounds that it was excessively religious and "enthusiastic" and insufficiently rational and philosophical. Thus, one of the most momentous events in British history is either ignored or consigned to the status of an anti-Enlightenment.[1]

The hostile tone of some later historians was anticipated as early as 1808 by Sydney Smith, who derisively lumped together the two Methodist societies, which by then had seceded from the Church of England, with the Evangelicals who remained within the church. "We shall use the general term of Methodism to designate these three classes of fanatic, not troubling ourselves to point out the finer shades and nicer discriminations of lunacy, but treating them all as in one general conspiracy against common sense and rational orthodox Christianity."[2] More than half a century later, the eminent Victorian Leslie Stephen, a self-described "agnostic" who had as little use for "rational orthodox Christianity" as for its less rational emanations, derided eighteenth-century Wesleyanism as "heat without light—a blind protest of the masses . . . a recrudescence of obsolete ideas." Nor did he have more respect for the Evangelicals: "We can admire their energy, though we cannot read their books. Throughout England sturdy sensible men, of the narrowest possible intellectual horizon, but the most vivid conviction of the value of certain religious teachings, were stirring the masses by addresses suited to indolent imaginations."[3] On the other hand, a contemporary of Stephen, W. E. H. Lecky, an ardent devotee of the rationalism whose history he chronicled, and no less contemptuous than Stephen of Wesley's belief in witchcraft and miracles, nevertheless paid tribute to him as "the greatest religious leader" of his century and as having had a "wider constructive influence in the sphere of practical religion" than anyone since the sixteenth century.[4]

Just as it took one Frenchman, Alexis de Tocqueville, to bring a new perspective to American democracy, so it took another Frenchman, Elie Halévy, to do the same for British religion and society. Halévy's thesis about "the miracle of modern England"—the fact that England was able to survive the economic revolution of the eighteenth century without succumbing to a political revolution—is best known as it appeared in his classic work *England in 1815* (published in France in 1913 and translated into English in 1924). But it was anticipated in two little-known articles, "The Birth of Methodism in England" (written in 1906 and translated only in 1971), which analyzed the religious movement that largely accounted for that miracle. The economic crisis of 1739, Halévy pointed out, coincided with the religious revival started that year by the brothers John and Charles Wesley and George Whitefield, reanimating a religious spirit that was no longer satisfied by either the Dissenting sects or the Church of England. Crowds numbering in the thousands and tens of thousands heard the Methodists (as they were soon called) propound an eclectic theology that was not always logically consistent but was eminently suited to the temper of the working classes in that early period of industrialism. Unlike the Calvinist doctrine of predestination, the Methodist amalgam of justification by faith and good works made salvation available to everyone. This creed was accompanied by an organizational structure in which hierarchy and egalitarianism were combined, as Halévy said, "in equal portions."[5]

Some English historians have assigned to Wesley an even more momentous role. J. H. Plumb, in an otherwise temperate account of eighteenth-century England, spoke of him in terms worthy of one of Hegel's "world-historical individuals": "Wesley himself was a great and complex character, one of the greatest known to modern times, a man in some ways comparable to Luther, Lenin, Gandhi, or even Napoleon. Few men have had his transcendental capacity to stir the heart; none has combined this with his genius for organization."[6] By providing the working classes with a means of emotional release as well as a sense of purpose and power, he helped make Methodism "a social force for good works." These admirable qualities, however, were more than outbalanced, Plumb found, by his autocratic leadership ("Pope John," his enemies called him), his repressive attitudes to children and education, and his "anti-intellectual" disposition.

> There was nothing intellectual about Methodism; the rational attitude, the most fashionable intellectual attitude of the day, was absolutely absent. . . . Everywhere in early Methodism one meets the prejudices of the uneducated, which always seem to be hardened by success. There was an anti-intellectual, philistine quality which attracted the dispossessed but was dangerous to society.[7]

The radical historian E. P. Thompson agreed that Methodism had a "strongly *anti-intellectual* influence," from which British popular culture, he said, had never recovered; it was nothing more than "a ritualized form of psychic masturbation."[8] But he was even more troubled by the Halévy thesis about revolution. Where Halévy commended Methodism for sparing England the ordeal of revolution, Thompson objected to it for precisely that reason, for repressing the working class and preventing it from pursuing its true interests. The early history of Methodism, Thompson conceded, had a democratic spirit that attracted working people, but once within the movement they were subjected to a "work-discipline" and authoritarian rule that stifled that spirit. Unlike Wesley's contemporaries (quoted by Thompson), who were worried about the democratic, even subversive influence of Methodism, Thompson deplored it as "reactionary, indeed, odiously subservient."[9] And unlike other radical historians who have praised Methodism for playing a large part in the trade union movement and the Labour Party, Thompson saw it as serving the interests of the new industrial bourgeoisie.[10]

Whatever else Wesley was—a world historical figure on the order of Luther, Lenin, Gandhi, or Napoleon, or a reactionary, repressive agent in the class struggle—he was not, for most historians, a force in the Enlightenment, because he lacked, as Plumb put it, that "most fashionable intellectual attitude," the "rational attitude." It remained for the American historian Bernard Semmel to bring Wesley and Methodism into the Enlightenment—not the Enlightenment of the French *philosophes,* to be sure, but that of the British moral philosophers.[11]

On the subject of religious toleration, Semmel pointed out, the Methodists were very much in the Enlightenment tradition, in spite of their deep personal religiosity. As "enthusiasts" they were naturally an object of suspicion for many contemporaries (as for most historians), but they were not zealots, still less fanatics, and they genuinely believed in religious toleration, for all sects as well as their own. (Like Locke and so many others, however, they did not extend that toleration to Catholics.) Their own creed was derived largely from Arminianism, with its doctrines of free will, divine grace, and universal salvation, but even that creed was not binding upon them. Methodists, Wesley said, "do not insist on your holding this or that opinion . . . they think and let think." What they did insist upon was the feeling and experiencing of their faith. Nor did they impose upon anyone "any particular mode of worship"; all that was required was the desire to save one's soul. This, Wesley boasted, was "true liberty of conscience," which no other religious sect, ancient or modern, had ever enjoyed.[12]

Methodism also shared the social ethos of the British Enlightenment. If there was, as has been said, a "rationalizing" of religion by the deists,[13] there was also a "socializing" of religion by the Wesleyans. Whatever the differences between the moral philosophers and the Methodists—philosophical, theological, temperamental—in important practical matters, they tended to converge. Wesley himself admitted a philosophical affinity with Francis Hutcheson, whose religious views he deplored but whose idea of a moral sense he recognized as akin to his own idea of an "internal sense," or "conscience," that made men relish the happiness of others.[14] While the philosophers were invoking the moral sense as the basis for the social affections, Methodist preachers were giving practical effect to that idea by spreading a religious gospel of good works, engaging in a variety of humanitarian causes, and welcoming the poor into their fold.

"The poor are the Christians," Wesley proclaimed, and proceeded to make of them his special mission. When the Anglican churches were closed to him, he made a virtue out of necessity by preaching in the open fields, thus reaching multitudes who were not welcome in churches or did not feel comfortable there. He assured the clergy that they need fear no competition from him. "The rich, the honourable, the great, we are thoroughly willing . . . to leave to you. Only let us alone among the poor." His poor, moreover, were not only the "deserving," "respectable" poor who were the likeliest candidates for conversion. He made a point of seeking out "the outcasts of men," the "forlorn ones," the "most flagrant, hardened, desperate sinner."[15] It was an article of his faith that no one was beyond salvation, no one too poor, benighted, or uncivilized to attain the spiritual and moral level deserving of the name Christian.

The poor were the objects of spiritual redemption, and, by the same token, of social and material amelioration. "Christianity is essentially a social religion," Wesley declared.[16] Denouncing the common assumption that the poor were poor because they did not want to work, he cited his own experiences among the poor in London: "I found some in their cells underground, others in their garrets, but I found not one of them unemployed who was able to crawl about the room. So wickedly, devilishly false is that common objection, they are poor only because they are idle."[17]

In one of his best-known and often repeated sermons, "The Use of Money," he propounded a new trinity: "Gain all you can," "Save all you can," "Give all you can." This trinity was the basis of moral life on earth and of eternal life in the hereafter. The prescription to gain, for example, was accompanied by the prohibition against gaining at the expense of one's own or another's bodily or mental health or subsistence.[18] Some of Wesley's injunctions—against usury, pawnbroking, or unfair competition—may seem anomalous to those historians who identify Methodism with Puritanism and thus with the capitalist ethic. In fact, there was a tension within the Methodist ethic, making it sometimes appear to be not so much anti-capitalist as pre-capitalist.[19] Wesley himself was acutely aware of this, and aware especially of its implications for religion. One of the purposes of religion, he insisted, was the inculcation of morality, which in turn was conducive to such other goods as industriousness and thus to the acquisition of wealth. But wealth, he suspected, was all too likely to subvert religion.

> I fear, wherever riches have increased, the essence of religion has decreased in the same proportion. Therefore I do not see how it is possible, in the nature of things, for any revival of true religion to continue long. For religion must necessarily produce both industry and frugality, and these cannot but produce riches. But as riches increase, so will pride, anger, and love of the world in all its branches. How then is it possible that Methodism, that is, a religion of the heart, though it flourishes now as a green bay tree, should continue in this state?[20]

It was to prevent just such a perversion of religion that Wesley proposed the trinity of Gain/Save/Give, with the stipulation that "to gain money, we must not lose our souls."[21] Setting an example for his followers, Wesley himself gave tirelessly of his own time, energy, and money. By the time of his death he had either given away or expended in his publication ventures virtually all of his considerable earnings from his books. He travelled and preached incessantly, even in the early years when he was suffering from tuberculosis. He made it a practice to rise at four in the morning and preach his first sermon at five, before the laborers had to go to work. (He claimed that it was this regimen that cured him of tuberculosis.) During the last fifty years of his life, he travelled some 225,000 miles and preached more than 40,000 sermons (an average of about fifteen a week), most in the open, often in rain and cold.[22]

It was not only the rich who were to assure their salvation by giving of their riches, or the preachers of their time and energy, but all members of the congregation, who were enjoined to contribute their pennies and, more important, their personal efforts to relieve the sufferings of those less fortunate than they. This gospel of charity and good works was a vital part of Methodism from the beginning. The movement had barely come into being when it was called upon to help alleviate the distress caused by the economic crisis of 1739–40. In the years that followed, Methodists took the initiative in the distribution of food, clothing, and money to the needy, paid visits to the sick and to prisoners in jail, and set up loan funds and work projects for the unemployed. Lest these projects seem condescending or patronizing to those who were being assisted, Wesley advised his stewards: "Put yourself in the place of every poor man, and deal with him as you would God should deal with you."[23]

Although the emphasis was upon the personal giving of charity and good works, the Methodists helped establish and support philanthropic enterprises and institutions of every kind: hospitals, dispensaries, orphanages, friendly societies, schools, and libraries. They also played a prominent part in the movement for the abolition of the slave trade. Wesley himself was passionate on the subject of "that execrable villainy," slavery. "An African," he wrote, was "in no respect inferior to the European"; if he seemed so, it was because the European had kept him in a condition of inferiority, depriving him of "all opportunities of improving either in knowledge or virtue."[24]

Conceding the humanitarian efforts of Wesley personally and of the Methodists in general, in respect to slaves, prisoners, the sick, and the poor, some historians have faulted them for their attitude toward children. E. P. Thompson went so far as to accuse them of "psychological atrocities" and "religious terrorism," because they filled the children's minds with lurid images of brimstone and fire.[25] Others have charged that they confined the education of the poor to the reading of the Bible and religious tracts, deliberately prohibiting the teaching of writing and arithmetic so as to make sure that they became a docile and profitable source of labor. Wesley himself shared the common Puritanical suspicion of amusements and leisure as especially treacherous to the souls of the young. In the school he founded in 1739 in the mining town of Kingswood (near Bristol), the pupils rose at four, and were allowed to sing, pray, meditate, study, and walk, but not to play, for "he that plays when he is a child," Wesley declared, "will play when he is a man."[26] Another school was established in London on similar principles. The charity schools that were supported by Methodists but catered to non-Methodists as well were less rigorous, and there is some evidence that the rules were relaxed for all the schools later in the century.

At a time when there was no clear conception of childhood as we now understand it, such a regimen was harsh enough. Yet it did not seem unduly harsh to parents who thought it a privilege to send their children to Methodist schools. (The Methodist Kingswood School exists to this day, as does an open-air chapel on the site where Wesley and Whitefield preached.) One item in this indictment is unfounded. It is not true, as is often said, that the children were taught only to read. According to Wesley's specific instructions, they were to learn to "read, write, and cast accounts," as well, of course, as to "know God, and Jesus Christ, whom he hath sent." This was also the curriculum for older children and for adults ("scholars of all ages, some of them grey-headed"), who were encouraged to attend the schools before or after work.[27]

The common criticism that Methodists restricted the education of the poor, like the charge of anti-intellectualism in general, is belied by the curriculum in their schools and, more important, by the ambitious program of publications supervised, supported, and in good part written by Wesley himself. These were intended for the edification not only of workers and the poor but for the preachers as well, most of whom came from the working classes. The publications included a short grammar and other primers; a host of tracts on medicine, electricity, natural history, and the like; abridgements, somewhat expurgated, of Shakespeare, Milton, Spenser, Locke, and other classics (eventually this project came to fifty volumes); and editions and translations of theological works. (The last were suprisingly ecumenical, including an abridgement by Wesley of a life of Mme Guyon, the French Catholic mystic.) Wesley's three-volume *Compendium of Natural Philosophy* paid effusive tribute to Francis Bacon, and the work itself, in spite of its subtitle (*A Survey of the Wisdom of God in the Creation*), was naturalistic and empirical rather than theological. Some of the books were practical manuals. Wesley's *Primitive Physick* prescribed remedies for 288 specific ailments; first published in 1747, it went through twenty-three editions by 1828, and was used by itinerant preachers who doubled as amateur doctors and pharmacists as well as book agents. In addition to the publication and distribution of these works, funds were also raised for the establishment of libraries in poor neighborhoods.

It is easy today to mock some of these enterprises—the bowdlerized versions of Shakespeare, for example (less bowdlerized, however, than those of Thomas Bowdler himself half a century later). But they may have done more, one historian has said, "to revive interest in Shakespeare and create a reading public than the higher literary criticism of Johnson and Coleridge."[28] The whole of this quite extraordinary publication industry, comprising books, pamphlets, and tracts on a variety of subjects and directed to different levels of literacy and interest, constituted something like an Enlightenment for the common man.

Wesley himself was by no means the anti-intellectual he has often been made out to be. Samuel Johnson, no mean intellectual himself, told James Boswell that he always enjoyed talking to Wesley, regretting only that the latter was so busy travelling and preaching that he did not allow himself the leisure of conversing.[29] Even Wesley's reliance upon feeling and personal experience as the source of faith, rather than upon reason or dogma, had a respectable counterpart in the empiricism of John Locke. Wesley never mentioned David Hume except to decry him as an infidel and skeptic, but he did cite Locke with approval. He even published long extracts from Locke's *Essay Concerning Human Understanding* in the *Arminian Magazine* which he edited. The *Essay,* he assured his readers, although it contained several mistakes of little importance, included many excellent truths by a "great master both of reasoning and language."[30]

If Wesley did not think to apply to his movement the label of "Enlightenment"—but then the moral philosophers did not use that label either—he certainly thought of himself as enlightened, and he believed his mission to be not only the spiritual salvation of the poor but also (which for him was the same thing) their intellectual and moral edification. He even appealed to reason as a corrective to excessive emotionalism and enthusiasm. On one occasion he rebuked a Methodist preacher (the leader of a group that later seceded from Methodism) for "overvaluing feelings and inward impressions . . . and undervaluing reason, knowledge and wisdom in general." To another correspondent, he enunciated his creed: "It is a fundamental principle with us, that to renounce reason is to renounce religion, that religion and reason go hand in hand, and that all irrational religion is false religion."[31] To yet another he wrote that it was only by "religion and reason joined" that "passion and prejudice," "wickedness and bigotry," could be overcome.[32]

Wesley's Enlightenment, however, was not a prescription for democracy, at least not in the political sense. Wesley himself was a firm believer in authority and monarchy. "I am a High Churchman," he declared, "the son of a High Churchman, bred up from my childhood in the highest notions of passive obedience and non-resistance."[33] Staunchly Tory in his political convictions (he opposed any move toward independence for America), he was also firmly authoritarian in his own church, rejecting, for example, the idea that church leaders and stewards be elected by the membership; they were chosen by him, as were the preachers who attended the annual church conference. "We are no republicans and never intend to be," he declared. "Do you honor and obey all in authority?" he asked his parishioners. "All your governors, spiritual pastors, and masters? Do you behave lowly and reverently to all your betters?"[34]* Vigorously affirming his loyalty to established authorities, he demanded the same loyalty from his congregants, perhaps to deter factions that threatened secession—the Calvinists, most notably, who did finally secede after the death of their leader, George Whitefield, in 1770.

Yet the movement was, in spirit if not formally, democratic. For a fee of a penny a week, the poor had the satisfaction of being members in good standing in a respectable and congenial "society," as it was called. (When Wesley was told

---

* These questions were immediately followed by others, making this part of a larger moral catechism: "Do you hurt nobody by word or deed? Are you true and just in all your dealings? Do you take care to pay whatever you owe? Do you feel no malice, or envy, or revenge, no hatred or bitterness to any man? If you do, it is plain you are not of God; for all these are the tempers of the devil."

that some congregants could not afford even a penny, he took it upon himself to pay their dues.) Methodism thus attracted a great number of people of the "lower orders" who might not otherwise have belonged to any church. In a typical society in Bristol in 1783, the largest single occupational group consisted of servants (of both sexes), followed by shoemakers and other tradesmen; a small group of "gentlemen and gentlewomen" was about equal to the number of the old and the very poor.

Within the church, there were few social distinctions. The lay preachers had no special educational or social qualifications. Laurence Sterne sneered that Methodist preachers were "much fitter to make a pulpit than to get into one."[35] Many of them were graduates from the movement itself, having been educated in Methodist schools and by their own publications, which constituted something like a "school without walls." And the organizational structure, however hierarchical, promoted a spirit of community and fraternity. The larger units of "societies" and "bands" were broken down into smaller groups of "classes" and "families," the latter consisting of "brothers" and "sisters" led by "fathers." (The "classes" later served as a model for the Chartists and other radical movements.) Members met once a week under the supervision of a leader whose duty it was to "advise, reprove, comfort or exhort, as occasion may require."[36]

The conspicuous number and active role of women in the movement was remarked upon at the time. In many congregations, more than half of the members, in some two thirds, were women, of whom nearly half were unmarried. And they were not passive members; as often as not they took the lead in prayer, counselling, and exhorting. More notable was the large contingent of women preachers, who had the same status and enjoyed the same respect as men. At a time when women were so often consigned to the domestic sphere, one historian observes, "Christian zeal brought them into prominence."[37]

In spite of a "political theology" that was conservative, the social ethic derived from that theology was democratic.[38] Unlike Calvinism, where the doctrine of predestination might be taken as limiting an individual's aspirations and potentialities, the Arminian doctrines of free will and universal salvation were an invitation to self-improvement and self-advancement. By working hard and saving, being temperate and responsible, people could better themselves—spiritually and morally in the first instance, but also materially and socially. It has been observed that Methodism was a powerful stimulus to social mobility. If the poor were enjoined to obey their masters, they were also encouraged to become masters and to be obeyed in turn. This ethic was all the more effective because it was not only social and religious but also, in important respects, individualistic. Derived from a powerful sense of the individual's relation to God, it promoted a sense of personal moral responsibility akin to the Puritan ethic, encouraging the virtues of thrift, diligence, temperance, honesty, and work. As Methodism joined the doctrines of free will and universal salvation with the social obligation of charity and good works, so it made "self-help" a correlative of helping others.

The ethic had the additional distinction of crossing both class and religious lines. By the end of the century, Wesleyanism had spawned an Evangelicalism that appealed largely to the middle and upper classes. William Wilberforce, perhaps the best known of the Evangelicals and the most prominent in the movement for the abolition of the slave trade, was a good friend of the Wesleys. Almost the last letter written by John Wesley was to Wilberforce: "Go on, in the name of God and in the power of His might, till even American slavery (the vilest that ever saw the sun) shall vanish away before it."[39] Even after Wesley's death, when the Methodists left the Church of England, they remained allies of the Evangelicals, helping Wilberforce get reelected to Parliament in 1806 and supporting their reforms and philanthropies.

Bernard Semmel has described Methodism as a "revolution"—the English counterpart of the "democratic revolution" that other historians have attributed to France.

> If Methodism muted the calls to liberty and equality in order to restrain enthusiastic, revolutionary propensities, the same motive made it stress fraternity. In the century of Voltaire's *sauve qui peut* and Smith's *laissez-faire,* when the paternalism of the traditional hierarchical society was breaking down, Methodism sought to endow the lower classes with a sense of their own worth, and to revive traditional religion as a source of warmth and solace, of comfort and joy.[40]

When Adam Smith, in the *Wealth of Nations,* described the "strict" or "austere" system of morality favored by the common people and promoted by the new religious sects, he also pointed out that the older Dissenting sects, led by "learned, ingenious, and respectable men," had lost much of their zeal for teaching and preaching. Thus it was that "the Methodists, without half the learning of the Dissenters, are much more in vogue."[41] At the time Smith wrote this, the official, dues-paying, churchgoing Methodist membership (not including the hundreds of thousands who had been exposed to Methodist teaching and preaching) was only a little more than 22,000.[42] What Smith did not anticipate was the quadrupling of that number by the end of the century. Nor did he foresee the extent or strength of Methodism among the middle classes in the form of Evangelicalism, nor that the latter would inspire the "Moral Reformation" and philanthropic movements that were so distinctive a part of the British Enlightenment.

6. "THE AGE OF BENEVOLENCE"

The "moral sense" or "moral sentiment," the "social virtues" or "social affections," the ideas of "benevolence," "sympathy," "compassion," "fellow-feeling"— these were the defining terms of the moral philosophy that was at the heart of the British Enlightenment. It was this social ethos that was the common denominator of the two Smiths and the two Burkes, of secular philosophers and religious enthusiasts, of Church of England bishops and Wesleyan preachers and missionaries. And it was this ethos that found practical expression in the reform movements and philanthropic enterprises that flourished during the century, culminating in what the Evangelical writer Hannah More described (not entirely in praise) as "the Age of Benevolence," and what a later historian called "the new humanitarianism."[1]

Early in the century, Bernard Mandeville objected to the social ethos that was already becoming prevalent in his country, attributing it to that "noble writer" Lord Shaftesbury, who "fancies that as man is made for society, so he ought to be born with a kind affection to the whole of which he is a part, and a propensity to seek the welfare of it."[2] Decades later, a London magistrate, distressed by what he regarded as the excessive leniency displayed toward criminals, also recalled Shaftesbury, rebuking Henry Fielding for "vulgarizing" him by reducing virtue to "good affections" and inventing "that cant phrase, goodness of heart, which is every day used as a substitute for probity and means little more than the virtue of a horse or a dog." The novel *Tom Jones,* he said, had done more toward corrupting the rising generation than any other work. "We live in an age," the magistrate complained, "when humanity is in fashion."[3]

Fielding was not only a novelist but also a justice of the peace and prison reformer. In 1740 (several years before the publication of *Tom Jones*), he praised the virtue of charity that "shone brighter in our time than at any period which I remember in our annals."[4] He might have justified that claim by citing a *History of London* published the year before, which gave a detailed account of the schools, hospitals, almshouses, and charitable societies flourishing in the metropolis. "As opulency and riches," William Maitland wrote, "are the result of commerce, so are learning, hospitality, and charity the effects thereof." Unlike other countries, he was pleased to report, England had a national, legal provision for relief, as well as a multitude of private charities supported by Englishmen of all ranks who raised vast sums of money to supplement public relief.[5] By 1756, when the second edition appeared, this section of the book had to be greatly expanded to accommodate the many new societies and institutions that had been established in the interim. Maitland then commended his countrymen for the "truly Christian spirit of benevolence, which at this time so generally prevails amongst us, to the great honour of this age and nation."[6]

Tocqueville did an injustice to Britain in identifying voluntary associations and civil society with the United States, as if they were unique to that country. The idea of "political association," he conceded, was imported from England, but the Americans were far more skillful and constant in their use of "civil association." This was the difference, he explained, between aristocratic and democratic societies. In aristocracies, there was less need for association because a few very powerful and wealthy individuals were capable of executing great undertakings by themselves, whereas in democratic societies, each individual was powerless by himself and therefore had the need to unite.[7]

In fact, there were a plenitude of such associations and a very lively civil society in Britain throughout the eighteenth century (and in the following century as well, when Tocqueville was writing). "Societies" existed for every kind of worthy purpose: "Promoting Christian Knowledge," "Bettering the Condition and Increasing the Comforts of the Poor," the "Reformation of Manners," the abolition of slavery, and the care of a variety of unfortunates including abandoned infants, sick and maimed seamen, orphans of clergymen, prostitutes, chimney sweeps, criminals, released criminals, and potential criminals (poor boys who might be tempted to a life of crime), the deaf, dumb, blind, and lame. (A "Humane Society" was devoted to the resuscitation of the drowned.) And it was not only the very powerful and wealthy, as Tocqueville thought, who were the moving forces in these enterprises. A lord or lady might lend his or her name to one or another society, but it was generally men and women of not very great wealth or social standing—industrialists, merchants, civil servants, members of Parliament, writers, clerics, retired military and naval men, and civic-minded women—who initiated, directed, and financed them.

The word "philanthropy," like "benevolence" and "compassion," was much in fashion, both in the original sense of "love of mankind" and as applied to the many charitable enterprises that flourished at the time. Over a hundred in-

stitutions and societies were established in the course of the
century, and scores of people contributed not only their
money but considerable time and energy to one or several
causes, making of philanthropy a profession, a full-time (or
very nearly full-time) calling.[8] Among the notable figures
identified as philanthropists were John Howard, Jonas Hanway, Thomas Gilbert, Henry Hoare, Thomas Coram, Grif-
fith Jones, Thomas Bernard, John and Henry Thornton,
Richard Reynolds, and Sarah Trimmer. In 1780, Edmund
Burke, in a speech supporting prison reform, paid tribute to
Howard, who travelled throughout Europe, Burke said, not
for personal or aesthetic pleasure but "to dive into the
depths of dungeons; to plunge into the infection of hospitals; to survey the mansions of sorrow and pain; to take the
gauge and dimensions of misery, depression, and contempt;
to remember the forgotten, to attend to the neglected, to
visit the forsaken, and to compare and collage the distresses
of man in all countries. . . . It was a voyage of discovery, a
circumnavigation of charity."[9] (Howard later died of an
infection received while attending a prisoner in Russia.)

Philanthropists were also, inevitably, reformers, exposing
wretched conditions in prisons and workhouses, proposing
varieties of social and legal reforms, and creating and subsi-
dizing new institutions. Between 1720 and 1750, five great
London hospitals and nine in the country were founded, and
the following half century saw the establishment of dispensaries, clinics, and specialized hospitals (maternity, infectious
diseases, insane asylums). An act providing nursing care in the
country for the infants of paupers, and such other measures as
the paving and draining of many London streets and the
clearing of some of its worst slums, resulted in a dramatic
reduction of the death rates, for children especially. In the
middle of the century, the proportion of burials of children
under the age of five to the number of infants christened was

almost 75 percent; by the end of the century, that proportion was just over 40 percent.[10]*

Philanthropists and reformers came in different sizes and shapes. William Hogarth is not usually included in that company, although he was surely one of them. His caricatures were powerful moral statements and were at least as effective—to judge by the extent to which they were plagiarized, pirated, and adapted for use in novels and plays—as the sermons of preachers and the more sober revelations of reformers.† "Gin Lane" depicts emaciated men and women in states of drunken abandon: one skeletal man is gnawing on a bone, another man has hanged himself, a besotted woman suckling an infant lets the child fall into the alley below. The inscription over the doorway of the liquor shop reads: "Drunk for a Penny, Dead Drunk for Twopence, Clean straw for nothing." An accompanying cartoon, "Beer Street," represents the salutary alternative to gin, with happy, corpulent men and women drinking beer; here the inn sign has merry harvesters dancing around a haystack. It was perhaps no accident that

---

* Roy Porter observes that the "culture of quantification" that produced such vital statistics was itself a by-product of the concern for public health on the part of physicians, actuaries, and officials. What were once regarded as accidents reflecting the arbitrariness of existence were now looked upon as physiological evidence of diseases that could be controlled.[11]

† They were, however, cartoons and should not be taken too literally. A modern historian, commenting on one of the more grotesque scenes in the "Industry and Idleness" series, says that it "probably gives a fair picture of the conditions in which poor people lived at the time"[12]—this of an image of the "idle apprentice" in bed with a prostitute, in a grotesquely filthy room, with a cat tumbling down the chimney in pursuit of a rat.

that same year, 1751, saw the passage of the act regulating the sale of cheap gin. Contemporaries recognized what historians have since affirmed, that this measure was a major event in the social history of London.

The series "Industry and Idleness" was even more unashamedly didactic. Hogarth explained that it followed the careers of two fellow apprentices, "the one, by taking good courses and pursuing those points for which he was put apprentice, becomes a valuable man and an ornament to his country; whilst the other, giving way to idleness, naturally falls into poverty and most commonly ends fatally."[13] Other moral messages emerged in the dozen plates of that series: the idle apprentice being driven to the place of his execution accompanied by the Methodist preacher who has apparently converted him, at least to the point where the apprentice joins him in singing a hymn; and the final plate where a huge crowd revels in the sight of his hanging at Tyburn—"Tyburn Fair," as it was mockingly called. The last scene reflected the outrage frequently expressed by his friend Henry Fielding at the "barbarous custom peculiar to the English of insulting and jesting at misery."[14] The series as a whole was, in a sense, a commentary on the life of another friend, Benjamin Franklin, who in his person seemed to represent the triumphal progress of the industrious apprentice. The last letter Hogarth received before his death, to his great satisfaction, was from Franklin.

In "The Four Stages of Cruelty," Hogarth dramatized an issue that had troubled Puritans in the seventeenth century and that emerged more prominently in the eighteenth. Hogarth's cartoons on the cruelty to animals had a double edge, first to expose "that barbarous treatment of animals, the very sight of which renders the streets of our metropolis so distressing to every feeling mind," and then to demonstrate the brutalizing effect of that barbarity upon the people inflicting it.[15] The boy who maltreats the animals in the first two scenes grows up to seduce a servant girl, incites her to robbery, and then murders her; the final panel shows his corpse, the hangman's noose still around his neck, being dissected from head to toe, with a dog nibbling at his intestines. Years later, after the passage of laws suppressing blood sports (bull- and bear-baiting, cock-throwing and dog-fighting), Hogarth was pleased to think that his work (another of his cartoons depicted the gaming scene on the cock-pit) had "checked the diabolical spirit of barbarity" that had once prevailed in the country.[16] A best-selling book for teenagers by "Tom Telescope," bearing the portentous title *The Newtonian System of Philosophy Adapted to the Capacities of Young Gentlemen and Ladies,* lectured its readers on the evils of cruelty to animals, and took the occasion to extend that lesson to slaves and other humans. "Kindness to animals, yes, but greater kindness to human beings" was the theme of Tom's final lecture.[17]

Discussing the campaign against blood sports, the historian Lawrence Stone related it to the upsurge of new attitudes and emotions inspired by the rise of "a new ideal type, namely the Man of Sentiment, or the Man of Feeling, the prototype of the late eighteenth-century Romantic."[18] Other historians have related the "culture of sensibility" to a "culture of reform" and a "cult of benevolence."[19] One does not normally think of Shaftesbury or Hutcheson, Smith, Hume, or Burke as romantics. Yet their philosophies, permeated with the ideas of sentiment and feeling, may well qualify them as such. The romantic sensibility gave both an aesthetic and an emotive dimension to their moral philosophy, so that the idea of virtue—social virtue as well as private virtue—had roots deeper than mere reason or even experience. "Pity," wrote the author of *The Man of Experience,* "is the greatest luxury the soul of sensibility is capable of relishing."[20]

137

Beauty was also associated with virtue. Shaftesbury set the tone by equating "taste" in the aesthetic realm with "sense" in the moral realm, "poetical truth" with moral truth, beauty with "a generous behavior, a regularity of conduct, and a consistency of life and manners."[21] So, too, Hutcheson, positing an inner sense of beauty akin to the inner sense of morality, found the "external beauty" of persons a reflection of their "concomitant virtue."[22] For Smith, the imagination was the source of sympathy—"it is by the imagination only that we can form any conception of what are his [the unfortunate's] sensations"—as well as of beauty. Indeed, it was the concern for "the beauty of order, of art and contrivance," that disposed men to those institutions that promoted the "public welfare."[23]

Burke's most important early work, which was highly regarded by his contemporaries, was on aesthetics. *A Philosophical Inquiry into the Origin of Our Ideas of the Sublime and Beautiful*—a youthful work, we are often reminded—has earned him a place in the annals of the Enlightenment, even among some historians who otherwise decry him as reactionary, for it is seen as a repudiation of classicism and a harbinger of romanticism.[24] A major theme of the book, the association of the sublime with terror, was the very epitome of romanticism, as expressed in the passage on Milton's conception of death: "All is dark, uncertain, confused, terrible, and sublime to the last degree."[25] Yet while asserting, in good romantic fashion, the primacy of the senses and passions over the classical principles of objectivity and perfection, Burke insisted that there were aesthetic standards that derived from "our common nature," a "sentiment common to all mankind." That common sentiment, the feeling of sympathy that motivated the social affections, applied as well to the arts, for "it is by this principle chiefly that poetry, painting, and other affecting arts transfuse their passions from one breast to another, and are often capable of grafting a delight on wretchedness, misery, and death itself." Thus, to understand literary tragedy, one must first understand real tragedy: "how we are affected by the feelings of our fellow-creatures in circumstances of real distress."[26]

In novels as well, sensibility was allied with morality. Samuel Richardson, Henry Fielding, Laurence Sterne, Oliver Goldsmith, Mrs. Radcliffe, and a host of other writers popular at the time and justly forgotten today, made this the heyday of what has been called the sentimental novel—a sentimentality heavily larded with morality. Rousseau's *La Nouvelle Héloïse* (published in 1761) is regarded as the preeminent sentimental-*cum*-moral novel. But Richardson's *Pamela* preceded it by two decades and went through five editions within the first year. And it was followed by scores of novels, plays, poems, and magazines (the *Lady's Magazine* and *Female Spectator*, for example) in a similar vein, where virtue asserted itself not by denying or subduing passion but by making passion virtuous.

Even the Methodists played their part in this culture. Wesley himself professed to be offended by the very title of Sterne's *A Sentimental Journey Through France and Italy.* "Sentimental! What is that? It is not English; he might as well say Continental. It is not sense. It conveys no determinate idea."[27] Yet he and his followers were as much part of that culture of sensibility as the novelists and philosophers. The Methodists published sentimental novels and poems (somewhat expurgated, to be sure), as well as sermons and tracts. And their theology had at its core feelings, sentiments, and emotions that were given expression in prayers, hymns, homilies, and, not least, in personal services for the sick and needy.

Others who were notably unsentimental and unromantic were sufficiently responsive to sentiment to find some humanitarian cause to elicit their sympathy. Daniel Defoe wrote a tract in favor of foundling hospitals; Mandeville approved of poor relief for the aged and sick; and Hannah

More was an enthusiastic supporter of Sunday Schools. In 1758, perhaps recalling the outpouring of money and sympathy to the victims of the Lisbon earthquake three years earlier (a generosity made more remarkable by the fact that the victims were foreigners and Catholics), Samuel Johnson wryly observed, "Every hand is open to contribute something, every tongue is busied in solicitations, and every art of pleasure is employed for a time in the interest of virtue."[28] Toward the end of his life, Wesley took the measure of the time: "While luxury and profaneness have been increasing on one hand, on the other, benevolence and compassion toward all forms of human woe have increased in a manner not known before, from the earliest ages of the world."[29]

Education does not normally come under the rubric of benevolence and compassion, still less of sentiment or sensibility. Yet education for the poor was an important part of the culture reflected in the British Enlightenment. The charity school movement had been started in 1699 by the Society for the Promotion of Christian Knowledge. Within three decades there were over 1,400 such schools catering to over 22,000 pupils.[30] To Addison and Steele, these schools represented the "glory of the age," the "greatest instance of public spirit the age has produced."[31] To Mandeville, they were yet further evidence of the insidious influence of Shaftesbury and his successors. The "enthusiastic passion" inspired by the schools prompted him to append to a new edition of *The Fable of the Bees* an essay about them that would confirm, he suspected, the prevailing opinion of him as "an uncharitable, hard hearted, and inhuman if not a wicked, profane and atheistical wretch." Undaunted, he proceeded to denounce the schools for promoting the very vices they were intended to correct. So far from abating crimes and other social disorders, as their defenders claimed, they had the effect of encouraging idleness by keeping the poor from working. And idleness was more responsible for "the growth of villainy" than "the grossest ignorance and stupidity."

> Reading, writing, and arithmetic are very necessary to those whose business require such qualifications, but where people's livelihood has no dependence on these arts, they are very pernicious to the poor, who are forced to get their daily bread by their daily labor. . . . Going to school in comparison to working is idleness, and the longer boys continue in this easy sort of life, the more unfit they'll be when grown up for downright labor, both as to strength and inclination.[32]

Mandeville had been quite right in anticipating that the worthies of the age would be outraged by his views. While he criticized the schools as "pernicious to the poor," Adam Smith condemned Mandeville's essay as "wholly pernicious."[33]

The charity school movement was succeeded by private educational endowments and, later in the century, the Sunday School movement. Started by a society consisting of both Anglicans and Dissenters, the Sunday Schools had the support of Methodists and Evangelicals as well. By the turn of the century, they had an enrollment of over 200,000.[34] Hannah More is often cited as expressing the prevailing view that instruction be confined to reading, especially of the Bible and religious tracts, on the theory that writing would encourage the children to rise above their station. In fact, even the early charity schools had a more liberal concept of education, as is evident from Mandeville's complaint that they were teaching such "pernicious" subjects as reading, writing, and arithmetic. That most of the Sunday Schools did so as well may be deduced from the records of expenditures on spelling books, slates, pencils, and desks. By 1795, 94,000 spelling books had been distributed; within a decade, that figure had doubled.[35] Sabbatarians objected to writing, but solely on religious grounds; in some cases, classes were held during the week to permit instruction in writing. Toward the end of the century, Sir Frederick Morton Eden, in his voluminous study *The State of the Poor,* dismissed the objections that had once been levelled against the education of the poor: "It is now admitted on all hands that intellectual acquisitions are beneficial to every class of the community, and that children of our laborers are not the less likely to become useful members of the state in that sphere of life for which they are destined, from having been instructed in reading, writing, and arithmetic."[36]

The Sunday Schools were as much a social phenomenon as a religious and educational one. Apart from educating the poor, they had the corollary effect of fostering the same kind of communal spirit that the Wesleyan movement did. School outings, teas, and clubs made them, as Thomas Laqueur, the leading historian of the movement, has noted, "a central feature of working-class community life"—all the more because the teachers often consisted of former students and parents. (This, too, is reminiscent of Methodism, where lay preachers were chosen from the congregation.) The schools were also the product, Laqueur observed, of "a new, more humane, more tolerant, indeed more optimistic view of childhood."[37] The movement for the education of the poor thus reflected the same sensibility and ethos that inspired such other philanthropic and reform movements as the campaign against cruelty to animals, for the abolition of slavery, for prison and legal reforms, and for the establishment of a multitude of societies that undertook to alleviate a variety of social ills.

These educational enterprises—indeed, the philanthropic and reform movements in general—were not inspired by the radicals. Indeed, their only contribution to educational reform involved children of the middle and upper classes. In

Thoughts on the Education of Daughters, Mary Wollstonecraft, who had once taught in a school for girls, proposed that girls be educated together with boys and in the same rational manner as boys, rather than in segregated boarding schools where they were thrown together and encouraged to develop the worst habits of the sex. The book is interesting in itself and is a fitting prelude to her *Vindication of the Rights of Woman* five years later. But neither then nor later did it enter into the discussions and debates about education. Nor did it prompt the radicals to put any of its ideas into effect, or to take any part in the educational experiments that were engaging so many of their compatriots.

The poor themselves were caught up in the same ethos that motivated the reformers and philanthropists, an ethos that combined a communal spirit with that of self-help. The Friendly Societies—insurance clubs, essentially—founded by workers for their mutual aid, were voluntary and independent, self-governing and self-supporting. Members would contribute regular sums (kept, in early years, in strongboxes or wooden chests), to be dispensed to those in need because of illness, infirmity, unemployment, or to pay for funerals and other emergencies; some groups engaged local doctors to attend to the sick. Like the Sunday Schools, the Friendly Societies served an important social function, bringing together people, sometimes in the local public house, for a common purpose and in a common spirit. In 1793, they acquired legal recognition in an act of Parliament providing for their "encouragement and relief." By 1801, a contemporary study estimated, there were 7,200 such societies with a membership of almost 650,000 adult males—this in a total population of 9 million.[38]

All of these private, voluntary enterprises, it must be remembered—charities, philanthropic institutions, Friendly

Societies—supplemented an elaborate system of public relief. By 1795, that system was expanded by the adoption in some counties of the "Speenhamland system," providing a family allowance not only for the indigent but for "every poor and industrious man" whose earnings fell below a level determined by the price of bread and the size of his family. A bill introduced by Prime Minister Pitt the following year, intended to establish relief as "a right and an honour," was finally withdrawn because so many additional benefits and supervisory agencies were added to it in committee that it became impracticable. But even without these additional provisions, the expenditure of public funds had grown considerably. In 1776, the annual cost of poor relief had been £1.5 million; by the end of the century, it was over £4 million.

It was no radical but Adam Smith, implicitly criticizing Price's famous sermon bearing that title, who wrote that "the love of our country" rests on two principles: a respect for the constitution and a concern for the good and happiness of others. "He is not a citizen who is not disposed to respect the laws and to obey the civil magistrate; and he is certainly not a good citizen who does not wish to promote, by every means in his power, the welfare of the whole society of his fellow-citizens."[39] And it was the Tory Samuel Johnson who said: "A decent provision for the poor is the true test of civilization. . . . The condition of the lower order, the poor especially, was the true mark of national discrimination."[40]*

Perhaps the most notable feature of this social ethic was its crossing of party, class, and religious lines. When Elie Halévy spoke of "the miracle of modern England"—the fact that

---

* Johnson also defies the conventional Tory stereotype by being a vigorous opponent of slavery. On one visit to Oxford, he proposed a toast to "the next insurrection of the negroes in the West Indies." His tract in 1775, *Taxation No Tyranny,* derided the Americans: "How is it that we hear the loudest yelps for liberty among the drivers of negroes?"[41]

England was spared the revolutions that wrought havoc on the continent—he gave Methodism a crucial role in that miracle.[42] But the Methodist ethos, he pointed out, was shared by others of different philosophical and religious persuasions. It was this convergence of thought and sensibility that proved decisive in this critical period of English history. By the second half of the eighteenth century, Halévy observed, "freethinkers in association with the philanthropists of the evangelical movement would work for the material and moral betterment of the poor. In the interval, they were 'converted' to philanthropy through the influence of Methodist preachers."[43]

Historians have quarrelled with one or another aspect of that "miracle," but few have challenged the role of Evangelicalism, the heir of Methodism, in the philanthropic movement. Indeed, the very word "philanthropist," it has been said, became very nearly synonymous with "Evangelical," and "philanthropy" was identified with those good works that appealed to Evangelical tastes.[44] Yet the movement, as Halévy said, extended well beyond the religious sphere. It reflected the dominant social ethic, which was a compound of the religious and the secular, the public and the private, the communal and the individual, the humanitarian and the romantic. If Evangelicalism played a large part in that ethic, so did the moral philosophy that gave it its philosophical rationale. And the two, however different in inspiration and disposition, worked together for what they took to be the common cause: the material as well as the "moral reformation" of the people.

By later standards, of course, the reforms, societies, and institutions reflecting this ethic seem woefully inadequate, and Hogarthian scenes of drunkenness and licentiousness, cruelty and misery continue to dominate the imagination, obscuring the humanitarian intentions behind those scenes (and obscuring, too, the occasional beneficent effects of those cartoons).

"The Age of Benevolence" obviously had its underside. If it produced a generation of reformers and humanitarians, it was partly because there was much to reform and even more to offend the sensibilities of a humane person. While one historian finds 1766 noteworthy as the year of publication of Jonas Hanway's *Earnest Appeal of Mercy to the Children of the Poor,* a tract that publicized infant mortality rates in the poorhouses and prepared the way for the boarding-out law, another cites that year as a time of an unprecedented number of food riots occasioned by a harvest failure—sixty riots in a three-month period, by one count.[45]

Yet another historian, David Owen, attributes the philanthropic movement to a complex of "Puritan piety, a benevolently humanitarian outlook, and a concern for national interest."[46] Others have been less generous, pointing to a mixture of motives in which public-spiritedness and good-heartedness served the interests of self-promotion and self-gratification.[47] "The beauty of such enlightened largesse," Roy Porter writes, "lay in fostering among the *bien pensants* the glow of a superior sensibility." But even he does not deny the practical effect of such largesse in the creation of hospitals, asylums, and other charitable establishments, and in the movements for penal reform and the abolition of the slave trade.[48]

This was the distinctive characteristic of the British Enlightenment, especially by comparison with the French. Benevolence was a more modest virtue than Reason, but perhaps a more humane one. And an Age of Benevolence was a more modest aspiration than an Age of Reason, but a more practical one. If that Age of Benevolence fell far short of what reformers at the time, and historians since, would have liked, it did represent—as, indeed, the very idea of Enlightenment did—a notable advance of spirit and consciousness, a "forward march of the human spirit," as Diderot put it in explaining his Enlightenment.[49]

THE FRENCH ENLIGHTENMENT:
THE IDEOLOGY OF REASON

J ust as Tocqueville brought to the study of America the perspective of a Frenchman, so he brought to the study of France the perspective gained from his experiences in both America and England. The contrast between the French *philosophes* and their English counterparts, he wrote in his work on the *ancien régime,* reflected the distinctive role of intellectuals in the two countries.

> In England writers on the theory of government and those who actually governed cooperated with each other, the former setting forth their new theories, the latter amending or circumscribing these in the light of practical experience. In France, however, precept and practice were kept quite distinct and remained in the hands of two quite independent groups. One of these carried on the actual administration while the other set forth the abstract principles on which good government should, they said, be based; one took the routine measures appropriate to the needs of the moment, the other propounded general laws without a thought for their practical application; one group shaped the course of public affairs, the other that of public opinion.[1]

He might have included America alongside England, for there the "writers on the theory of government and those who actually governed" not only cooperated with each other but actually were one and the same, so that the practical and the theoretical were even more closely related.

There were, of course, a multitude of reasons for the disparities among the three Enlightenments: the very different political characters of the countries and the relationship of classes within those political systems; the nature and authority of the churches and their role in the state; economies at various levels of industrialism and subject to different kinds and degrees of government regulation; and all the other historical and social circumstances that were unique to each country and helped shape its temper and character. The *philosophes,* living in a country that was neither autocratic nor free, that was erratic in its exercise of censorship and prosecution, that had never experienced the kind of reform of either church or state which might encourage another generation of reformers, could hardly aspire to influence policy as their counterparts in Britain or America could. What they could aspire to was bold and imaginative thinking, unconstrained by such practical considerations as how their ideas might be translated into reality. They were, in effect, all the more free to theorize and generalize precisely because they were less free to consult and advise.

The *Encyclopédie* embodied the spirit of the French Enlightenment, as *The Federalist* did the American. The initial edition of the *Encyclopédie,* published between 1751 and 1772, consisted of seventeen volumes of text and another eleven of engraved plates; seven supplementary volumes appeared between 1776 and 1780. The subtitle was ambitious enough, *Dictionnaire raisonné des sciences, des arts et des métiers,* but the prospectus was still more ambitious: it was to be a systematic analysis of the "order and interrelations of human knowledge."[2] In the article "Encyclopedia," Denis Diderot, its principal editor, went beyond even this; its mission was "to collect all the knowledge that now lies scattered over the face of the earth, to make known its general structure to the men among whom we live, and to transmit it to those who will come after us," thus making men, of this time and of all time, not only wiser but also "more virtuous and more happy."[3]

The Federalist had no such grand pretensions. Designed for a specific purpose and a specific country, the papers did take the occasion to reflect upon human nature and society and even aspired to formulate the principles of a science of politics, but such speculations grew out of immediate, practical concerns and were advanced modestly and even tentatively. In the final paper Hamilton warned his countrymen against "the chimerical pursuit of a perfect plan." "I never expect to see a perfect work from imperfect man," and the collective work of many men (he was speaking of the Constitution, but it applied to the *Federalist* itself) was all the more likely to be imperfect, a compound of "the errors and prejudices, as of the good sense and wisdom," of individuals of diverse interests and inclinations.[4]

REASON AND RELIGION

It was not only the *philosophes'* penchant, as Tocqueville said, for abstract principles that made them unique. It was a particular principle: reason. That word, repeated constantly and in the most varied contexts, served almost as a mantra, a token of good faith and right-mindedness.* Long before Paine

---

* The two notable exceptions, as will be seen, were Montesquieu and Rousseau, who did not share the *philosophes'* reverence for reason and who had therefore an uneasy and anomalous relationship with them. Montesquieu was treated with personal respect although his ideas were either ignored or rejected, while Rousseau was dismissed by Voltaire as a "Judas" and by Diderot as an "anti-*philosophe*."[5]

declared his age to be the "Age of Reason," Diderot had defined the *Encyclopédie* as the instrument of "a reasoning age," "a philosophical age."[6] This article was nicely complemented by another which made the *philosophe* not only the spokesman of that philosophical age but something more as well. The reader was reminded of the familiar adage (pedantically attributed to the emperor Antoninus): "How happy the people would be if kings were philosophers or philosophers were kings."[7]

The idea of reason had as its converse the idea of religion. "Reason is to the philosopher," the *Encyclopédie* declared, "what grace is to the Christian. Grace moves the Christian to act, reason moves the philosopher."[8] Here, as elsewhere, reason was not just pitted against religion, defined in opposition to religion; it was implicitly granted the same absolute, dogmatic status as religion. In this sense, reason was the equivalent of the doctrine of grace. There is much truth in the familiar assertion that the *philosophes'* animus against religion was a by-product of their hostility to the Catholic Church, a church that was seen as authoritarian and repressive in itself, and even more so as the accomplice of an authoritarian and repressive state. This was, certainly, a dominant factor in their thinking. But it does not entirely account for the "studious ferocity," as Tocqueville put it, of their attack on religion.[9] What was at stake for the *philosophes* was nothing less than reason. And reason illegitimized not only the Catholic Church but any form of established or institutional religion, and beyond that any religious faith dependent on miracles or dogmas that violated the canons of reason.

Some of the articles commissioned or written by Diderot—on "Conscience," "Fanaticism," "Irreligion," "Tolerance," "Intolerance"—rather than taking issue with religion as such, made the case for religious toleration, the liberty to profess other religions than Catholicism, or, it may be, no religion at all. In "Irreligion," Diderot argued that such liberty would have no serious consequences for society because morality was independent of religion. Other articles, by the Baron d'Holbach notably, were overtly anti-religion; "Priests" and "Theocracy" suggested that religion was an invention by clever clerics who imposed it on the ignorant and intimidated masses. Still others made just enough concessions to orthodoxy to forestall censorship and prosecution.

Diderot's article on "Reason" was typically and deliberately ambiguous, paying lip service to religion by conceding an area in which revelation was entitled to "complete assent from the mind," and then hastening to add that this did not limit or undermine reason but rather confirmed reason in all matters where there was "a clear and distinct idea." In such cases, reason was the only "true and competent judge"; revelation could confirm judgments based upon reason but could not invalidate them. "We are men before we are Christians," Diderot reminded his readers. Decrying the doctrinal and ceremonial extravagances of most religions, he concluded that religion, "which is the honor of humanity and the most excellent prerogative of our nature over beasts, is often the area where men appear to be most irrational."[10]

Outside the *Encyclopédie,* some of the *philosophes* were less restrained. Holbach, Claude Helvétius, and Julien de Lamettrie were avowed atheists and materialists, while others professed to believe in some form of Christianity, rejecting only the authority and institutions of the church. Voltaire, a deist or proponent of natural religion, was above all a believer in religious toleration. But his hatred of *l'infâme* (he once announced that he intended to end his letters with what had become his signature, "*Ecrasez l'infâme*") went well beyond the cause of toleration. It was directed not only against intolerance and fanaticism, and not only against the institutions and authority of the Roman Catholic Church, but against Christianity itself. Diderot said that he spoke for most of the *philosophes* when he paid tribute to Voltaire as the "sublime, honorable, and dear Anti-Christ."[11] The historian Peter Gay, himself an admirer of Voltaire, described Voltaire's "distaste" for Christianity as "almost an obsession." Repeatedly and passionately, Voltaire returned to the theme: "Every sensible man, every honorable man, must hold the Christian sect in horror."[12]

"Every sensible man, every honorable man"—but not the common people, who, in the eyes of some eminent *philosophes* were neither sensible nor honorable because they were in thrall to Christianity. In his article on the *Encyclopédie,* Diderot made it clear that the common people had no part in the "philosophical age" celebrated in this enterprise. "The general mass of men are not so made that they can either promote or understand this forward march of the human spirit."[13] In another article, "Multitude," he was more dismissive, indeed, contemptuous, of the masses. "Distrust the judgment of the multitude in matters of reasoning and philosophy; its voice is that of wickedness, stupidity, inhumanity, unreason, and prejudice. . . . The multitude is ignorant and stupefied. . . . Distrust it in matters of morality; it is not capable of strong and generous actions . . . ; heroism is practically folly in its eyes."[14]

Diderot might have argued—and this may well have been the intention of other *Encyclopédistes*—that the masses were in this unhappy condition because they were still in bondage to religion and the church, and that the progress of enlightenment would liberate them from that benighted state. It would have been a plausible mission of the *Encyclopédie* to extend the "march of the human spirit" to the "general mass of men." Yet that was not the argument of either the article on the *Encyclopédie* or that on the "Multitude." Diderot's rebuke to

Helvétius, that a man was "destined by nature for a given function,"[15] was a milder version of his remarks to Voltaire. The poor, he told Voltaire, were "imbeciles" in matters of religion, "too idiotic—bestial—too miserable, and too busy" to enlighten themselves. They would never change; "the quantity of the *canaille* is just about always the same."[16]

Voltaire agreed, with a typically Voltairean proviso. Religion, he wrote Diderot, "must be destroyed among respectable people and left to the *canaille* large and small, for whom it was made." This was the point of his famous witticism: "I want my lawyer, my tailor, my servants, even my wife to believe in God, because it means that I shall be cheated and robbed and cuckolded less often. . . . If God did not exist, it would be necessary to invent him." Almost as an afterthought, he added: "But all nature cries out to us that he does exist"[17]—thus making God complicitous in the creation of those benighted souls.

Voltaire was a deist, unlike some of his confreres—Holbach, most notably—who were outright atheists. It was not, however, because of his theological differences with Holbach that he and d'Alembert (who was in substantial agreement with Holbach) opposed the publication of Holbach's atheistic writings. In spite of their commitment to religious toleration, they argued, in the time-honored tradition of prudent philosophers, that such views should circulate privately but not publicly. In his *Philosophical Dictionary,* Voltaire raised the question of whether "a nation of atheists" could exist. "It seems to me," he replied, "that one must distinguish between the nation properly so called, and a society of philosophers above the nation. It is very true that in every country the populace has need of the greatest curb." Princes, he conceded (although not, presumably, philosophers), also had need of restraint, but it was the people especially who required a "Supreme Being, creator, ruler, rewarder, revenger."[18]

Without religion, he wrote elsewhere, the lower classes would be nothing but "a horde of brigands like our thieves"; they would "pass their miserable lives in taverns with fallen women"; each day would begin anew "this abominable circle of brutalities."[19]

One historian has described the *philosophes'* belief in the social utility of religion as a "paradox," a "contradiction," a "lag in their social thought" caused by their inability to create an organic, unitary conception of society based upon their secular beliefs.[20] But there could be no such organic, unitary conception so long as the classes were divided, as the *philosophes* thought, by the chasm not only of poverty but, more crucially, of superstition and ignorance. For the British philosophers, that social chasm was bridged by the moral sense and common sense that were presumed to be innate in all people, in the lower classes as well as the upper. The *philosophes,* allowing to the common people neither a moral sense nor a common sense that might approximate reason, consigned them, in effect, to a state of nature—a brutalized Hobbesian, not a benign Rousseauean, state of nature—where they could be controlled and pacified only by the sanctions and strictures of religion.

Although Voltaire thought Holbach's profession of atheism so imprudent as to warrant suppression, he himself made no effort to conceal, in public as in private, his "horror" of Christianity—or, even more, his horror of Judaism.[21] The Old Testament for him was nothing else than a chronicle of cruelty, barbarism, and superstition. It has been suggested that he used Judaism as a surrogate for Christianity, his tirades against the former being a convenient disguise for his animus against the latter.[22] But his obsession with Judaism went beyond that subterfuge. Moreover, it was not only the Judaism of the Old Testament, the foundation of Christianity, that he decried. Many of the entries in the *Philosophical Dictionary* were on modern as well as ancient Jews, vilifying them, in the classical mode of anti-Semitism, as materialistic, greedy, barbarous, uncivilized, and, again and again, usurious. (The last charge is all the more egregious because Voltaire himself staunchly defended the principle of usury against the Catholic Church, which condemned it.) The Jews had deserved their expulsion from Spain, Voltaire said, because they had controlled all the money and commerce in the country. And they still aspired to do so, making usury their "sacred duty."[23]

In one letter to d'Alembert, Voltaire grudgingly conceded that although Jews had a history of persecuting others, nevertheless they themselves deserved to be tolerated because enlightened men must be tolerant at all costs. But this was written at the height of the Calas affair when he was making the case for toleration for the Huguenots. Half a dozen years later he had so far forgotten that argument that he gave vent to diatribes (not in private letters but in published writings) that are especially chilling in the light of recent history: "I would not be in the least surprised if these people [Jews] would not some day become deadly to the human race. . . . You [Jews] have surpassed all nations in impertinent fables, in bad conduct, and in barbarism. You deserve to be punished, for this is your destiny."[24]

While some historians today ignore or belittle Voltaire's anti-Semitism, contemporaries were well aware of it. Anti-Jewish pamphleteers quoted him approvingly, and Jewish writers counted him as their enemy. His views, moreover, were shared in large part (although less passionately and obsessively) by Diderot, Holbach, and others. Perhaps uneasy about this patent violation of the principle of toleration, Diderot assigned the article "Jew" to Louis de Jaucourt, who wrote an altogether sympathetic account of Jews and Judaism. Apart from Jaucourt, however, and Montesquieu, who was very nearly philo-Semitic, most of the *philosophes* were far more derogatory of Judaism than of Christianity.★

LIBERTY AND REASON

If reason heads the list of qualities defining the French Enlightenment, liberty is not far behind. Reason may have been the impulse behind the appeal for religious toleration—reason refusing to be bound by the strictures of religion—but the ostensible principle supporting that appeal was liberty, the liberty to follow one's conscience, interest, and will. The idea of liberty, however, although often invoked, did not elicit anything like the passion or commitment that reason did. Nor did it inspire the *philosophes* to engage in a systematic analysis of the political and social institutions that would promote and

---

★ Anti-Semitism was present in Britain as well, but in a milder and less insistent form. Shaftesbury found in the Jewish heroes of the Bible the embodiment of the worst characteristics of human beings. And Burke spoke casually of "money-jobbers, usurers, and Jews," and described Lord George Gordon, the anti-Catholic agitator responsible for the Gordon riots, who later converted to Judaism, as the "heir to the old hoards of the synagogue . . . the long compound interest of the thirty pieces of silver." But Gordon could redeem himself, Burke added, by meditating on the Talmud until he learned to conduct himself in a manner "not so disgraceful to the ancient religion" he had embraced.[25] Hume, on the other hand, was notably sympathetic to the Jews and critical of the "egregious tyranny" that had been responsible for their persecution and expulsion from England in the thirteenth century.[26] So far from being vilified as usurers, Jews were often praised (after their readmission to England by Cromwell) for their contributions to commerce and the economy. In Britain, it was generally men of letters and public figures who were well disposed to the Jews, favoring, for example, the bill passed by Parliament in 1753 providing for the naturalization of foreign-born Jews. That bill was repealed several months later because of popular pressure.

protect liberty.[27] Two notable exceptions were Turgot and his fellow physiocrats, who inquired seriously into the conditions of economic liberty, and Montesquieu, whose *Spirit of the Laws* was the seminal work (for America, although not for France) on political liberty.

A long article by Diderot on "Political Authority," in the first volume of the *Encyclopédie,* opened promisingly: "No man has received from nature the right to command others. Liberty is a gift from heaven, and each individual of the same species has the right to enjoy it as he enjoys the use of reason."[28] But it went on to deal only in the most general terms with the relation between subjects and monarchs. Another lengthy article on "Liberty" treated it entirely as a metaphysical problem, a question of free will and determinism. This was followed by half-page articles on "Natural Liberty" (liberty in the state of nature), "Civil Liberty" (liberty under law), and "Political Liberty" (on legislative and executive bodies), and a considerably longer article on "Liberty of Thought" (primarily on religion).

On the subject of liberty, as on religion, the *philosophes* may have been less than forthright for prudential reasons. A more concrete and extensive analysis of liberty could well have invited censorship, prosecution, and imprisonment. This was, in fact, the experience of several *philosophes* at one time or another. Diderot was briefly imprisoned early in his career, Rousseau and Voltaire had to take temporary refuge abroad, and d'Alembert felt obliged to resign the editorship of the *Encyclopédie* (which continued to be published under Diderot's editorship, even after it was formally suppressed in 1759). In spite of these measures, however, the *philosophes* did manage to discuss at some length and with great passion the no less sensitive subject of religion, with the usual euphemisms and concessions, to be sure—stratagems that might have been adapted to the subject of liberty as well.

Censorship and public condemnation, while inhibiting and

intimidating booksellers as well as authors, were less formidable than one might suppose. They sometimes even redounded to the favor of the writers. Montesquieu's *Persian Letters,* published anonymously in Amsterdam in 1721, was easily smuggled into France, where it sold so well that eight new editions came out in as many years—all without appearing in the booksellers' catalogues. (The double device, of fictional letters about an exotic country, was adopted by many imitators to evade the censors.) In 1748, *The Spirit of the Laws* was even more successful, in spite of the fact that the work was placed on the Index. The public burning of Voltaire's *Philosophical Letters* in 1734, on the grounds that the work was subversive and sacrilegious, helped make it an immediate success and may have inspired the author to greater feats of audacity. In 1765, so far from being discouraged by the burning of his *Philosophical Dictionary* and its proscription by Rome, Voltaire spent the next five years reprinting, revising, and enlarging it. Helvétius's *De l'esprit* was condemned by the Sorbonne and publicly burned (and, as an additional bonus, criticized by Voltaire, Rousseau, and others), whereupon it became famous in France and was translated into every European language.

The case of Montesquieu illustrates, perhaps more dramatically than anything else, the equivocal role of liberty in the thinking of the *philosophes.* Rousseau is often regarded, with good reason, as the odd man out among them. But in important respects, Montesquieu was even more so. Although *The Spirit of the Laws* was quoted in the *Encyclopédie,* it did not inform the thinking of the *philosophes,* as it did the authors of *The Federalist,* where it was cited frequently and appreciatively. Montesquieu himself, although he was asked to contribute to the *Encyclopédie,* did not do so; he finally agreed to write one article, on "Taste," but died before it was completed. (D'Alembert wrote his eulogy in the *Encyclopédie.*)

Apart from Jaucourt, who genuinely admired him, Montesquieu had few followers among the *philosophes* and many critics. When he died, only Diderot attended his funeral, as a mark of personal respect rather than sympathy with his ideas.

Unlike his confreres, Montesquieu did not appeal to reason as the fundamental principle of politics and society. Instead, he approached these subjects sociologically, making the political forms and institutions of a country dependent on the "spirit" of the regime and its physical and historical circumstances: "Mankind are influenced by various causes, by the climate, by the religion, by the laws, by the maxims of government, by precedents, morals, and customs; whence is formed a general spirit of nations."[29] Conspicuously absent from this list of causes was reason. And conspicuously present was religion. Montesquieu was not uncritical of the church in France, but he was more dismissive of atheism, preferring an established church suitable to the character of the country—the Catholic Church for France, the Anglican for England.

This sociological mode was hardly congenial to *philosophes* who believed that the function of reason was to produce universal principles independent of history, circumstance, and national spirit. "A good law," Condorcet protested, "ought to be good for all men, just as a true proposition is true for all."[30] The abbé Sieyès voiced a common complaint when he said that Montesquieu was concerned with "what is" rather than "what ought to be," thus violating the basic purpose of a "true political science."[31] Rousseau similarly criticized Montesquieu, in the name of the "science of political right," for dealing with the "positive right of established government" instead of the "principles of political right."[32] Helvétius went further, rejecting everything in *The Spirit of the Laws* that derived from the British model, most notably the separation of powers that Montesquieu regarded as the genius of the British constitution and the prerequisite of political liberty. Helvétius thought so ill of the book that he urged Montesquieu not to publish it, warning him that it would hurt his reputation.[33] Voltaire, in his *Commentary on the Spirit of the Laws,* while ostensibly praising its brilliant author, was sharply critical of the work itself. "Hardly has he established a principle, when history opens before him and shows him a hundred exceptions." (Montesquieu reciprocated in kind. "Sound judgment is better than brilliance," he said of Voltaire.)[34]

Among Voltaire's other objections, shared by almost all the *philosophes,* was Montesquieu's adherence to a theory that today may seem esoteric and academic but was of great political significance at the time. This was the *thèse nobiliaire,* the idea that the essential power in the French system of government, and the safeguard against monarchical despotism, resided with the nobility and the institutions it controlled, the *parlements* and judiciary. It is interesting that the alternative theory espoused by most of the *philosophes* was not a *thèse bourgeoise,* still less a *thèse prolétaire,* but the *thèse royale,* which insisted upon the fundamental authority of the king and denigrated the aristocracy as a self-seeking and disruptive force. "As to our aristocrats and our petty despots of all grades," Helvétius wrote to Montesquieu, "if they understand you, they cannot praise you too much, and this is the fault I have ever found with the principles of your work."[35]★

★ It may be said that Montesquieu had a personal stake in the *thèse nobiliaire,* having been born into the *noblesse de robe.* By the same token some of the adherents of the *thèse royale* may also have been personally motivated, either because of their relations with enlightened monarchs or their positions, pensions, and grants, which were dependent on the court. (Thirty-eight of the *Encyclopédistes* belonged to the prestigious Royal Academies, which were salaried posts, and fifteen were longtime employees in the civil or military administration.) Voltaire had a special reason for resenting Montesquieu and his theories. Just as he was completing his *History of Louis XIV,* with its defense of the *thèse royale,* *The Spirit of the Laws* was published, undermining that thesis (which was also being discredited by the weakness of Louis XV).

These alternative theories had the largest implications. For Montesquieu, the nobility was a countervailing force to the monarchy, thus an essential part of the separation and balance of powers which he took to be the fundamental principle of political liberty. For the *philosophes,* that limitation of sovereignty was unacceptable, not only because it gave too much power to petty aristocrats but also because it threatened the authority and power of an enlightened, or potentially enlightened, monarch.

ENLIGHTENED DESPOTISM AND THE GENERAL WILL

The predilection of the *philosophes* for "enlightened despotism" (the expression was a contemporary one, not the invention of historians) was more than an exercise of vanity, a response to monarchs who flattered them by consulting, fêting, and even supporting them financially, as if they were indeed philosopher-kings. Voltaire was engagingly candid about this: "How does one resist a victorious king, a poet, musician, and philosopher, who affected to appear to love me!"[36] But beyond this was a serious philosophical principle. Enlightened despotism was an attempt to realize—to enthrone, as it were—reason as embodied in the person of an enlightened monarch, a Frederick enlightened by Voltaire, a Catherine by Diderot. "There is no prince in Europe," Diderot once rejoiced, "who is not also a philosopher."[37] When Voltaire left Prussia in 1753 after spending two years there, it was not he who was disillusioned with Frederick but Frederick who made it clear that Voltaire was no longer welcome at the court (among other reasons, because of his illegal speculation in government bonds). Almost twenty-five years later, Voltaire defended Catherine's Russia against Montesquieu, who had criticized it for being despotic. Her government, Voltaire reported, "seeks to destroy anarchy, the odious prerogatives of the nobles, the power of the magnates, and not to establish intermediate bodies or to diminish its authority."[38]

If some of the *philosophes* later expressed qualms about absolute power in the hands of an enlightened despot, it was not because of any principled commitment to liberty, but because they began to suspect that good despots were rare and that even enlightened ones might fail to use their power wisely or justly. Diderot's relations with Catherine were more amiable than Voltaire's with Frederick, but even he was later moved to doubt. "If reason governed sovereigns," Diderot wrote, ". . . peoples would not need to bind the hands of the sovereigns." Unfortunately, that was rarely the case. The qualities that made for "a good, resolute, just, and enlightened master" were rare enough separately, still more so combined in a single person.[39] Two or three reigns of a "just and enlightened despotism," he told Catherine, would be a great misfortune, for they would reduce the subjects to the level of animals habituated to blind obedience. (He made this point in a private communication with Catherine, and repeated it briefly in his last published and little-known essay on the emperors Claudius and Nero.)[40]

Even utilitarians like Helvétius and Holbach, whose ultimate principle was the happiness of the people, did not welcome the separation of powers. On the contrary, they were as devoted to the *thèse royale* as Voltaire and as opposed to any idea of the separation of powers. Indeed, they were all the more eager to vest power in a "legislator" (a generic term that included a monarch) who would ensure that individual interests were made consonant with the greatest good of all. "The legislator," the article of that title in the *Encyclopédie* explained, "in all climates, circumstances, and governments [the allusions to Montesquieu are obvious] must propose to change private and property interests to community interests. Legislation is more or less perfect, according to what extent it leads to this goal."[41] The utilitarians had no principled objections to enlightened despotism, only practical ones. It was a failure of character and will, not of liberty, that gave them pause. Holbach, having dedicated one of his books to Louis XVI and spoken approvingly of his "absolute power," later had second thoughts: "Absolute power is very useful when it means to destroy abuses, abolish injustice, reprove vice, and reform morals. Despotism would be the best of governments if one could be promised that it would always be exercised by a Titus, a Trajan, or an Antoninus; but it usually falls into hands incapable of using it wisely."[42] However desirable unlimited power would be in the hands of an enlightened despot, Holbach concluded, such power finally "corrupts the mind and heart and perverts the best disposed men."[43] Even then, however, he was not moved to reconsider his opposition to limited sovereignty or the separation of powers.

"In the kind of universe which Helvétius depicts," Isaiah Berlin has observed, "there is little or no room for individual liberty."[44] He might have said the same of other Enlightenment thinkers—the physiocrats, for example, who, in the name of reason, argued in favor of both free trade and enlightened despotism. Men do not make laws, François Quesnay wrote, they only discover those laws which conform to "the supreme reason which governs the universe."[45] And that supreme reason was more readily discovered and acted upon by a single sovereign than by a multitude of individuals in a parliament reflecting different interests and ideas. Mercier de la Rivière coined the term "legal despotism" in place of "enlightened despotism" to make it clear that the authority of the despot derived from the natural law that was the basis of his sovereignty. Later, the term became a liability and even Mercier abandoned it, but at the time it was taken up favorably by Diderot, Mirabeau, and others (although not by Turgot, who thought it impolitic). It was Mercier who made the famous pronouncement deifying Euclid which has become the epigram of this school:

Euclid is the true type of despot. The geometrical ax-
ioms which he has transmitted to us are genuine
despotic laws; in them the legal and the personal despotism of the legislator are one and the same thing, a
force evident and irresistible; and for that reason the
despot Euclid has for centuries exercised his unchallenged sway over all enlightened peoples.[46]★

Because of their precept *"laisser faire, laisser passer,"* the
physiocrats have been identified with Adam Smith; one historian has described them as "Smith's acknowledged inspiration."[47] But while Smith agreed with them on the issue of
free trade, he disagreed not only with the primacy they gave
to agriculture as against industry and commerce but also with
their conception of the state and political authority. Where
Smith's theory of natural liberty applied to the polity as much
as the economy, the physiocrats allowed for individual liberty
only in the marketplace, arguing that the absolute sovereignty
of a monarch was necessary to establish the conditions for
economic liberty. Contrasting the physiocrats (*économistes,* he
called them) with Smith, Walter Bagehot described them as
being "above all things anxious for a very strong government;
they held to the maxim, everything *for* the people—nothing
by them; they had a horror of checks and counterpoises and
resistances; they wished to do everything by the *fiat* of the
sovereign."[48]

★ The mathematical paradigm was compelling for most of the *philosophes,*
which is why Isaac Newton was idolized. D'Alembert was a mathematician of some distinction, the author, at the age of twenty-six, of a *Treatise
on Dynamics* that elaborated upon Newton's laws of motion. So, too,
Condorcet made his mark as a mathematician with his work on probabil-
ity, long before he applied that mode of thought to social and political
affairs.

. . .

What the enlightened despot was to some of the *philosophes*—the supreme arbiter and legislator—the general will was to others. The concept of the general will has always, and properly so, been identified with Rousseau's *The Social Contract,* published in 1762. But Rousseau himself, seven years earlier, in his article "Political Economy" (a misnomer, because it dealt entirely with politics and not at all with economics), attributed it to Diderot's article "Natural Law" in the same volume of the *Encyclopédie.*★ It is curious to find the two articles on ostensibly different subjects making the same point, in almost the same words, about the subservience of individual wills to the general will. Diderot's article is worth dwelling upon, partly because it shows that the idea of the general will was not, as is sometimes thought, confined to Rousseau, and partly because Diderot associated it, as Rousseau did not, with the idea of reason.

"We must reason about all things," Diderot wrote, "because man is not just an animal but an animal who reasons." There were different ways of arriving at the truth, but whoever refused to seek it renounced the very nature of man and "should be treated by the rest of his species as a wild beast." And once the truth had been discovered, whoever refused to accept it was "either insane or wicked and morally evil."[49] Without freedom, there was no good or evil, right or wrong. But it was not the individual who had "the right to decide about the nature of right and wrong." Only "the human race" had that right because only it expressed the general will. And the general will was always paramount.

★ The question of priority is murky. Rousseau had used the idea of the general will, although not the term, in his *Second Discourse* in 1754. But he had had access, the previous autumn, to a draft of Diderot's "Natural Law" article.

Individual wills are suspect; they can be good or evil. But the general will is always good. It is never wrong, it never will be wrong. . . . It is to the general will that the individual must address himself to know how far he ought to be a man, a citizen, a subject, a father, a child, and when it is suitable to live or to die. It is for the general will to determine the limits of all duties. . . . If you therefore meditate carefully on the above, you will remain convinced: 1) that the man who listens only to his individual will is the enemy of the human race; 2) that the general will in each individual is a pure act of understanding that reasons in the silence of the passions about what man can demand of his fellow man and what his fellow man can rightfully demand of him; 3) that this consideration of the general will of the species and of the common desire is the rule of conduct relating one individual to another in the same society. . . .

After several other such propositions, Diderot concluded by invoking once again the authority of reason: "All these conclusions are evident to anyone who reasons, and . . . whoever does not wish to reason, renouncing his nature as a human being, must be treated as an unnatural being."[50] In effect, the theory of the general will was a surrogate for the enlightened despot. It had the same moral and political authority as the despot because it, too, was grounded in reason, a reason that was the source of all legitimate authority.

If the idea of reason lent itself to theories of enlightened despotism and the general will, it was also invoked in support of such classically liberal causes as religious toleration and legal reforms. These two issues came to a dramatic head in the notorious Calas affair. The conviction and execution in 1762 of Jean Calas, a Huguenot charged with murdering his son ostensibly because of the young man's desire to convert to Catholicism, became an international *cause célèbre* when Voltaire took it up. For him, as Peter Gay says, the case was perfect: If Calas had murdered his son, it was a specimen of Protestant fanaticism; if the state had murdered the father, it was a specimen of Catholic fanaticism. "One way or the other," Voltaire wrote, "this is the most horrible fanaticism in the most enlightened century."[51] When he began to inquire into the circumstances of the case, after the execution of Calas *père,* Voltaire concluded that the father was innocent, the victim of a state-sponsored inquisition on behalf of the church—yet another example of the ubiquitous *l'infâme.*

For Voltaire, as for most of the *philosophes,* the immediate lesson to be drawn from the Calas affair was the need for religious toleration; the secondary lesson was the reform of a legal system that permitted this miscarriage of justice. Long before this, Montesquieu had taken up the cause of legal reform. In *The Spirit of the Laws,* he proposed a number of measures designed to liberalize the law. Sacrilege, heresy, and "the crime against nature" (homosexuality) should no longer be prosecuted as crimes; "indiscreet speech" should not be chargeable as high treason; the death penalty should be used more discriminately; and punishment in general (and of debtors in particular) should be less harsh and proportionate to the crime.[52] Whatever their differences with Montesquieu, the *philosophes* were entirely in agreement with him on these reforms. And whatever their differences with the English on the separation of powers and the role of Parliament, they favored the adoption of such other British institutions as trial by jury, habeas corpus, and royal reprieves. (Condorcet went so far as to favor an internationally uniform code of law.) They also vigorously opposed slavery and the slave trade; most called for the immediate emancipation of slaves, others for its gradual abolition.

LE PEUPLE AND LA CANAILLE

On other social issues, however, the *philosophes* were far removed from the British. Just as there was nothing like the concept of a general will among the British philosophers, so there was nothing among the French like the "condition of the people" problem (as the British called it). The Americans, to be sure, were also less concerned than the British with this problem, perhaps because poverty in America, with all its attendant conditions, was far less exigent than in Britain. In France, however, the situation was, if anything, worse than in Britain. It might be said that the *philosophes* were inhibited from inquiring into social problems by the threat of censorship and prosecution. Yet that threat was far more serious in respect to religion, and it did not deter them from speculating and writing about that subject.

It is as if the *philosophes* expended so much intellectual capital on the exalted idea of reason that they had little thought left, and even less sympathy, for the common people. Diderot professed great admiration for Shaftesbury, whose book he had translated. But Shaftesbury would never have said, as Diderot did in one article, that a man who did not wish to reason must be treated as an "unnatural being," a "wild beast,"[53] or, in another, that "the common people are incredibly stupid."[54] The moral sense and common sense that the British attributed to all individuals gave to all people, including the common people, a common humanity and a common fund of moral and social obligations. The French idea of reason was not available to the common people and had no such moral or social component.

Holbach was obviously criticizing Adam Smith (and the moral philosophers in general) when he said that what moralists called "sympathy" was only an act of imagination. For some people, he observed, the sentiment of pity simply did not exist, or existed in a very feeble state. Indeed, most people were unmoved by the distress of others—princes by the misfortunes of their subjects, fathers by the plaints of their wives and children, greedy men by the plight of those they had reduced to misery. So far from lending a helping hand to the unfortunate, they fled from the spectacle of misfortune. Worse yet, they deliberately added to the ills of others. "I must go beyond this," Holbach warmed to his theme. "Most men feel themselves entitled by the weakness or misfortune of others to inflict further outrages upon them without fear of reprisal; they take a barbarous pleasure in adding to their afflictions, in making them feel their superiority, in treating them cruelly, in ridiculing them."[55]

In an essay ironically entitled "Discourse on Happiness," Lamettrie described the happiness of ordinary people as consisting, in effect, of making other people unhappy. "Man in general seems a deceitful, tricky, dangerous, perfidious animal; he seems to follow the heat of his blood and passions rather than the ideas which were given to him in childhood and which are the basis of natural law and remorse." This observation was prefaced by the even more cynical comment: "Let it not be said that I am urging people to crime. I am urging them only to be tranquil in crime."[56] Helvétius was no less harsh. Ignorance was more dangerous than ambition, he wrote, and men in general were "more stupid than wicked."[57] So, too, Voltaire, who never concealed his disdain for the people—"*la canaille*" (the rabble), as he habitually called them. "As for the *canaille,*" he told d'Alembert (much as Diderot had said to him), "I have no concern with it; it will always remain *canaille.*"[58]★

★ It may be said that the English had their equivalent of the *canaille* in the Irish immigrants. Yet while there was much indignation over the vagrancy, drunkenness, and lawlessness of some of the immigrants, this was often accompanied by expressions of pity for the wretched conditions in which they lived in England and the more desperate conditions in their own country from which they had fled.

The nearest British equivalent to this kind of misanthropy was Bernard Mandeville, and even he did not express himself quite so sharply. And Mandeville was hotly repudiated by the Enlightenment community in Britain, whereas in France, Diderot, Voltaire, Holbach, Helvétius, and Lamettrie were leading lights in the Enlightenment, valued contributors to the *Encyclopédie,* and frequenters of the Paris salons. (Holbach, the richest of the *philosophes,* presided over the most lavish salon.)

It is curious that just as the term "Enlightenment" has been claimed for the French, so has the word "compassion." Yet it was the English who introduced that word into the social vocabulary long before the French and made it the central theme of their moral philosophy, as the French did not. In the *Encyclopédie,* "Compassion" earned an entry of only several sentences, concluding with the observation that the more miserable one is, the more susceptible to compassion—which is why, d'Alembert wryly concluded, the people love to watch executions.[59] "Beneficence" fared somewhat better, a single column containing the usual platitudes, with an added qualification that gave primacy to reason: "It is not simply goodness of soul that characterizes beneficent people; that would only make them sensitive and incapable of harming others. It is a superior reason that brings that to perfection."[60] Rousseau, who is generally credited with the idea of compassion (or pity, as he more often spoke of it),[61] gave it an ambiguous role in society. Unlike the British, for whom compassion was a social virtue, a quality natural to individuals in society, in Rousseau's *Discourse on the Origin of Inequality,* pity appeared as a "natural sentiment" only in the state of nature, where it contributed to the preservation of the species by moderating the force of *l'amour de soi* (self-love). In civil society, pity was replaced by the "factitious" sentiment of *l'amour propre* (vanity, the corruption of self-love), which destroyed both equality and freedom and subjected mankind to "labor, servitude and misery."[62] Reviewing the *Discourse* (four years before his own *Theory of Moral Sentiments* appeared), Smith criticized Rousseau for sharing Mandeville's asocial conception of human nature, which assumed that "there is in man no powerful instinct which necessarily determines him to seek society for its own sake." The absence of that moral instinct, in Rousseau as in Mandeville, meant that the laws of society had no moral validity; they were nothing but "the inventions of the cunning and the powerful, in order to maintain or to acquire an unnatural and unjust superiority over the rest of their fellow creatures."[63]

In his novel *Emile*, Rousseau did posit an "inner senti- ment," as the basis, however, not of compassion but of self- love. "When the strength of an expansive soul makes me identify myself with my fellow, and I feel that I am, so to speak, in him, it is in order not to suffer that I do not want him to suffer. I am interested in him for love of myself [*l'amour de moi*]." This in turn was the source of justice: "Love of men derived from love of self [*l'amour de soi*] is the principle of human justice."[64] The social virtues did not come naturally to Emile. He had to learn them by becoming involved with those less fortunate than he. But he had also to learn that "his first duty is toward himself."[65] And he was instructed to exercise the social virtues not in relation to particular individuals but to the "species," the "whole of mankind."

> The less the object of our care is immediately involved with us, the less the illusion of particular interest is to be feared. The more one generalizes this interest, the more it becomes equitable, and the love of mankind is nothing other than the love of justice. . . . It is of little importance to him [Emile] who gets a greater share of happiness provided that it contributes

to the greatest happiness of all. This is the wise man's first interest after his private interest, for each is part of his species and not of another individual.

To prevent pity from degenerating into weakness, it must, therefore, be generalized and extended to the whole of mankind. Then one yields to it only insofar as it accords with justice, because of all the virtues justice is the one that contributes most to the common good of men. For the sake of reason, for the sake of love of ourselves, we must have pity for our species still more than for our neighbor.[66]

Whatever Rousseau's differences with the *philosophes* (and they were many), they had this in common: the tendency to "generalize" the virtues, to elevate "the whole of mankind" over the "individual," the "species" over one's "neighbor." When Francis Hutcheson spoke of the "greatest happiness for the greatest numbers," he meant this in the most prosaic, quantitative sense; when Rousseau spoke of the "greatest happiness of all," he meant it in some transcendent, metaphysical sense, a "common good of men" that was something other than the sum of the goods of individual men.

The "common good of men" did not necessarily mean the good of the common man. It did not even mean the education of the common man. In *Emile,* Rousseau's great work on education, the common man figured not at all. Emile himself was of "noble birth," and his education was undertaken by a private tutor. "The poor man," Rousseau observed, "does not need to be educated. His station gives him a compulsory education. He could have no other."[67] The same message appeared in *Julie, ou La Nouvelle Héloïse:* "Those who are destined to live in country simplicity have no need to develop their faculties in order to be happy. . . . Do not at all instruct the villager's child, for it is not fitting that he be instructed; do not instruct the city dweller's child, for you do not know yet what instruction is fitting for him."[68]

In his article "Political Economy," Rousseau spoke of the need for public education, not in the prosaic sense of reading, writing, and arithmetic but as a moral and social discipline. Education in this larger sense, he explained, was too important to be left to the "understanding and prejudices" of mortal fathers, for "the state remains, and the family dissolves." Thus, the public authority had to take the place of the father and assume the responsibility of imbuing children with "the laws of the state and the maxims of the general will." Only then would children learn "to cherish one another mutually as brothers, to will nothing contrary to the will of society, to substitute the actions of men and citizens for the fruitless and vain babbling of sophists, and to become one day the defenders and fathers of the country of which they will have been so long the children."[69] It was in the same spirit, seventeen years later, that Rousseau recommended to the new government of Poland a system of education that would inculcate children in the love of country. "It is education which must give souls the national form, and so direct their opinions and their tastes that they are patriots by inclination, by passion, by necessity. A child, on opening his eyes, should see his country, and until he dies he should see nothing but his country." Under such a regimen, children would not be allowed to play separately and privately but only together and in public, so that they would all aspire to a common goal.[70]

It may be said that Rousseau withheld education, in the ordinary sense, from the common man in the belief that natural man had his own natural virtue and wisdom, which would only be corrupted by education. But that would not account for the other *philosophes,* who had no such faith in natural man. It is remarkable that the leading lights of the Enlightenment should

have paid so little attention to the kind of elementary education that would be the necessary prelude to enlightenment in
its loftier sense. The proposals for popular education that were
circulated at the time did not come from the major *philosophes*
and did not have the imprimatur of the *Encyclopédie*. When the
Encyclopédie did raise the subject, it dealt with it in moral and
political terms rather than the commonplace sense of literacy.
The article on "School" defined it simply as a public place
"where one teaches languages, humanities, sciences, arts, etc.,"
followed by one short paragraph on the etymology of the
word.[71] Another, on "Education," explained that for every
order of citizens some kind of education was appropriate. Just
as there were schools that teach the verities of religion, so there
should be those that teach the "exercises, the practices, the
duties and the virtues of their state."[72] Yet another article gave
to the "Legislator" the task of educating children as a means
"of attaching the people to the country, of inspiring them with
community spirit, humanity, benevolence, public virtues, private virtues, love of honesty, passions useful to the state, and
finally of giving them and of conserving for them the kind of
character, of genius that is suitable to the country."[73]

Voltaire did raise the subject of education in the usual
sense of that word, conceding that some few children, the
offspring of skilled artisans, might be taught to read, write,
and calculate. But, like Rousseau, he saw no such need for
the children of agricultural laborers: "The cultivation of the
land required only a very common kind of intelligence." He
mocked the *Frères des Ecoles Chrétiennes* who made it their
mission to establish schools in the countryside, praised the
author of one book on education that opposed schooling for
the masses, and assured the misguided author of another,
who supported a system of national education, that the
people would never have the capacity to learn. "They will die
of hunger before they become philosophers. It seems to me
essential that they be ignorant beggars."[74] To d'Alembert, he

wrote, "We have never pretended to enlighten shoemakers and servants; that is the job of the apostles."[75]

Diderot's contribution to the subject came not in the *Encyclopédie* but in private letters to Catherine the Great for the reform of Russia, in one of which he suggested that publicly supported schools be established in the cities and villages. When Catherine protested that it was impossible to educate a large population, he replied that he did not know of any country, however populous, that could not have small schools for poor children where they would be fed as well as taught reading, writing, arithmetic, and "the moral and religious catechism."[76] It is ironic that Diderot's proposal for schools in Russia resembled those run by the church in France, which is perhaps why he never recommended any such public system for his own country. In any case, his communications with Catherine were private (the correspondence was not published until 1920), so that this proposal was not available to his countrymen. What was public, enshrined in the *Encyclopédie,* was his image of the "ignorant and stupefied" multitude, whose voice was that of "wickedness, stupidity, inhumanity, unreason, and prejudice."[77]

The argument kept coming back to this—the great enemy, *l'infâme.* The people were uneducable because they were unenlightened. They were unenlightened because they were incapable of the kind of reason that the *philosophes* took to be the essence of enlightenment. And they were incapable of reason because they were mired in the prejudices and superstitions, the miracles and barbarities, of religion. Moreover, the very idea of popular education was suspect because the institutions of education were in the hands of the church, so that the expansion of education would only further stupefy and stultify the people.

If some of the poor did in fact become educated in pre-revolutionary France, it was not because of the *philosophes,* the historian Daniel Roche points out, but in spite of them.

"Most Enlightenment thinkers opposed teaching peasants how to read and write, while the Church and especially the lower clergy favored it."[78] Early in the century, ordinances had been passed making schooling compulsory—not, to be sure, out of solicitude for education but as part of the campaign against Protestantism. Although these rules were not always carried out, literacy rates (defined as the ability to sign one's name) rose from 29 percent in 1700 to 37 percent in 1790, as a result of the church-run schools for which the *philosophes* had such contempt.[79] It is also ironic, Alan Kors observes, that the church had not only educated the *philosophes* (most, like Voltaire, attended Jesuit schools), but had created the reading public for the *Encyclopédie*.[80]

The *Encyclopédie* prided itself on its treatment of the "mechanical arts." It included copious drawings, diagrams, and plates illustrating those arts, and professed great respect for the artisans who practiced them. But it exhibited little patience and less regard for the great mass of the people who were not artisans, and its pages contain few practical proposals to alleviate their condition. In a very brief article on the "Indigent," Diderot protested against the division of society into the opulent and the miserable, concluding with the cryptic observation, "There are no indigent among savages."[81]★ But he did not explain why that was so or how civi-

---

★ Tocqueville once made a similar statement, not about savages but about poorer countries. There were more indigent, he explained, in England than in Portugal, partly because the standard of indigence (what was regarded as necessary for bare existence) was higher in England, and partly because the English were more desirous of relieving the condition of the indigent, thus permitting more people to qualify as indigent.[82] Diderot may have meant something like this in his statement about savages and the indigent.

lized society could cope with its indigents. Other articles complained about the gross inequalities in society and the unfortunate situation of the very poor, without offering any practical proposals for reform.

Turgot was the rare *philosophe* who was also a reformer. As intendant of Limoges, one of the poorest provinces in France, he introduced new agricultural methods and crops, promoted local free trade, encouraged industry, and provided measures of relief for the poor. Later, in his brief tenure as France's comptroller-general of finance, he tried to enact reforms on a larger scale, abolishing some sinecures and monopolies, immunities from taxation, guild privileges, and compulsory labor on the roads. (After his forced resignation, most of these reforms were repealed.) As a prominent physio-crat, he advocated a policy of free trade, which would have been (as Smith also pointed out) to the ultimate advantage of the poor as well as to the national economy. He was unsym-pathetic, however, even hostile to charity, not only because it was administered by the church but also because he deplored its practical effects. The poor, he wrote in the *Encyclopédie,* had "incontestable rights on the abundance of the rich," and charitable foundations were meant to alleviate their miseries. The result of such endeavors, however, was unfortunate, for those countries where charity was most abundant were also those where misery was most widespread. The reason was simple: "To permit a large number of men to live free of charge is to encourage laziness and all the disorders that fol-low; it is to render the condition of the idler preferable to that of the man who works. . . . The race of industrious citi-zens is replaced by a vile population composed of vagabond beggars free to commit all sorts of crimes."[83]

Diderot echoed these sentiments, criticizing the *hôpitaux* (poorhouses as much as hospitals) as refuges for professional beggars. Nor was the situation outside the poorhouses much better, for there were masses of "young and vigorous idlers who, finding in our ill-conceived charity easier and more generous sustenance than they could get by work, fill up our streets, our churches, our grand boulevards, our market-towns, our cities, and our countryside"; they were the "vermin" produced by a state that did not value real men.[84] Jaucourt was one of the few contributors to the *Encyclopédie* who made a point of distinguishing between beggars—"vagabonds by profession . . . who demand alms for idleness and sloth, rather than earn their livelihood by work"—and those who were indigent because of sickness or old age. Unlike Diderot, he recommended that workhouses be established for the needy in conjunction with the *hôpitaux*.[85] In another article, making a similar distinction between beggars and the common people, he disputed the prevalent idea that the latter would work and be docile only if they were kept in poverty.[86]

It is interesting that no serious thought was given to the English example of the Poor Laws. D'Holbach did mention them, only to criticize them for the same reasons that he disapproved of religious foundations and charities in general, because they encouraged laziness and idleness.[87] Even Montesquieu, otherwise so well disposed to the English, was opposed to the English system. At one point he seemed to favor something like a state provision for the poor: "The alms given to a naked man in the street do not fulfil the obligations of the state, which owes to every citizen a certain subsistence, a proper nourishment, convenient clothing, and a kind of life not incompatible with health." He went on, however, to argue not only against a state system of relief but also against organized, private charitable institutions. Transient help, he insisted, was much better than permanent foundations. "The evil is momentary; it is necessary, therefore, that the succor should be of the same nature, and that it be applied to particular accidents."[88]

Being wary of charity and charitable institutions (and not just because they were administered by the church), the *philosophes* produced neither the community of philanthropists nor the multitude of private societies that were so prominent in Britain. The article on "Philanthropy" in the *Encyclopédie* consisted of one short paragraph distinguishing between two kinds of philanthropies: the first designed to make oneself loved for one's virtues, and the second, common in polite society, meant to gain the approval of others; in the latter case, "it is not men that one loves but oneself."[89] The *philosophes* were fond of the word *bienfaisance,* but they themselves (with the notable exception of Turgot) were not personally involved in benevolent enterprises or practical reforms. Just as there was no "Age of Reason" in Britain, so there was no "Age of Benevolence" in France.

ENLIGHTENMENT AND REVOLUTION

It is often said that the *philosophes* did not foresee or want revolution, that they preferred to have change come about by means of an enlightened monarch rather than an unenlightened mob. On one occasion, however, when he was feeling especially aggrieved, Voltaire confessed that he looked forward to a popular revolution.

Everything I observe [he wrote to a friend in 1764] is sowing the seeds of a revolution that will inevitably come to pass and which I shall not have the pleasure of witnessing. The French always get there late but at last they do arrive. By degrees enlightenment has spread so widely that it will burst forth at the first opportunity, and then there will be a grand commotion. The younger generation are lucky; they will see some great things.[90]

Of the better known *philosophes,* only Condorcet was "lucky" enough to see the Enlightenment burst forth into revolution. Helvétius died in 1771, Voltaire and Rousseau in 1778, d'Alembert and Diderot in 1783 and 1784, Holbach in 1789 on the eve of the Revolution (but he had been ill and inactive for several years before that). Condorcet did live to see the Revolution and had the highest hopes for it, until he was forced to flee from the Terror and died in jail in 1794. A number of lesser contributors to the *Encyclopédie* survived. A dozen or so participated in the local assemblies that drew up the *cahiers,* the letters of grievance submitted to the States-General in May 1789, but they expressed no desire to abolish the nobility or monarchy. They were not, in fact, revolutionaries or republicans, and were disaffected very early in the course of the Revolution. Some fled from Paris or emigrated; four were imprisoned by the Terror; one was executed.[91]

Yet the ideas of the Enlightenment did have resonance in the Revolution, if not quite that which their creators might have desired. The most obvious legacy of the Enlightenment was anti-clericalism. The *philosophes* would surely have approved of the disestablishment of the church, the emancipation of Protestants and Jews, and the legalization of civil marriage and divorce. But they might have had cause for disquiet about some of the other consequences of the disestablishment. They had been opposed to the charities run by the church, but the elimination of those charities left the indigent with no resources at all. The remedies hastily improvised by the Revolution—workshops and laws regulating prices, wages, and the production of food—proved unwieldy and ineffectual, leaving the poor, most historians agree, worse off at the end of the Revolution than at the beginning.[92]

Similarly, the church-run schools were abolished with nothing to replace them. In 1791, Condorcet wrote a report for the Assembly recommending the establishment of village schools, but it was put off for discussion, perhaps because of the outbreak of war the following year. When he returned to the subject, in his *Sketch for a Historical Picture of the Progress of the Human Mind* (written while he was in hiding from the Terror and published posthumously), he devoted a single paragraph to the purposes of such an education, starting with the management of the household and concluding with the ability to exercise one's rights and reason, but containing no concrete proposal for schooling. In 1793, Robespierre presented a plan for compulsory education in boarding schools, where the children would be protected from the insidious influence of reactionary parents. Although this was passed by the Convention, its essential provisions were eliminated. Only after Thermidor did the Directory promulgate an educational code providing for a minimal elementary education to be paid for by parents.

One cannot fairly saddle the Enlightenment with responsibility for all the deeds, or misdeeds, of the Revolution. Yet there were unmistakable echoes of the *philosophes,* of Rousseau especially, at every stage. The famous pronouncement by the abbé Sieyès in the pamphlet published on the eve of the Revolution, *What Is the Third Estate?,* might have been coined by his hero Rousseau. "The nation," Sieyès declared, "is prior to everything. It is the source of everything. Its will is always legal; indeed it is the law itself."[93] The first sessions of the National Assembly in 1789 were devoted to drafting the Declaration of the Rights of Man and the Citizen, which included references to the social contract taken almost verbatim from Rousseau's book. The following year, a bust of Rousseau was installed in the Assembly Hall, together with a copy of the *The Social Contract,* and a law was passed calling for the erection of a statue of him. Effigies, busts, and images of him were common, and items reputedly belonging to him (his walking stick, for example) were sold many times over. When Paris was divided into electoral districts, one section was named *"Contrat Social."* And when his body was transferred to the Panthéon, it was together with a copy of *The*

Social Contract resplendent on a velvet cushion. A member of the National Convention reported on this event: "It is not the *Social Contract* that brought about the Revolution. Rather, it is the Revolution that explained to us the *Social Contract*."[94]

Rousseau's influence on Robespierre was even more pronounced. The opening lines of *Emile,* "Everything is good as it leaves the hands of the Author of things; everything degenerates in the hands of man," were echoed by Robespierre: "Man is good, as he comes from the hands of nature . . . if he is corrupt, the responsibility lies with vicious social institutions."[95] Robespierre might also have been invoking the general will when he contrasted the "people" to "individuals": "The people is good, patient, and generous. . . . The interest, the desire of the people is that of nature, humanity, and the general welfare. . . . The people is always worth more than individuals. . . . The people is sublime, but individuals are weak."[96]

Robespierre explicitly paid tribute to Rousseau when he proclaimed the Festival of the Supreme Being ushering in the "Republic of Virtue" (the euphemism for the Terror). In the *Encyclopédie,* Rousseau had called for the establishment of "the reign of virtue" that would make "particular wills" conform to the "general will."[97] He did not use the expression "reign of virtue" in *The Social Contract,* but he did introduce, in the final chapter of that work, the idea of a civil religion that would inaugurate, in effect, such a reign. That religion was to be based on a "civil profession of faith" prescribing the "social sentiments without which a man cannot be a good citizen or a faithful subject." No one, Rousseau added, would be compelled to believe the dogmas of that religion, but anyone who did not believe them would be banished from the state—banished not for impiety but as an "anti-social being, incapable of truly loving the laws and justice, and of sacrificing, at need, his life to his duty."[98] And anyone who, after professing to believe those dogmas, acted as if he did not believe them, would be put to death. The dogmas themselves seem banal, even innocent: the existence of an almighty and beneficent deity, immortality, the happiness of the just and punishment of the wicked, and the sanctity of the social contract and laws. But the idea of a civil religion, with all the solemnity and strictures attached to it, was anything but innocent, for it was meant to carry out the purpose of the new regime, as Rousseau understood it, which was nothing less than the radical reshaping not only of society but of humanity:

> He [the sovereign, or "legislator"] who dares to undertake the making of a people's institutions ought to feel himself capable, so to speak, of changing human nature, of transforming each individual, who is by himself a complete and solitary whole, into part of a greater whole from which he in a manner receives his life and being; of altering man's constitution for the purpose of strengthening it; and of substituting a partial and moral existence for the physical and independent existence nature has conferred on us all.[99]

It was as if Robespierre, in instituting the Republic of Virtue, were responding to Rousseau's challenge, taking upon himself, as the supreme legislator, the task of "changing human nature" and "transforming each individual." "I am convinced," Robespierre said of his proposal for the education of the young in boarding schools, "of the necessity of bringing about a complete regeneration, and, if I may express myself so, of creating a new people."[100]

This was Tocqueville's reading of the Revolution: "The ideal the French Revolution set before it was not merely a change in the French social system but nothing short of a regeneration of the whole human race." And again: "They [the revolutionists] had a fanatical faith in their vocation—that of transforming the social system, root and branch, and regenerating the whole human race."[101] A modern French historian agrees. The idea of "regeneration," Mona Ozouf says, was a key concept of revolutionary discourse. "People began to speak only of regeneration, a program without limits, at once physical, political, moral, and social, which aimed for nothing less than the creation of a 'new people.'" This idea, so fervently affirmed by Rousseau, was often invoked by the revolutionists, which was "one of the reasons why the Revolution was all his from the beginning."[102]

An alternative view of the Revolution stops short of the idea of a regenerated human nature, seeing it instead as a thoroughgoing social revolution. For Hannah Arendt, the Revolution was "born out of compassion" for the "low people," *les misérables*. First articulated by Rousseau and carried out by his disciple Robespierre, this "passion for compassion" inevitably culminated in the Terror, for compassion responded only to "necessity, the urgent needs of the people," leaving no room for law or government, for liberty or even reason.[103] This is a moving but, I believe, fanciful reading of history. The French Revolution was not a social revolution, and the Terror was instituted not out of compassion for the poor but for purposes of "public safety," the safety of the regime. *Le peuple,* in whose name Robespierre established the republic, was not the people in any ordinary sense, still less *les misérables,* but a singular, abstract people, represented by an appropriately singular and abstract general will.

"Ah," Robespierre proclaimed, in paying homage to Rousseau, "if he had witnessed this revolution of which he was the precursor and which has carried him to the Pantheon, who can doubt that his generous soul would have embraced with rapture the cause of justice and equality?"[104]

"Justice and equality"—not, notably, "liberty." One wonders how Rousseau, or for that matter the other *philosophes,* would have fared had they been "lucky" enough (as Voltaire put it) to live to see that Revolution. Not well, to judge by the fate of Condorcet and some of the *Encyclopédistes,* who lived to see it—and to die from it. And, of course, there was Robespierre himself, the disciple of Rousseau, who became the victim of his own Terror.

THE AMERICAN ENLIGHTENMENT:
THE POLITICS OF LIBERTY

I n Britain, the social virtues were in the forefront of philosophical speculation and social policy, the primary condition of the public good. In America, they were in the
background, the necessary but not sufficient condition. What
was in the forefront was liberty. And not the natural liberty that
Smith saw as the basis of a free economy and society, but artificial liberty, so to speak—political liberty, the principles and
institutions appropriate to the new republic. It was in the name
of liberty—religious liberty—that many of the first settlers
came to America. (Some, to be sure, came for their own liberty, although not for that of others.) And it was in the name
of liberty—political liberty—that they later declared their
independence from Britain. "An empire of liberty," John
Adams described his vision of the America of the future, an
empire comprising "twenty or thirty millions of freemen,
without one noble or one king among them."[1]

The American *novus ordo saeclorum* was a new political
order, not a new social or human order.* As it was liberty that

---

* The distinction between the political and social is reflected in the common (but not explicit or consistent) distinction between liberty and freedom, liberty being primarily a political and legal concept, freedom a
social and psychological one. In his famous essay "Two Concepts of Liberty," Isaiah Berlin denies this distinction, making a point of using both

was the driving force of the American Enlightenment, so it was political theory that inspired the Constitution designed to sustain the new republic. Gordon S. Wood has commented on the curious situation in which the Americans found themselves on the eve of the Revolution. For almost a century, they had basked in the glory of the British constitution: "the best model of government that can be framed by mortals," "the glorious fabric of Britain's liberty," "the palladium of civil liberty," "the most perfect form of government." Even as the Revolution approached, the Americans prided themselves that they had the British constitution on their side, that their Revolution was justified by "both the letter and the spirit of the British constitution."[3] Sir William Blackstone's *Commentaries on the Laws of England,* published less than a decade before the Revolution, was often cited as the authoritative source for their own principles and institutions, as was Montesquieu's *The Spirit of the Laws,* which drew so heavily upon the example of Britain. Yet within a few years the Americans were denouncing that government, Parliament as well as king, as corrupt and tyrannical. It was then that they applied themselves to the creation of what *The Federalist* called a new "science of politics," a science designed to create a republic *de novo.*[4]

"We have it in our power to begin the world over again," Thomas Paine exulted in 1776; and after the French Revolution, he rejoiced in "seeing government begin, as if we had lived in the beginning of time."[5] The more sober and conservative John Jay was no less enthusiastic: "The Americans are the first people whom Heaven has favored with an opportunity of deliberating upon, and choosing, the forms of

words interchangeably.[2] Yet much of his discussion of negative and positive liberty—in effect, liberty and freedom—would be clarified by recognizing that distinction.

government under which they shall live."[6] Yet the Founders did not come to their task *de novo*. They were practical men of affairs who had actually been involved in the workings of government, indeed, had been the principal actors in public life, as they were also the principal theorists.

Perhaps more important, the citizens themselves had had practical experience in governing—in self-governing. Many years later, Adams observed: "The Revolution was effected before the war commenced. The Revolution was in the minds and hearts of the people; a change in their religious sentiments of their duties and obligations."[7] At the time, however, he found the roots of that Revolution not in religion but in politics. It was in their "bodies politic," their town halls and assemblies, that Americans "acquired from their infancy the habit of discussing, of deliberating, and of judging of public affairs"; and it was there that "the sentiments of the people were formed in the first place."[8] Because of the prior existence of these political institutions and sentiments, the Revolution did not return the people to civil society (as Locke would have had it), still less to a state of nature (as Hobbes thought), but to a political society, a polity—a less organized, certainly a less centralized one than the Constitution was to give them, but a polity nevertheless.

REVOLUTION AND CONSTITUTION

This political experience and temper was reflected in a body of literature that had no equivalent in either France or Britain. *The Federalist* (a misnomer in that singular form, yet that was the title originally given to it) consisted of eighty-five newspaper articles appearing over the course of ten months from October 1787 to August 1788 (published in two volumes while the serial papers were still being issued). Written by Alexander Hamilton, John Jay, and James Madison, the articles debated all the issues pertinent not only to the Constitution but to the very idea of a republican government. Some were rebuttals to the Anti-Federalists, whose writings were equally impressive and even more voluminous (six tomes in the latest edition, plus an introductory volume). In addition, there were a multitude of pamphlets, sermons, editorials, and essays; speeches delivered in the state assemblies, ratifying conventions, and the Constitutional Convention; and private letters by the Founders that were serious commentaries on ideas and public affairs. This corpus of political literature was an extraordinary intellectual achievement for a country that was, as Bernard Bailyn has said, "provincial," thousands of miles removed from the center of civilization.[9]

What is remarkable is that *The Federalist,* written by three men who often disagreed with each other, composed hastily in response to the pressing issues of the moment or recycled from letters and speeches, should have commanded the attention and respect it did—and, even more remarkably, still does. Against the powerful arguments of the Anti-Federalists, the Federalists defended the essential principle of the Constitution: a strong central government with a due regard for the rights and liberties of both individuals and the states. No subject was too large or too small to engage their attention: taxation and representation, war and commerce, foreign relations and domestic affairs, the separation of powers and checks and balances. In one way or another, they attempted to reconcile what many believed to be unreconcilable, the sovereignty of the state and the liberty of the individual—and, what was even more difficult, to reconcile them within the context of a large, commercial republic.

If there were few references in *The Federalist* to the ancient republics (and those were mainly unfavorable or dismissive), it was because the work was intended for a specific purpose and a uniquely modern situation. In this sense, it was, like the Constitution itself, a consciously modern document. It was also, one might say, a consciously post-revolutionary work, putting the Revolution behind it and going on to the next stage of history: the *novus ordo saeclorum* that was to succeed and transcend—or, as Hegel might say, "negate"—the Revolution. In effect, it was a rebuttal to those, like Jefferson and Paine, who did not want to put the Revolution behind them, who wanted to perpetuate not so much the memory or glory of the Revolution as the continuing fact and reality of revolution.

Like revolutionaries of a later generation, Jefferson and Paine adhered to something like a theory of "permanent revolution," of perpetual dissent and renewal. Almost the very day that Hamilton, with Shays's Rebellion in mind, was cautioning the readers of *The Federalist* against "domestic factions and convulsions,"[10] Jefferson, then minister to France, was writing from Paris to an American (Adams's son-in-law, as it happened) praising the rebellion that was "so honorably conducted." "God forbid we should ever be twenty years without such a rebellion. . . . What signify a few lives lost in a century or two? The tree of liberty must be refreshed from time to time with the blood of patriots and tyrants. It is its natural manure."[11] Only a little less sanguinary was Jefferson's earlier letter to Abigail Adams, who had been appalled by his recommendation that the rebels be pardoned. "The spirit of resistance to government is so valuable on certain occasions, that I wish it to be always kept alive. It will often be exercised when wrong, but better so than not to be exercised at all. I like a little rebellion now and then. It is like a storm in the atmosphere."[12]

Two years later, writing to Madison from Paris, perhaps inspired by the French Declaration of the Rights of Man and the Citizen that had just been issued, Jefferson enunciated the famous principle: "No society can make a perpetual constitution or even a perpetual law. The earth belongs always to the living generation." At first Jefferson seemed to be limiting that principle to material goods. It was property, the "usufruct" of the earth, that belonged to the living—and not only property as such but debts, which could not be passed on from one generation to another. But he soon went well beyond that, applying the principle to laws and constitutions as well, so that the people in one generation were masters of their own property and "masters too of their own persons, and consequently may govern them as they please." Jefferson even specified the exact definition of generation, setting it initially at thirty-four years and then, consulting the actuarial tables, revising it downward to nineteen years. Thus, no law or constitution would be valid beyond nineteen years, unless expressly reenacted by the people. This condition was not satisfied, he insisted, by a provision for the repeal or amendment of laws, because there were too many impediments to such actions.[13]

Madison responded to Jefferson's proposal with great gravity. Would not such a government be "too subject to the casualty and consequences of an interregnum?" Would it not become "too mutable and novel to retain that share of prejudice in its favor which is a salutary aid to the most rational govt?" And would it not "engender pernicious factions . . . and agitate the public mind more frequently and more violently than might be expedient?" After a series of other objections, Madison concluded, as if to soften their impact, that he did not mean to impeach the utility of Jefferson's principle in specific cases or to deny its importance "in the eye of the philosophical legislator." Unfortunately, he added, the spirit of philosophical legislation was not much in fashion in America or in its legislative body.[14]

Madison himself was not especially respectful of the "philosophical legislator." Nor was Jefferson always so critical of the idea of a constitution. He had, in fact, drawn up a draft of a constitution for Virginia in 1776 (reprinted six years later in his *Notes on the State of Virginia*), designed to establish "the fundamental laws and principles of government," including a provision for the repeal or amendment of parts of the state constitution. Later, in *The Federalist,* Madison went so far as to criticize that repeal clause. By suggesting that there was a defect in the government and appealing to the people to correct it, the clause deprived the constitution of "that veneration which time bestows on every thing, and without which perhaps the wisest and freest governments could not possess the requisite stability." Reason alone, like man alone, Madison reminded his readers (and his friend Jefferson), was "timid and cautious," and had to be fortified by the opinions of others.

> In a nation of philosophers, this consideration ought to be disregarded. A reverence for the laws would be sufficiently inculcated by the voice of an enlightened reason. But a nation of philosophers is as little to be expected as the philosophical race of kings wished for by Plato. And in every other nation, the most rational government will not find it a superfluous advantage to have the prejudices of the community on its side.[15]

Only two years later Burke and Paine, responding to the French Revolution, were to engage in a similar dialogue. In the *Reflections,* Burke protested against the "metaphysicians" who sought to create a government based upon reason and failed to appreciate the role of opinion and prejudice in the affairs of men. Paine replied by deriding this legitimization of opinion and prejudice. Like Jefferson, he declared each generation sovereign, bound by nothing but its own reason and rights. "Every age and generation must be as free to act for itself, *in all cases,* as the ages and generations which preceded it. The vanity and presumption of governing beyond the grave is the most ridiculous and insolent of all tyrannies." Just as every child was born anew, the world "as new to him as it was to the first man that existed," so every generation was a new "creation."[16]

By this time, the issue was moot. Indeed, it had never been a serious option. The American republic, the *novus ordo saeclorum,* was created *de novo,* to be sure. But the Founders never doubted that they were not only creating but "founding" a republic, not for their generation alone but for an untold number of future generations. This was the meaning of the Constitution, in which they had invested so much thought and effort. It was meant to settle "the fundamental laws and principles of government," as Jefferson said of the constitution he had proposed for Virginia. And the amendment clause was designed to allow for the new circumstances that would inevitably arise, while reaffirming those fundamental laws and principles.

LIBERTY AND VIRTUE

The "politics of liberty" that was the animating spirit of the Founders was, in a sense, a corollary of the "sociology of virtue." It was only because virtue—the will and capacity to put the public interest over the private—was insufficient to maintain liberty that politics had to perform that function. "I think with you," John Adams wrote to his cousin Samuel Adams, "that knowledge and benevolence ought to be promoted as much as possible; but, despairing of ever seeing them sufficiently general for the security of society, I am for seeking institutions which may supply in some degree the defect." Nor was the love of liberty itself sufficient. "We must not, then, depend alone upon the love of liberty in the soul of man for its preservation. Some political institutions must be prepared to assist this love against its enemies."[17]

The relationship between social virtue and political liberty was at the heart of the quarrel between the Federalists and the

Anti-Federalists. Virtue was the principal concern of the Anti-Federalists, and corruption (the kind of corruption they saw in England) their principal worry. If the Federalists were enamored of Montesquieu principally for his views on the separation and balance of powers—he was by far the most quoted author in *The Federalist* and in the debates on the Constitution—the Anti-Federalists revered him for his definition of virtue in a republic: "the love of the laws and of our country," "a constant preference of public to private interest."[18] Like him, they believed that a virtuous people could thrive only in a republic that was small, homogeneous, and predominantly agrarian.★

There was nothing utopian or even optimistic in this view of virtue or human nature. On the contrary, it was because the Anti-Federalists were so pessimistic (or realistic) that they were anxious about the destabilizing and demoralizing effects of industry, commerce, and urban society. A commercial society, they believed, "begets luxury, the parent of inequality, the foe to virtue, and the enemy to restraint."[19] Jefferson was adamant on the subject. Manufacturing, he insisted, should be resorted to only of necessity, not choice, because a people engaged in industry were dependent on the caprice of customers, and such dependence "begets subservience and venality, suffocates the germ of virtue, and prepares fit tools for the designs of ambition." Agriculture, on the other hand, was a prescription for virtue. "Those who labor in the earth are the chosen people of God, if ever he had a chosen people. . . . Corruption of morals in the mass of cultivators is a phenomenon of which no age nor nation has furnished an example."[20]

★ Jefferson filled twenty-eight pages of his *Commonplace Book* with extracts from *The Spirit of the Laws,* more space than he devoted to any other author. He and Madison later became critical of Montesquieu—Jefferson because Montesquieu was too well disposed to English institutions, Madison because of Montesquieu's insistence that a republic could be sustained only in a small territory.

Once the euphoria of revolution wore off, the Anti-Federalists predicted, both the people and their leaders would fall prey to venality and corruption, and the republic itself would be endangered. In the hope of recalling the country to the moral basis of the regime, they sought to have a Bill of Rights incorporated in the body of the Constitution, complete with a statement of ethical principles. In this, as in much of the rest of the Constitution, the Federalists prevailed. The Bill of Rights (recommended by Jefferson but actually written by Madison) appeared in the form of amendments, without the "aphorisms," as *The Federalist* disparagingly put it, more appropriate to an ethical treatise than a constitution.[21]

In his insistence on natural rights and a contract between the people and the government, Jefferson may be thought of as a disciple of Locke. (He had read Locke's *Treatise on Government* three times.) Yet he believed no less ardently in the moral sense that the Scottish philosophers favored and that Locke would have repudiated.★ In a dialogue between "Head" and "Heart" in 1786, in which he took upon himself the role of "Heart," Jefferson asserted that "morals were too essential to the happiness of man to be risked on the uncertain combinations of the head. She [nature] laid their foundation therefore in sentiment, not science."[23] A letter to his nephew the following year (repeated almost verbatim to John Adams twenty-eight years later) might have been penned by a professor of moral philosophy at the University of Glasgow.

> Man was destined for society. His morality therefore was
> to be formed to this object. He was endowed with a

★ The conflation of Lockean and Scottish views, as if they were entirely compatible, was so common at the time that it defies the attempts of historians to characterize the American Enlightenment as either Lockean or Scottish.[22]

sense of right and wrong merely relative to this. This sense is as much a part of his nature as the sense of hearing, seeing, feeling; it is the true foundation of morality. . . . The moral sense, or conscience, is as much a part of man as his leg or arm. It is given to all human beings in a stronger or weaker degree, as force of members is given them in a greater or less degree. It may be strengthened by exercise, as may any particular limb of the body. This sense is submitted indeed in some degree to the guidance of reason; but it is a small stock which is required for this: even a less one than what we call common sense.[24]

The Federalists were no less pessimistic (or realistic) than the Anti-Federalists. Having little confidence in the ability of a people to sustain the kind of public-spiritedness that was identified with virtue, they sought a surrogate for public virtue in interest—or rather, in the "opposite and rival interests" that would naturally emerge in a large commercial republic. It was to foster such a multiplicity and diversity of interests, together with the parties and sects representing those interests, that they wanted to encourage commerce and enlarge the republic. Like Adam Smith and Hume (and unlike Jefferson), the Federalists looked upon an expansive, "progressive" commercial and industrial economy as the condition for moral and material self-betterment. "The assiduous merchant," Hamilton wrote, "the laborious husbandman, the active mechanic, and the industrious manufacturer—all orders of men look forward with eager expectation and growing alacrity to the pleasing reward of their toils."[25]

By the same token, it was to prevent corruption and preserve the Union that they were so insistent upon the separation of powers and checks and balances. "It may be a reflection on human nature that such devices should be necessary to control the abuses of government. But what is government itself, but the greatest of all reflections on human nature?" This observation prompted the memorable epigram: "If men were angels, no government would be necessary."[26] Because men were not angels, government had to exploit their lower natures by pitting interest against interest and ambition against ambition. These countervailing forces, Madison said, were the "republican remedy for the diseases most incident to republican government."[27] This was the essential difference between the two parties: where the Anti-Federalists were fearful of the diseases incident to republican government, the Federalists found remedies precisely in those diseases.

"If men were angels . . ." But they were not devils either. As the Anti-Federalists are identified with Montesquieu, so the Federalists have been with Hobbes.[28] Theirs was not, however, a Hobbesian view of human nature and society. Nor was it entirely, or perhaps even predominantly, a Lockean view. Montesquieu was repeatedly quoted in *The Federalist,* Locke not at all, and the final quotation in that work was a cautionary note from Hume on the inevitable mistakes in any endeavor such as theirs. Echoes of Hume may also be heard in the Federalists' arguments (*pace* Montesquieu) in favor of a large republic—a government, Hume had said, with "compass and room enough to refine the democracy."[29] (But Montesquieu could also be quoted, as Hamilton did, on a "Confederate Republic" as a means of enlarging the area of republican government.)[30]

The Founders were not about to rely upon the moral sense, any more than upon reason, in creating the political institutions for their new republican government. But they did assign to virtue—individual as well as social virtue—a crucial part in shaping the *moeurs* of the people as the basis of a sound polity. The new governments, John Adams told his wife, would require "a purification from our vices and an augmentation of our virtues, or they will be no blessings."[31] Samuel

Adams agreed: "We shall succeed if we are virtuous. I am infinitely more apprehensive of the contagion of vice than the power of all other enemies."[32] So, too, Benjamin Rush: "Liberty without virtue would be no blessing to us."[33]

The Federalists, as much as the Anti-Federalists, believed that a republic had to assume the existence of virtue in the citizenry, even if its political institutions were based upon the diversity of interests and factions. "As there is a degree of depravity in mankind which requires a certain degree of circumspection and distrust, so there are other qualities in human nature which justify a certain portion of esteem and confidence. Republican government presupposes the existence of these qualities in a higher degree than any other form."[34] Indeed, republican government not only presupposed those qualities; it called them forth, bringing into office citizens "whose wisdom may best discern the true interest of their country, and whose patriotism and love of justice will be least likely to sacrifice it to temporary or partial considerations."[35] Virtue and wisdom would be found in the representatives of the people because they were present in the people, who were themselves virtuous and wise enough to choose them.

> I go on this great republican principle [Madison said], that the people will have virtue and intelligence to select men of virtue and wisdom. . . . Is there no virtue among us? If there be not, we are in a wretched situation. No theoretical checks, no form of government, can render us secure. To suppose that any form of government will secure liberty or happiness without any virtue in the people is a chimerical idea. If there be sufficient virtue and intelligence in the community, it will be exercised in the selection of these men; so that we do not depend on their virtue, or put confidence in our rulers, but in the people who are to choose them.[36]

RELIGION AND VIRTUE

Virtue was a presupposition of the Constitution, but it did not appear in the document itself. Nor did religion. Both were omitted for the same reason: because they were presumed to be rooted in the very nature of man and as such were reflected in the *moeurs* of the people and in the traditions and informal institutions of society. To make either virtue or religion the direct objects of government—and of the national government especially—would be counterproductive, undermining the natural impulses that gave birth to them and kept them alive. Education, not government, was the proper instrument for the diffusion of virtue. For Rush, it was an education rooted in religion. "The only foundation for a useful education in a republic," he wrote, "is to be laid in religion. Without it there can be no virtue, and without virtue there can be no liberty, and liberty is the object and life of all republican governments."[37] (It is noteworthy that the Constitution said nothing about education either, leaving that, like virtue and religion, to individuals and the states.)

Religion did make fleeting appearances in the Declaration of Independence: in the "laws of nature and of nature's God," in the "self-evident" truth that men are "endowed by their Creator with certain unalienable rights," and in the appeal to the "supreme judge of the world" and "divine Providence" (the latter added by Congress to Jefferson's draft).★ But it was permitted to have only a negative role in the Constitution, in the prohibition of religious tests and an established church. (Some of the state constitutions gave a

---

★ There might have been another religious note in the Declaration had Franklin not changed Jefferson's phrase, "We hold these truths to be sacred and undeniable," to the more secular dictum, "We hold these truths to be self-evident."[38]

more positive role to religion; the Declaration of Rights of Massachusetts, for example, called for "the public worship of God" and "public instructions in piety, religion and morality.")[39] Most of the delegates, whatever their personal views, wanted to avoid what would have been a controversial and divisive subject. Those who would have preferred to pay some tribute to the God who had guided them to victory might have consoled themselves with the thought that religion was so "self-evident," so firmly entrenched in society, that it did not require the imprimatur of government. It was Franklin, surprisingly, the least religious of the Founders, who wanted some mention to be made of God in the Constitution and who proposed that the proceedings of the Convention begin with a daily prayer.

Although religion was not in the Constitution, it was firmly embedded in society, which was itself the infrastructure of government. Tocqueville later explained that in writing about America, he seldom mentioned France, but he hardly wrote a page without having her in mind.[40] This was most obvious on the subject of religion. The *philosophes,* he wrote, believed that "religious zeal . . . will be extinguished as freedom and enlightenment increase." America disproved that theory. The first thing that struck him on his arrival in the United States was the religious nature of the country. "Among us [the French] I had seen the spirit of religion and the spirit of freedom almost always move in contrary directions. Here I found them united intimately with one another: they reigned together on the same soil." Thus, the country where Christianity was most influential was also "the most enlightened and the most free."[41]

Tocqueville was writing half a century after the establishment of the republic, but his observations were as true of the colonial period as well. The first Great Awakening, the religious revival of the 1730s and early 1740s, paralleled the Methodist revival in Britain. Even more than in Britain, it affected the larger religious landscape, revitalizing and evangelizing, so to speak, other creeds, and influencing the political climate as well. By 1750, the Awakening had begun to peter out; the number of churches declined (proportionate to the population), and few of the revolutionary leaders were evangelical. But while evangelical zeal diminished (to be revived again in the 1790s), religion in general continued to be a powerful support for republicanism.[42]★ "Deists and Unitarians," Mark Noll points out, "were joined in embracing republicanism by Protestant theological conservatives representing the older British churches, by rambunctious promoters of new-breed evangelicalism, by spokesmen for traditional Protestant faiths from the Continent, by Roman Catholics, and even by representatives of what was then the tiny community of American Jews."[46]

Other scholars have given religion a large part in the creation of the republic even within this supposed period of evangelical decline. One study sees religion as experiencing a "vigorous growth and luxuriant development," a renewal on a smaller scale of the first Great Awakening.[47] Another describes the period between the two Awakenings as a "convergence of millennial and republican thought," a joining of "republican history" and "Christian eschatology."[48] Martin Marty has a graphic image of two simultaneous revolutions:

★ The statistical evidence on churches is ambiguous and contradictory. One table actually reveals an increase in the number of churches between 1770 and 1790, with no indication of when, during that twenty-year period, that growth started.[43] From other statistics showing a low rate of church membership in 1776, the authors conclude that "the vast majority of Americans had not been reached by an organized faith."[44] Another survey, however, has between 71 percent and 77 percent of people in church one Sunday in 1776, suggesting a quite respectable degree of religious observance.[45]

the first an inward, spiritual revolution that made American religion evangelical; the second an outward, political one that made American society republican. Inspiring both revolutions was a new kind of millenarianism, gradual and reformist rather than (like Priestley's) cataclysmic and apocalyptic. In this uniquely American vision of a "city upon a hill," Marty observes, piety and the Enlightenment coincided, a Christian America and a republican America coming together in the common pursuit of happiness.[49]

The abiding strength and influence of religion was such that even those who were not themselves believers respected not only the religious beliefs of others but the idea of religion itself. Again, Tocqueville's observations were as true of this period as of the later one. "All differ in the worship one must render to the Creator, but all agree on the duties of men toward one another. Each sect therefore adores God in its manner, but all sects preach the same morality in the name of God." What was important was not so much that "all citizens profess the true religion but that they profess a religion."[50] The contrast with France was implicit. In seeking respite from the religious passions of the Old World, the Americans did not, like the French, turn against religion itself. Instead, they incorporated religion, of almost every degree and variety, into the mores of society. They "moralized" and "socialized" religion, even as they observed the rituals and dogmas of their particular church—or even when they did not observe those rituals and dogmas.

The Americans did this, moreover, without formalizing or institutionalizing the role of religion, let alone providing for an established church. Indeed, the First Amendment prohibited just such an establishment. That clause has been variously interpreted: as intended to protect state-established churches from displacement by a national establishment; or as part of a larger federalist principle declaring religion, like so many other matters, not a national concern and therefore not subject to the police powers of the national government; or as precluding the imposition of any established church but not preventing the government, national or state, from supporting voluntary religious activities. Today, a common interpretation of that clause goes beyond these scholarly ones, prohibiting not only a religious establishment but any "intrusion" of religion in any "public square," national, state, or local. This last reading cites as its authority Jefferson's "wall of separation between church and state," enunciated in his famous New Year's Day letter of 1802 to the Danbury Baptist Association. Yet Jefferson may not have meant by that wall what it is often taken to mean today. Two days after that Danbury letter, the first Sunday of the new year, Jefferson attended a service not in the local church that he normally attended but in the House of Representatives, a custom he continued for the next seven years. One scholar goes so far as to say that on Sundays in Washington, during his presidency, "the state became the church."[51]

Long before his presidency, Jefferson had displayed a more subtle and appreciative attitude toward religion than is generally attributed to him. His cavalier dismissal of religion in *Notes on the State of Virginia* is often quoted: "It does me no injury for my neighbor to say there are twenty gods or no god. It neither picks my pocket nor breaks my leg." But only a few pages later he wrote: "Can the liberties of a nation be thought secure when we have removed their only firm basis, a conviction in the minds of the people that these liberties are the gift of God? That they are not violated but with his wrath?"[52] This was before Jefferson's supposed conversion to Unitarianism under the influence of Priestley, when he came to recognize Jesus as a moral preceptor and saviour. As president, he was even more respectful of Christianity as the bulwark of liberty and public morality. A friend happened to meet him on his way to church one Sunday morning carrying his large red prayer book. "You going to church Mr. J. You do not believe a word in it." "Sir,"

Jefferson replied, "no nation has ever yet existed or been governed without religion. Nor can be. The Christian religion is the best religion that has been given to man and I as chief Magistrate of this nation am bound to give it the sanction of my example. Good morning Sir."[53]

The separation of church and state, however interpreted, did not signify the separation of church and society. On the contrary, religion was all the more rooted in society because it was not prescribed or established by the government. This is why, Tocqueville explained, religion and liberty coexisted and reinforced each other. And this is the meaning of one of his most profound paradoxes: "Religion, which among Americans, never mixes directly in the government of society, should therefore be considered as the first of their political institutions; for if it does not give them the taste for freedom, it singularly facilitates the use of it." Religion was "the first of their political institutions" because it was the prerequisite of both freedom and morality—thus of republican government itself.

> Freedom sees in religion the companion of its struggles and its triumphs, the cradle of its infancy, the divine source of its rights. It considers religion as the safeguard of mores; and mores as the guarantee of laws and the pledge of its own duration.[54]

> At the same time that the law permits the American people to do everything, religion prevents them from conceiving everything and forbids them to dare everything.[55]

> Despotism can do without faith, but freedom cannot. . . . How could society fail to perish if, while the

political bond is relaxed, the moral bond were not tightened? And what makes a people master of itself if it has not submitted to God?[56]

Finally, most eloquently:

I do not know if all Americans have faith in their religion—for who can read to the bottom of hearts?—but I am sure that they believe it necessary to the maintenance of republican institutions. This opinion does not belong only to one class of citizens or to one party, but to the entire nation; one finds it in all ranks.[57]★

It is curious that Tocqueville, who often cited *The Federalist* on other subjects, never quoted the Founders on religion. Washington's "Farewell Address" is eminently quotable: "Of all the dispositions and habits which lead to political prosperity, religion and morality are indispensable supports." As if to warn his countrymen that enlightenment was no substitute for religion, Washington advised them not to "indulge the supposition that morality can be maintained without religion. Whatever may be conceded to the influence of refined education on minds of peculiar structure, reason and experience both forbid us to expect that national morality can prevail in exclusion of religious principle."[59]† John Adams made the

★ As Tocqueville had no illusions about democracy, so he had none about religion. Even in its excesses and perversions, he saw religion as preferable to its alternative. "I would judge that its citizens risk brutalizing themselves less by thinking that their soul is going to pass into the body of a pig than in believing it is nothing."[58]

† Washington went further than Madison in favoring the public recognition and practice of religion, but he was careful to preserve the principles of religious liberty and pluralism. Thus, he provided for military chaplains

point more pithily: "Our constitution was made only for a moral and religious people. It is wholly inadequate to the government of any other."[61] The French Revolution's attempt to establish a secular republic drew from him the famous comment: "I know not what to make of a republic of thirty million atheists."[62] Benjamin Franklin, himself a deist, agreed: "If men are so wicked as we now see them with religion, what would they be if without it?"[63]

Even those of the Founders who were not devout believers, or those who were most wary of the government's support of religion (Madison most notably), respected religion in general and the religious beliefs of their countrymen. It is sometimes said, in disparagement, that the Founders had a utilitarian or functional view of religion, valuing it as a social and political asset. But this view of religion is not in itself unworthy. To look upon religion as the ultimate source of morality, and hence of a good society and a sound polity, is not demeaning to religion. On the contrary, it pays religion—and God—the great tribute of being essential to the welfare of mankind. And it does credit to man as well, who is deemed capable of subordinating his lower nature to his higher, of venerating and giving obeisance to something above himself.

If the Founders did not look upon religion as the enemy of liberty, neither did the churches look upon liberty as the enemy of religion. The various denominations and sects had an obvious stake in religious liberty, and they appreciated, as Tocqueville did, the relationship between religious and political liberty. Most of them, especially after the passage of the Stamp Act, were enthusiastic supporters of republicanism and

to be paid by the government, but specified that there were to be chaplains for each denomination. And while he did not hesitate to invoke the deity in his public declarations, he did so in non-denominational language—"Almighty Being," or "Great Author."[60]

of the Revolution.* And they arrived at that position not by attenuating or secularizing their religion but by spiritualizing politics itself. "Far from removing political culture from the domination of religious concepts," one historian writes, "ministers extended the canopy of religious meaning so that even the cause of liberty became sacred."[64]

RELIGION AND ENLIGHTENMENT

Religion, then, was not seen as a threat to liberty. Nor was it seen, and this is perhaps more notable, as a threat to enlightenment—to reason, science, and the life of the mind in general. Cotton Mather is today remembered for his fiery sermons about witchcraft and satanic possession, which helped provoke the Salem witch trials (of which he did not entirely approve). But he was also an enthusiastic student of astronomy and of the Copernican system, and (like Wesley in England) a persistent advocate, in the face of great popular resistance, of inoculation against smallpox. Well informed in the natural sciences, he was the first native-born American to be named a fellow of the Royal Society, and was awarded an honorary doctorate of divinity by the University of Glasgow, the heart of the Scottish Enlightenment. Disappointed in his desire to become the president of Harvard (his alma mater), he took an active part in the founding of Yale.

So, too, Jonathan Edwards, the leading light of the Great Awakening, was far from being the stereotypically retrograde

---

* Before the war and in its early stages, many Methodists were loyalists, perhaps out of deference to Wesley, who, as a good Tory, supported his country in the struggle against the colonies. By the end of the war, however, they had rallied to the American cause and were respected as good citizens and patriots.

and repressive religious fanatic. A graduate and, for a time, head tutor at Yale, he read widely and eclectically, admiring Newton, as everyone did, but also Locke, Hutcheson, and other Scottish philosophers. Impressed by Locke's *Essay on Human Understanding,* he adapted its psychological and epistemological principles to his own interpretation of Calvinism. He was also much taken with the statistical methods that had become fashionable in the scientific world, using them to arrive at the cheerful conclusion that the millennium would lead to so rapid an increase of the birth rate that the percentage of the saved would far outweigh that of the damned. Although he fell out of favor with his own parish because he was excessively rigorous doctrinally, he was sufficiently respectable in the lay world to be appointed president of the College of New Jersey (later Princeton). He had barely taken office before he died, in 1758, from a smallpox inoculation.

Other university presidents exhibited the same combination of religious devotion and secular learning. In 1768, the presidency of the College of New Jersey was assumed by John Witherspoon, a Scottish Calvinist cleric (a member of the more rigorous of the two Calvinist sects in Scotland), who was persuaded to come to America by Benjamin Rush, an evangelical who was then a student at Edinburgh. Witherspoon brought to the college not only his religious beliefs but also the commonsense philosophy of Thomas Reid, both of which were reflected in his popular course on moral philosophy. (Among his students was Madison, who developed and retained a serious interest in theology.) That combination of Scottish philosophy and Calvinism, modified in the course of time, pervaded the college, making it a major intellectual center in America, and making Witherspoon himself a public figure of note—indeed, one of the signers of the Declaration of Independence. The president of Yale, Ezra Stiles, was more eccentric but no less learned, lecturing on astronomy, theology, and philosophy, and conducting experiments in electricity (with equipment provided by Benjamin Franklin). Politically more radical than his colleagues, he described himself as a democrat (using the word favorably, unlike most of his contemporaries), and was an enthusiastic supporter of the French Revolution, undaunted by the Terror.

The association of science with secularism is generally epitomized in the figure of Benjamin Franklin, the most celebrated scientific entrepreneur and inventor abroad as well as in America. Yet he was a deist, believing not only in a Supreme Being but also in a future state in which rewards and punishments would be meted out to the just and unjust. In his *Autobiography,* he recalled the first time he heard George Whitefield preach. Resolved not to contribute to the collection, he found, as the sermon went on, that he was so taken with it that he thought to give him some coppers, then a few silver dollars, and ended by giving him five gold pieces.★ Although he withstood Whitefield's attempts to convert him, they remained good friends until Whitefield's death. Franklin himself became more religious as he grew older. "The longer I live," he said in a speech proposing that each meeting of Congress open with a prayer, "the more convincing proofs I see of this truth—that God governs in the affairs of men. And if a sparrow cannot fall to the ground without His notice, is it probable that an empire can rise without His aid?"[66]

★ Yet Franklin was not so overawed by Whitefield's oratory as to be unmindful of its more mundane aspects. Listening to him preach one evening in Philadelphia, Franklin was curious about the number of people who were present and could hear him. By walking through the streets, Franklin determined how far he could be heard, and then, allowing for two square feet for each person within that area, he computed that Whitefield could be heard by more than thirty thousand people. This satisfied Franklin that the newspaper accounts of his preaching to twenty-five thousand people in the fields were accurate.[65]

Intensely religious men were no less respectful of, even enthralled by, science. Benjamin Rush, an ardent evangelical, had some notable "firsts" to his credit: he was the first professor of chemistry in America (later a professor of medicine at the University of Pennsylvania), established the first free dispensary, and helped found the first anti-slavery society. As a practicing doctor, he made strenuous attempts to improve medical services in the army, and at great risk to his own health, tended the sick during the yellow fever epidemic in 1793. If his cure for that disease (the bleeding and purging of patients), as well as his theory of its cause (the effluvia rising from open sewers and fetid marshland), were faulty, his recommendations for sanitary measures and public health were entirely salutary.

The temper of the country was reflected in its two preeminent intellectual institutions: the American Philosophical Society established by Franklin in 1744 (and reorganized in 1768), and the American Academy of Arts and Sciences founded by John Adams in 1780. Both were intended primarily to encourage the pursuit of science, theoretical and practical, and both consisted of clergymen of every denomination as well as scientists, doctors, and prominent public figures. Witherspoon's son-in-law and successor at the College of New Jersey, Samuel Stanhope Smith, a Presbyterian clergyman, was elected to the American Philosophical Society when he assumed the presidency of the college in 1786. (His address to the society the following year, on the "Variety of the Human Species," maintained that blacks were not inferior to whites and that, because of the climate and environment, they were getting whiter all the time.) In one memorable period in the history of the societies, Jefferson was president of the American Philosophical Society when he was elected president of the United States—at the same time that John Adams, his opponent for the presidency, presided over the rival American Academy of Arts and Sciences.[67]

The historian Henry May, documenting the religious sensibility that pervaded the American Enlightenment, ruefully remarked: "One can perhaps regret that there was so little place in America for the Skeptical Enlightenment"—the anti-religious Enlightenment, that is, of the *philosophes*.[68] John Adams, who founded the American Academy of Arts and Sciences on the model of the French Academy of Sciences, would not have agreed. He admired the scientific disposition of the French Enlightenment but not at all its skeptical disposition. He admired even less the ideas of human nature and perfectibility that he found in the *philosophes*. To Jefferson, who was partial to Helvétius, Adams wrote: "I have never read reasoning more absurd, sophistry more gross . . . than the subtle labors of Helvétius and Rousseau to demonstrate the natural equality of mankind. *Jus cuique,* the golden rule, do as you would be done by, is all the equality that can be supported or defended by reason or common sense."[69] He was even more outraged when he read that d'Alembert had told Frederick the Great that "had he [d'Alembert] been present when God created the world, he could have given Him some good advice." "Thou louse, flea, tick, ant, wasp, or whatever vermin thou art," Adams raved, "was this stupendous universe made and adjusted to give you money, sleep, or digestion?"[70]

This was Adams later in life, when he could have comforted himself with the thought that the skeptical Enlightenment *à la France* had had virtually no influence on America in its formative years. The *Encyclopédie* was in the major university libraries as well as the private libraries of some of the Founders, but was rarely referred to, still less quoted. Voltaire was the only *philosophe* well known in America before the Revolution, but it was his histories of Louis XIV and Charles XII that were popular, not his polemical and anti-religious works, which became available only later. Madison had read Voltaire's *Letters Concerning the English Nation* in college, and was fond of repeating his quip about the salutary effect of a multiplicity of sects.[71] But this was the pro-English Voltaire, not the *"Ecrasez l'infâme"* crusader. Rousseau became known in America only after the Revolution, and even then it was *Emile,* not the *Social Contract,* that was generally read (and not always in approval).

THE DISADVANTAGED AND THE DISENFRANCHISED

If the American Enlightenment was notably deficient in that skeptical spirit, it was because it was more beholden to the British moral philosophers than to the French *philosophes.* Yet it did not translate the moral sense into anything like a "sociology of virtue," and it did not produce the plethora of charitable enterprises, philanthropic societies, and proposals for social reform which were so conspicuous in Britain.

That social dimension was less prominent in America because the country was focused upon more immediate political concerns—upon the "politics of liberty" rather than the "sociology of virtue." Morover, America did not have the serious social problems Britain had, or at least did not experience them with the same urgency. Poverty was less intrusive in a land so expansive and with a population so mobile. Indeed, many thoughtful people, not only Anti-Federalists, regarded luxury as more of a social problem than poverty. The French émigré to America J. Hector St. John de Crèvecoeur, writing as an "American Farmer" (with the comparison of France in mind), reported that agricultural laborers in America lived in relative "comfort." Everyone had bread and meat, the elderly and infirm were provided for by the township in which they resided, and "as for the real poor, we have none in this happy country."[72] In his *Notes on the State of Virginia,* Jefferson observed that he had never seen a native American begging in the streets or highways; what beggars there were were usually foreigners who had no settlement in a parish and therefore received no relief from it.[73]★ Writing from Paris a few years later, he was struck by the contrast between the two countries. "Of twenty millions of people supposed to be in France, I am of opinion there are nineteen millions more wretched, more accursed in every circumstance of human existence than the most conspicuously wretched individual of the whole United States."[75] Crèvecoeur and Jefferson may have been unduly optimistic, but they did testify to a common perception that poverty was not a serious problem and that what poverty there was was being adequately relieved by local agencies and private charities.

Nor was literacy regarded as a problem, which was why more attention was paid to higher education than to elementary education. In New England, where elementary education was provided by law, there was almost universal male literacy; John Adams observed that an illiterate was as rare as a Jacobite or Catholic. Jefferson did propose a uniform course of elementary education for Virginia, but he did not pursue it or develop it with anything like the passion and dedication he gave to the University of Virginia. Nor was Jefferson alone in furthering the cause of higher education. In a relatively short period of time, other colleges were founded which rivalled in quality the ancient British institutions.

Nor did philanthropy loom as large in America as in Britain. Quakers and Methodists were active in the reform of prisons and asylums, in varieties of charitable causes, and, most notably, in the abolitionist movement. But there was nothing like the flourishing profession of philanthropy that

---

★ In his "revisal" of the laws of Virginia, however, Jefferson proposed an ambitious plan of poor relief (which was never acted on), including provisions for the apprenticeship of poor children and for schools much like the pauper schools in Britain.[74]

was notable in Britain. The most ambitious philanthropic enterprise was the founding of the colony of Georgia in 1732 by James Oglethorpe. Subsidized by Parliament, it was meant to provide a haven for "the most distressed, virtuous and industrious."[76] (Immigrants from Germany and Italy were allowed, but neither Jews nor Catholics.) The colony was bound by rigid regulations governing the ownership, sale, and use of the land—the trustees, for example, could not personally profit from it—and by detailed rules for the production of silk, which was the principal industry. Slavery in the colony was prohibited, as was the sale and consumption of liquor. Within two decades, the experiment, including the silk industry, proved to be a failure and the charter was handed back to the Crown, whereupon the restrictions, economic and moral, were lifted and the colony prospered.

America was, however, saddled with two problems that Britain was happily spared, the Indians and slavery, both of which proved to be very nearly intractable. For economic if for no other reasons, the displacement of the Indians was the precondition for the very existence of the settlers. The native occupations of hunting and subsistence farming were incompatible with a more sophisticated agricultural economy, to say nothing of industry and commerce. Individual settlers and communities coped with the situation as best they could, with no firm principles or policies to guide them. What they did have, in addition to a clear recognition of their own interests and needs, was a strong sense of their superiority, as human beings, as Christians, and as citizens. "Savages," in popular parlance, was almost synonymous with Indians, signifying a people without laws, morals, or anything resembling civilization. The Declaration of Independence expressed the view of enlightened America when it complained that Britain was inciting "the merciless Indian savages, whose known rule of warfare is an undistinguished destruction of all ages, sexes and conditions."★

Like all his countrymen, George Washington had no doubt that the future lay with the superior civilization, but he wanted to bring about that future as peacefully as possible. In 1783, he recommended purchasing land from the Indians rather than driving them out by force of arms. Several years later, in his message to Congress, he reminded his country-men that they had a special responsibility for this "unenlight-ened race." "A system corresponding with the mild principles of religion and philanthropy towards an unenlightened race of men, whose happiness materially depends on the conduct of the United States, would be as honorable to the national character as conformable to the dictates of sound policy."[78] Later still, in a speech to the Cherokees delivered shortly be-fore his Farewell Address, Washington assured them that he had given much thought to the problem and had come up with only "one path" that would permit Indians and whites alike to enjoy the good things of life. This was the path of assimilation. The Indians had to give up their traditional habits and occupations (hunting, for example) and adopt those of the whites. On a moving personal note, he told them that just as he himself was about to retire from public life, so he was asking them to retire as a nation.[79]

Confronting the same problem when he became presi-dent, Jefferson insisted that the best interests of both whites

---

★ Many years later, speaking of the War of 1812, Jefferson repeated the charge that England had "seduced" the Indians to massacre the whites, thus preventing the amalgamation of the two peoples and leading to "the brutalization, if not the extermination of this race in America." This was yet another instance, Jefferson bitterly noted, of the "Anglo-mercantile cupidity" that had deluged the earth with blood, in Ireland and Asia as well as America.[77]

and natives would be served if the Indians converted to an agricultural economy, thus making the most economical use of the land. He looked forward to a time when the two peoples would learn to "meet and blend together, to intermix, and become one people," with the Indians full citizens of the United States. This idea was so novel that he feared it would shock the Indians (the Indians, he said, not the whites) were it even hinted to them. But they might be gradually familiarized with it by being encouraged to sell their land to the government as a first step in the "natural progress of things." In the meantime, he counselled his correspondent to keep that bold thought to himself.[80]

While Washington appealed to the "national character" of Americans to behave honorably to the Indians, others worried that the American character was not up to the task, indeed, that it was already degraded by the struggle with the Indians. John Jay warned his countrymen that they were being reduced to the level of "white savages," murdering Indians in cold blood for nothing else but their land. Would it not be better, he asked, for the whites to extend their settlements gradually, rather than pitching their tents in the wilderness remote from each other and from the amenities of civilization? He foresaw dire consequences if whites persisted in their present course. "Shall we not fill the wilderness with white savages, and will they not become more formidable to us than the tawny ones who now inhabit it?"[81]

The problem of slavery was even more formidable than that of the Indians. There the one path of assimilation did not seem to present itself. Quakers and Methodists, to be sure, did have a solution and a host of pamphleteers and preachers agreed with them; this was nothing less than the abolition of slavery. Slavery, the minutes of the Methodist Conference declared in

1780, "is contrary to the laws of God, man, and nature, and hurtful to society, contrary to the dictates of conscience and pure religion." Methodist preachers agreed to free their own slaves and persuaded many of their parishioners to do so as well; in one county, in the last two decades of the century, the Methodists were responsible for almost 750 manumissions.[82] Their congregations were also notably hospitable to blacks (as they were to the poor); by 1790, blacks constituted a fifth of the membership.

Most people, including thoughtful and well-intentioned men like Patrick Henry, inveighed against the "lamentable evil" of slavery while believing that the "inconvenience" of living without slaves was so great as to make abolition impractical.[83] Too much was at stake for too many people, and not only for reasons of "inconvenience" (a euphemism for economics), but for political reasons as well. While the war was being waged and a new government was being forged, it was thought divisive and therefore imprudent to conduct a serious debate on the issue, let alone attempt to resolve it. That belief persisted well after the new government was firmly established, so that Washington, even as he was drawing up his will providing for the freeing of his slaves—not upon his own death but upon the death of his wife—was also preparing his Farewell Address in which he was careful not to mention the subject of slavery (except, interestingly, as a metaphor, in which a nation was said to be "a slave" to its passions if it ignored its interests and duties).[84]

The Founders, like historians since, were well aware that the Constitution failed to carry out the bold affirmation of the Declaration that "all men are created equal" and endowed with the "unalienable rights" of "life, liberty, and the pursuit of happiness." The violation of that precept was flagrant, first in the provision equating five slaves with three white men (for purposes of representation and taxation), then in permitting the importation of slaves (for twenty years), and requiring the return of escaped slaves to their owners. That the Founders were profoundly uneasy about these clauses is evident from the care they took never to use the word "slaves" (or even "blacks" or "negroes") in the Constitution. The euphemism "other persons" as distinct from "free persons" in the three-fifths clause, or "person held to service" in the fugitive slave clause, permitted them to salve their conscience by giving the slaves the status of human beings, even while denying both their equality and their liberty. *The Federalist* put the best face on these provisions, accepting the argument that the three-fifths clause recognized the slave "as a moral person, not as a mere article of property," and defending the twenty-year slave trade clause as better than the alternative that would have prescribed no limit. "It ought to be considered, as a great point gained in favor of humanity," Madison declared, that the "unnatural traffic" of slavery might be terminated after twenty years, and that in the interim it would be discouraged by the federal government and perhaps abolished by some states.[85]

Yet, as in the case of the Indians, there was more to the issue of slavery than interest or prudence. There was also a widespread and deeply held conviction of the ineradicable differences of the races and the inferiority of the blacks. When Hamilton proposed, during the war, that black soldiers be encouraged to enlist by giving them "their freedom with their muskets," he knew that this suggestion would be strongly opposed for reasons of "prejudice and self-interest."[86] And when the Quakers, after the adoption of the Constitution, petitioned Congress first to end the importation of slaves and then to abolish slavery, the only name that commanded respect on their petitions was that of the aged and ailing Benjamin Franklin. (The Quakers were in any case suspect because they had not fought in the war.) Hamilton, although an abolitionist, did not support the petition because it distracted from his own agenda on finance, and Madison favored the abolition of the slave trade but was ambivalent about slavery itself.

More equivocal, and perhaps unexpectedly so, was Jefferson. In his constitution for Virginia, Jefferson proposed that the slaves be emancipated and then, suitably equipped and armed, sent abroad to colonize elsewhere as a "free and independent people"; to replace them, an equal number of white people would be induced to emigrate to America. Such a costly and cumbersome transfer of population was warranted, he said, because of the deep-rooted prejudices of whites, the memories of blacks of the injuries they had sustained, and the "physical and moral" qualities of the blacks, which would always divide the races and "produce convulsions which will probably never end but in the extermination of the one or the other race."[87] Forty years later, in his *Autobiography*, Jefferson repeated this proposal:

> Nothing is more certainly written in the book of fate than that these people are to be free. Nor is it less certain that the two races, equally free, cannot live in the same government. Nature, habit, opinion has drawn indelible lines of distinction between them. It is still in our power to direct the process of emancipation and deportation peaceably and in such slow degree as that the evil will wear off insensibly, and their place be pari passu filled up by free white laborers.[88]

At the time, this idea did not seem quite as bizarre as it now appears to be. Only two years earlier, Madison had endorsed a similar proposal that was being circulated by a philanthropic society. Where the society had sought to transport only freed slaves to Africa, Madison suggested that the policy be extended to all blacks and that the government bear the cost of transportation because it was to the advantage of the entire nation.[89]

It was on the issue of slavery that the politics of liberty dramatically clashed with the sociology of virtue. The political philosopher Herbert Storing has attempted to reconcile the two. The primary purpose of the Founders, he reasoned, was the creation of a union destined to be the "greatest instrument of liberty ever made." Although the idea of liberty was grievously violated in the case of the blacks, the union itself, dedicated to the idea of liberty, would eventually prove to be the instrument of their liberation. Thus, slavery, admittedly an evil, was "an evil to be tolerated, allowed to enter the Constitution only by the back door, grudgingly, unacknowledged, on the presumption that the house would be truly fit to live in only when it was gone, and that it would ultimately be gone."[90]

If this was the strategy of the Founders, it did finally succeed—but only after a bloody and traumatic Civil War, a war that was, perhaps more than the Revolution, the most cataclysmic event in American history. Abraham Lincoln, it might be said, pursued the same strategy, waging a war that had the dual purpose of preserving the union and abolishing slavery—preserving the union, it might be said, *in order to* abolish slavery. In this sense, Lincoln was the true heir of the Founders. The politics of liberty that had established the union resulted, more than half a century later, in the abolition of slavery.

In *The Federalist,* Madison asked those who had raised objections to one or another clause of the new Constitution that they should keep in mind the defects of the old. "It is not necessary," he reasoned, "that the former [the new constitution] should be perfect: it is sufficient that the latter [the old] is more imperfect."[91] The opening words of the preamble to the Constitution confirmed that principle: "We the people of the United States, in order to form a more perfect union. . . ." Not *the perfect* union, which might have been the aim of a "philosophical legislator," but only *a more perfect* union. The British moral philosophers would have endorsed that modest sentiment. The French *philosophes,* aspiring to be philosophical legislators, might not have done so.

EPILOGUE

I n America today, the Enlightenment is alive and well.
Biographies—by reputable historians, not hagiogra-
phers—of the Founders ("Founding Fathers," as they
were once known) have become a virtual industry, flooding
the bookstores and appearing regularly on the best-seller lists.
The Federalist, available in several editions, is assigned as a
textbook in political science courses, and cited regularly, and
more frequently as time goes on, in legal debates and decisions, by liberals and conservatives alike.* The Revolution
that was the culmination of the Enlightenment is celebrated
as a national holiday, as is the birthday of George Washington, whose Farewell Address is read annually on that date in
the U.S. Senate. These tributes to history are not the ceremonial rites of a sentimental or romantic people. They are part
of a living history, as is evident from the Constitution itself,
which, more than two centuries later, is the unchallenged
basis of the law and government of the oldest republic. Even
that other most notable, and far more bloody, event, the Civil

---

* Bernard Bailyn estimates that in the 210 years of the Supreme Court's
existence (to January 2000), *The Federalist* was cited 291 times: once in the
eighteenth century, 58 times in the nineteenth, 38 in the first half of the
twentieth, and 194 in the second half.[1]

War, is seen as a sequel to the Revolution, fulfilling the premises of the Enlightenment and the founding.

Tocqueville, that most perspicacious of all commentators, had a momentary lapse when he confessed doubts about the permanent viability of the American republic:

> I want very much to put faith in human perfectibility; but until men should have changed in nature and have been completely transformed, I shall refuse to believe in the longevity of a government whose task is to hold together forty diverse peoples spread over an area equal to half of Europe, to avoid rivalries, ambition, and conflicts among them, and to unite the action of their independent wills toward the accomplishment of the same designs.[2]

Toward the end of this chapter, however, after expounding on the diverse nature of the component parts of the Union, Tocqueville came to exactly the opposite conclusion:

> A time will arrive, therefore, when one can see one hundred fifty million men in North America, equal among themselves, who all belong to the same family, who have the same point of departure, the same civilization, the same language, the same religion, the same habits, the same mores, and through whom thought will circulate in the same form and be painted in the same colors. All the rest is doubtful, but this is certain.[3]

Tocqueville was being unduly pessimistic in the first instance, and perhaps excessively optimistic in the second. Successive waves of immigration, as well as a population almost double that anticipated by him, have diminished the sameness of civilization, language, religion, habits, mores. But in spite of all the pressures toward a multiculturalist society, the social and political institutions of the country have remained intact. All the rest, as Tocqueville said, may be doubtful, but this is certain. It is surprising, however, to find him saying that only a "faith in human perfectibility" could have persuaded him of the longevity of the United States. No one knew better than he that it was precisely a belief in human *im*perfectibility, and the civic and political arrangements deriving from that belief, which sustained the country—a united country—through all the turmoil of its history.

As the founding was unique to the United States, so was the Enlightenment upon which it was based. And so is the enduring commitment to the Enlightenment, the "habits of the mind" and "habits of the heart" that inspired the Founders and that are still a source of inspiration today. There is nothing like it in France or Britain. The literature on the French Enlightenment is vast, but it is largely an academic literature, of passionate interest to historians but of little relevance to contemporary affairs—except, perhaps, as a cautionary tale. If the French Enlightenment did inspire the French Revolution, and the Revolution the Terror, that is cause for disquiet rather than satisfaction. Indeed, the republic that came in the wake of the Enlightenment—the First French Republic, as it has gone down in history—has long since been superseded by other republics and even by monarchies, so that it can hardly be the subject of celebration or veneration. Today, in the early years of the new millennium, the office of the French foreign minister is adorned with portraits not of Voltaire or Rousseau but of Napoleon, who transformed the republic into an empire and then presided over its ignominious downfall. The "glory" of military adventure and defeat—that is hardly the spirit of the French Enlightenment, to say nothing of being a curious ideal for a minister of state.

The fortunes of the British Enlightenment have been no less strange. Finally, after centuries of neglect, it has come into its own as a historical subject—but only as that. Adam

Smith is much admired, even revered in some circles, but his authority is rarely invoked in Britain today. That authority, indeed, was undermined within a decade after his death, with the publication in 1798 of Thomas Malthus's *Essay on the Principle of Population*. Malthus's "principle of population," asserting that population is always kept down to the level of the means of subsistence, was presented as a law of nature with all the inevitability of a biological law (it was derived from the two primary characteristics of human beings: sexual passion and the need for food), and with all the certainty of a mathematical law (the geometric increase of population compared with the arithmetic increase of subsistence). Malthus wrote his book as a refutation of the idea of perfectibility advanced by Godwin and Condorcet. But it was as effective a refutation of Smith's more modest idea of progress. Where Smith's system of natural liberty promoted the well-being of "the lowest ranks of the people," the principle of population condemned those lowest ranks to perpetual "misery and vice."[4]

Malthus's principle was soon followed by David Ricardo's "iron law" of wages, the combination of the two having the effect of de-moralizing political economy and vitiating the moral philosophy once associated with it. Toward the end of the nineteenth century, Alfred Marshall, who had been a lecturer in "Moral Science" before taking up the study of economics, tried to restore the moral dimension of economics by basing it upon a Kantian conception of man, a man possessed, by nature and by reason, of a moral instinct akin to the golden rule. "It's all in Adam Smith," Marshall is reported to have said of his own work.[5] But Marshall, and Smith still more, were soon overwhelmed by the very different ethos expressed in the famous remark of a Liberal member of Parliament, cynically echoed by the Prince of Wales, "We are all socialists now."[6]

Almost a century later, Margaret Thatcher tried to restore

an old ethos by reviving the idea of "Victorian values." She was accused of glorifying the individual at the expense of society, indeed, of denying the reality of society. Had she gone back further in time, to Smith and the moral philosophers, she would have come upon the moral sense that was the genesis of those values and that gave them an undeniably social character.

The British moral philosophers, even the better known of them, Smith and Hume, do not enjoy today the reputation or stature of their predecessors, Hobbes and Locke, let alone of the classical philosophers. And for good reason. Their works are surely wanting in the profundity and gravity of great philosophy. And the social virtues they esteemed—sympathy, compassion, benevolence—lack the grandeur of the classical virtues: heroism, courage, wisdom. Yet their moral philosophy is deserving of serious consideration and respect. It was, as Tocqueville said in another connection, "of all philosophic theories the most appropriate to the needs of men in our time." Tocqueville made that comment about self-interest "properly understood," but it applies as well to the moral sense, again, properly understood.

> [It] is a doctrine [Tocqueville said of self-interest] not very lofty, but clear and sure. It does not seek to attain great objects; but it attains all those it aims for without too much effort. . . . [It] does not produce great devotion; but it suggests little sacrifices each day; by itself it cannot make a man virtuous; but it forms a multitude of citizens who are regulated, temperate, moderate, farsighted, masters of themselves; and if it does not lead directly to virtue through the will, it brings them near to it insensibly through habits. . . .
> If [it] came to dominate the moral world entirely,

extraordinary virtues would without doubt be rarer. But I also think that gross depravity would then be less common. . . . [It] perhaps prevents some men from mounting far above the ordinary level of humanity; but many others who were falling below do attain it and are kept there. Consider some individuals, they are lowered. View the species, it is elevated.

I shall not fear to say that [it] seems to me of all philosophic theories the most appropriate to the needs of men in our time. . . . The minds of the moralists of our day ought to turn, therefore, principally toward it. Even should they judge it imperfect, they would still have to adopt it as necessary.[7]

Like self-interest, the idea of a moral sense, innate or habituated in human beings, was "not very lofty, but clear and sure." It did not elevate a few individuals "far above the ordinary level of humanity," but it did permit many more who might have fallen below it to attain and retain that level. It did not encourage individuals to "extraordinary virtues," but it did encourage them to ordinary virtues and discouraged them from "gross depravity." It was, in short, an eminently human and humane idea. Especially at a time of great economic, social, and political turmoil, it was, as Tocqueville said of self-interest, "most appropriate to the needs of men."

It is ironic that that philosophy has more resonance in the United States today than in Britain. Having derived a good deal of its own Enlightenment from the mother country, the United States is now repaying Britain by perpetuating the spirit of her Enlightenment. We are often reminded of the theme of American "exceptionalism." America was exceptional at the time of its founding, and continues to be so today. Europeans complain that the United States is unduly individualistic, religious, and moralistic (the last meant invidiously). And so it is, by European standards, including British standards, today. But not by British standards of old. If America is now exceptional, it is because it has inherited and preserved aspects of the British Enlightenment that the British themselves have discarded and that other countries (France, most notably) have never adopted.

The United States, more than any other country, has retained Adam Smith's vision of political economy, a system of natural liberty that governs the polity as well as the economy. Libertarians protest that the United States is insufficiently liberal, in their rigorous, individualistic sense of that word. But Smith was never a libertarian in that sense. He was a moral philosopher as well as a political economist, and it is this amalgam that characterized Britain then, as it does the United States today. Americans take for granted what Europeans regard as an inexplicable paradox: that the United States is the most capitalistic and at the same time the most moralistic of countries.

So, too, the United States is far more religious today—religious in observance and in conviction—than any European country. A wise French historian, François Furet, once told me that France had become so secular that it was no longer anti-clerical. (This was before the Muslim immigrants were seen as a threat to French *laicisme*.) The same might be said of Britain today, which has no disestablishment movement because the established church has accommodated itself so entirely to the popular ethos that there is no incentive for disestablishment. So, too, the Dissenting churches are a shadow of their former selves, not a power to be reckoned with or to be resisted. In the United States, by contrast, evangelicalism is a serious social as well as religious force.

America has, in effect, superimposed on the politics of liberty something very like a sociology of virtue. After decades of disuse, virtue is once again a respectable part of the political and social vocabulary, accepted as an idea and ideal even when, as often happens, it is violated in practice. And the revival of the idea of virtue in the private sense has been accompanied by its revival in the public sense—the social virtue of compassion. That idea was the unique contribution of the British Enlightenment. What had been a religious virtue was transmuted into a secular one, and a private duty became a public responsibility. This was the achievement not only of the British philosophers who made so much of the idea of compassion but also of the Methodists and Evangelicals who put that idea into practice in the form of philanthropy and good works. It was in Britain that the "passion for compassion" (in Hannah Arendt's memorable phrase) first arose. In France, Peter Gay explains, the campaign to abolish torture, like that to expel the Jesuits, was part of "the struggle to impose man's rational will on the environment."[8] In Britain, the campaign to abolish slavery, like the other reform movements, was motivated not by "rational will" but by humanitarian zeal, by compassion rather than reason.

Revived in the United States today, this ethic has crossed political party lines. Long the preserve of liberals, for whom it served to justify every act of social engineering, the "politics of compassion" was derided by conservatives as a softhearted and, worse, soft-minded approach to social problems, in which sentiment prevails over reason, intentions over results, and feeling good over doing good—all having the effect of enlarging the scope of government and the state. Yet today, "compassionate conservatism" has been embraced not only by many conservatives (indeed, the reigning party of conservatives) but by many liberals as well, who seek to strengthen civil society and thus reduce the role of the state by channeling the sentiment of compassion into voluntary and communal endeavors. This is the purpose of the much-publicized proposals to replace welfare with "workfare" and to integrate faith-based charities into the larger system of relief. The ultimate purpose is to enhance the moral sense of giver and receiver alike, to encourage the social affections of the one while respecting the moral dignity and integrity of the other.

The sociology of virtue, the ideology of reason, the politics of liberty—the ideas still resonate today. But they carry with them the accretions of more than two centuries of historical experiences and memories. And other ideas now compete for our attention: equality, most notably, but also nationality and ethnicity, class and gender, cultural diversity and global homogeneity. If the three Enlightenments ushered in modernity—or at least a new stage in modernity, or new variations on modernity—the postmodernists may be justified in calling this a postmodern age. Yet the ideas of virtue, liberty, and reason did not originate in modernity; nor have they been superseded or superannuated by postmodernity. We are, in fact, still floundering in the verities and fallacies, the assumptions and convictions, about human nature, society, and the polity that exercised the British moral philosophers, the French *philosophes,* and the American Founders.

NOTES

1. The Castel Gandolfo lecture, delivered August 10, 1996, was printed in German in *Klett-Cotta Sonderdruck* (1997). The British Academy lecture, of May 15, 2001, was published in the *Proceedings of the British Academy* (2001) under the title "Two Enlightenments: A Contrast in Social Ethics." A much revised version of the British Academy lecture, "The Idea of Compassion: The British vs. the French Enlightenment," appeared in *The Public Interest* (Fall 2001).

PROLOGUE

1. I capitalize "Enlightenment" when it refers to the historical schools or movements of thought associated with the eighteenth century, and lowercase it when speaking of it in a non-historical context.

2. John Gray, *Enlightenment's Wake: Politics and Culture at the Close of the Modern Age* (London, 1995), p. viii.

3. Daniel Gordon, introduction to *Postmodernism and the Enlightenment: New Perspectives in Eighteenth-Century French History*, ed. Gordon (New York, 2001), p. 1. Gordon, and the contributors to this volume, defend the Enlightenment against the postmodernists, but always in the shadow of the postmodernist critique. There is by now a considerable literature on the "Enlightenment project," as it is called (generally pejoratively), starting with one of the sources of this critique, Michel Foucault, "What Is Enlightenment?" *The Foucault Reader*, ed. Paul Rabinow (New York, 1984). For more recent contributions to this debate, see *What's Left of Enlightenment? A Postmodern Question*, ed. Keith Michael Baker and

Peter Hanns Reill (Stanford, Calif., 2001); Nicholas Capoldi, "The Enlightenment Project in Twentieth-Century Philosophy," in *Modern Enlightenment and the Rule of Reason,* ed. John C. McCarthy (Washington, D.C., 1998); James Schmidt, "What Enlightenment Project?" *Political Theory* (December 2000), and the ensuing exchange between Christian Delacampagne and Schmidt, *Political Theory* (February 2001). Richard Rorty distinguishes between the politics of the Enlightenment, which he endorses, and its metaphysics, which he repudiates (*Objectivity, Relativism, and Truth: Philosophical Papers* [Cambridge, 1991], I, 21 ff.).

4. A sophisticated version of this approach is Daniel Roche, *France in the Enlightenment* (Cambridge, Mass., 1998).

5. Robert Darnton, "The High Enlightenment and the Low-Life of Literature," in *The Literary Underground of the Old Régime* (Cambridge, Mass., 1982). *The Business of Enlightenment: A Publishing History of the* Encyclopédie (Cambridge, Mass., 1979) is Darnton's pathbreaking book on the publication of the *Encyclopédie,* but his mode of cultural history is best exemplified in his volumes of essays, *The Great Cat Massacre and Other Episodes in French Cultural History* (New York, 1984); *The Kiss of Lamourette* (New York, 1990); and *The Forbidden Best-Sellers of Pre-Revolutionary France,* with its companion volume *The Corpus of Clandestine Literature in France, 1769–1789* (New York, 1995). For a spirited critique of Darnton and defense of intellectual history, see Dominick LaCapra, *History and Criticism* (Ithaca, N.Y., 1985), pp. 87–94.

6. I have not attempted to deal with the Enlightenments in Italy, Germany, Spain, Russia, and elsewhere. Excellent brief accounts of these appear in *The Enlightenment in National Context,* ed. Roy Porter and Mikulas Teich (Cambridge, Mass., 1981).

7. Alexis de Tocqueville, *Democracy in America,* trans. and ed. Harvey C. Mansfield and Delba Winthrop (Chicago, 2000 [1st French ed., 1835, 1840]), p. 275 (vol. I, pt. 2, ch. 9). The concept of *moeurs,* Tocqueville said, was foremost in his mind, the "common truth," the "central point," the "end of all my ideas" (p. 295).

8. Ira O. Wade, *The Intellectual Origins of the French Enlightenment* (Princeton, 1971), dates the Enlightenment from the Renaissance. In his later book, *The Structure and Form of the French Enlightenment,* Vol. I: *Esprit Philosophique* (Princeton, 1977), he modifies this by recognizing a "turning point, though not a break" at the time of the death of Louis XVI (p. xii). Jonathan I. Israel, *Radical Enlightenment: Philosophy and the Making of Modernity, 1650–1750* (Oxford, 2001), also takes the Enlightenment back to the seventeenth century, giving Spinoza a major role. I take a narrower view of the Enlightenment, confining it to the eighteenth century,

where it emerged not only as an episode in the history of philosophy but as an intellectual and social movement, a historic event with political and social consequences.

9. Peter Gay, *The Enlightenment: An Interpretation,* Vol. I: *The Rise of Modern Paganism* (New York, 1975 [1st ed., 1966]), pp. x, 3, 7–8, 10. See also Gay's *The Party of Humanity: Essays in the French Enlightenment* (New York, 1971).

10. The criticism of this view of the unity of the Enlightenment was first voiced by Betty Behrens in the *Historical Journal* (1968). For a pluralistic view of the Enlightenment, emphasizing the national differences, see *The Enlightenment in National Context,* ed. Roy Porter and Mikulas Teich (Cambridge, Mass., 1981); Roy Porter, *The Creation of the Modern World: The Untold Story of the British Enlightenment* (New York, 2000); J. G. A. Pocock: "Post-Puritan England and the Problem of the Enlightenment," in *Culture and Politics from Puritanism to the Enlightenment,* ed. P. Zagorin (Berkeley, 1980); J. G. A. Pocock, *Barbarism and Religion,* vol. I of *The Enlightenments of Edward Gibbon* (Cambridge, 1999); Charles R. Kesler, "The Different Enlightenments: Theory and Practice in the Enlightenment," in *The Ambiguous Legacy of the Enlightenment,* ed. William A. Rusher and Ken Masugi (Lanham, Md., 1995); and Arthur Herman, *How the Scots Invented the Modern World: The True Story of How Western Europe's Poorest Nation Created Our World and Everything in It* (New York, 2001).

11. Georg Wilhelm Friedrich Hegel, *The Philosophy of History,* trans. J. Sibree (New York, 1944 [1st trans. by Sibree, 1899]), pp. 436–37.

12. Ibid., p. 86.

13. Ibid., pp. 453–54.

14. Hannah Arendt, *On Revolution* (New York, 1963), p. 49.

15. Jean le Rond d'Alembert, "Preliminary Discourse," in *Denis Diderot's The Encyclopedia: Selections,* ed. and trans. Stephen J. Gendzier (New York, 1967), p. 12. (In citing the texts of the French Enlightenment, I have used translations where available.)

16. Franco Venturi, *Utopia and Reform in the Enlightenment* (Cambridge, 1971), pp. 126–27, 132–33.

17. Caroline Robbins, *The Eighteenth-Century Commonwealthmen: Studies in the Transmission, Development and Circumstance of English Liberal Thought from the Restoration of Charles II Until the War with the Thirteen Colonies* (Cambridge, Mass., 1959), pp. 3, 381, 383.

18. Quoted in Porter, "The Enlightenment in England," p. 5.

19. Jean-Jacques Rousseau, *Confessions* (1781, 1788), trans. and ed. M. Hedouin (London, n.d.), p. 98 (bk. III).

20. Rousseau, *Emile* (1762), trans. Allan Bloom (New York, 1979), p. 450.

21. John Morley, *Diderot and the Encyclopaedists* (New York, 1878), p. 163.

22. Immanuel Kant, "What Is Enlightenment?" in *The Philosophy of Kant: Immanuel Kant's Moral and Political Writings,* ed. Carl J. Friedrich (New York, 1949), p. 138. For the context of this debate, see *What Is Enlightenment? Eighteenth-Century Answers and Twentieth-Century Questions,* ed. James Schmidt (Berkeley, 1996).

23. James Schmidt, "Inventing 'the Enlightenment': Stirling, Hegel, and the *Oxford English Dictionary,*" *Journal of the History of Ideas* (forthcoming).

24. Edmund Burke, *Reflections on the Revolution in France* (New York, Dolphin ed., 1961 [1st ed., 1790]), pp. 86, 155, 208, 259. For other references to "enlightened," see pp. 78, 100, 101, 129, and 155. The word appeared in Burke's very first work, *A Vindication of Natural Society* (1756), in *The Works of Edmund Burke* (London, 1909), I, 38.

25. Schmidt, "Inventing 'the Enlightenment,'" p. 7.

26. Morley, *Diderot and the Encyclopaedists,* pp. 6, 117. "Enlightenment," not capitalized and not in the sense of a school of movement, appeared once, in a quotation from Friedrich Grimm, the German philosopher and friend of the *philosophes* (p. 373). Morley occasionally used the adjective "enlightened" (pp. 87, 401).

27. Hegel, *Philosophy of History,* p. 438. The *Oxford English Dictionary* records the earliest usage of "Enlightenment," as translations of *Aufklärung,* in books on Hegel by J. H. Sterling in 1865 and on Kant by Edward Caird in 1889 (*A New English Dictionary on Historical Principles* [Oxford, 1897], vol. III, pt. 2, p. 191). See Schmidt, "Inventing 'the Enlightenment,'" for an analysis of the controversy over this entry in the *OED,* particularly the misrepresentation of the quotation from Caird. A rare instance of "Enlightenment" appears in 1894 in the translation of Wilhelm Windelband's *Geschichte der Philosophie.* That work also has the distinction of paying tribute to England as the progenitor of the Enlightenment (Schmidt, "Inventing 'the Enlightenment,'" p. 7).

28. Schmidt, "Inventing 'the Enlightenment,'" p. 15.

29. *Encyclopaedia Britannica: A New Survey of Universal Knowledge* (14th ed., London, 1929), VIII, 613.

30. Paul Wood, "Introduction: Dugald Stewart and the Invention of 'the Scottish Enlightenment,'" in *The Scottish Enlightenment: Essays in Reinterpretation,* ed. Wood (Rochester, N.Y., 2000), p. 1. Wood attributes the term to William Robert Scott in 1900, but points out that the idea of

such a school originated with Dugald Stewart, himself a member of that school. (Stewart succeeded Adam Ferguson to the chair of moral philosophy at Edinburgh, and was the biographer and editor of Adam Smith.) John Lough has the term originating with Hugh Trevor-Roper as late as 1967 (Lough, "Reflections on Enlightenment and Lumières," *British Journal of Eighteenth-Century Studies* [Spring 1985], p. 9). Reflecting on the confusion in the use of the terms "Enlightenment" and *Lumières,* and on the disparate thinkers and ideas embraced in those terms, Lough proposes abandoning them entirely, for France as well as other countries (p. 14).

31. Franco Venturi, *Utopia and Reform in the Enlightenment* (Cambridge, 1971), pp. 126–27, 132–33 (see above, p. 9); Herman, *How the Scots Invented the Modern World,* pp. 225–26.

32. Alfred Cobban, *In Search of Humanity: The Role of Enlightenment in Modern History* (London, 1960), p. 7. I am indebted to Arthur M. Wilson, "The Enlightenment Came First to England," in *England's Rise to Greatness, 1660–1763,* ed. Stephen B. Baxter (Berkeley, 1983), for this and the following quotations. Wilson's own essay, however, entitled "The Enlightenment Came First to England," focuses entirely on such thinkers as Locke, Hobbes, Milton, and the deists, arguing that its existence has been obscured because "almost all of it occurred during the seventeenth century" (p. 4). Thus, he, too, leaves the eighteenth-century Enlightenment to the French.

33. Wilson, "The Enlightenment Came First," p. 3, quoting Robert R. Palmer, article on Turgot in *Journal of Law and Economics* (1976).

34. Ibid., p. 17, quoting Henry Steele Commager, *The Empire of Reason: How Europe Imagined and America Realized the Enlightenment* (Garden City, N.Y., 1977), p. 242. Yet Commager himself, in that same book, dates "the Old World Enlightenment" from the founding of the Royal Society in 1660 and the publication of Newton's *Principia* in 1687 (p. 4).

35. See the articles and books by Pocock and Porter in note 10 above. One critical review of Porter's book, under the title "Unenlightened England," argues that there was no Enlightenment in England because there was no understanding of "modern, commercial societies" (this of a country whose statesmen and thinkers revered Adam Smith), and no group of philosophers notable for their views of "government, economy and society" (*pace* Burke and Gibbon, Paine and Price) (John Robertson, "Unenlightened England," *Prospect* [January 2001], p. 62).

36. Edmund Burke, *An Appeal from the New to the Old Whigs* (1791), in *Works,* III, 113.

37. Venturi, *Utopia and Reform,* p. 73.

38. John Lough, *The* Encyclopédie *in Eighteenth-Century England and*

Other Studies (Newcastle, 1970), p. 14. On the subject of the relations between English and French intellectuals, see also Wade, *Structure and Form of the French Enlightenment,* I, 120–71.

39. *On Moral Sentiments: Contemporary Responses to Adam Smith,* ed. John Reeder (Bristol, 1997), p. 5.

40. Adam Smith, "Of the Nature of That Imitation Which Takes Place in What Are Called the Imitative Arts," in Smith, *Essays on Philosophical Subjects,* ed. W. P. D. Wightman and J. C. Bryce (Oxford, 1980), p. 198.

41. Adam Smith, *The Theory of Moral Sentiments,* ed. D. D. Raphael and A. L. Macfie (Oxford, 1976 [reprint of 6th ed., 1790]), pp. 214–15 (pt. VI, sect. 1).

42. "*Philosophe,*" in *Encyclopédie,* XII, 509. By giving Spinoza a major role in his book *Radical Enlightenment,* Jonathan Israel identifies the "Radical Enlightenment" with the attack on religion.

43. Ernst Cassirer, in his seminal work on the Enlightenment, saw reason as the "homogeneous formative power" of the time: "'Reason' becomes the unifying and central point of this century, expressing all that it longs and strives for, and all that it achieves. . . . The eighteenth century is imbued with a belief in the unity and immutability of reason. . . . Reason is the same for all thinking subjects, all nations, all epochs, and all cultures." In this context, the Enlightenment "mind" was essentially French, taking its model from Newton but finding expression most coherently in the *Encyclopédie.* (See Cassirer, *The Philosophy of the Enlightenment,* trans. Fritz C. A. Koelln and James P. Pettegrove [Princeton, 1951 (1st German ed., 1932)], pp. 5 6.)

44. William Kristol, "The Politics of Liberty, the Sociology of Virtue," in Mark Gerson, ed., *The Essential Neo-Conservative Reader* (Reading, Mass., 1996), pp. 434ff. The expression "sociology of virtue" is more often associated with the late nineteenth-, early twentieth-century French syndicalist philosopher Georges Sorel. See, for example, John L. Stanley, *Sociology of Virtue: The Political and Social Theories of Georges Sorel* (1981), and Arthur L. Greil, *Georges Sorel and the Sociology of Virtue* (1981). The sociologist Robert Nisbet blended the two terms when he described conservatism as the "politics of liberty" or the "search for political virtue." (Nisbet, *Conservatism: Dream and Reality* [Minneapolis, 1986], p. x). "Ideology of reason" is my own formulation.

45. Quoted by Terence Marshall, "Rousseau and Enlightenment," in *Rousseau Papers,* ed. Jim MacAdam, Michael Neumann, and Guy La France (Montreal, 1980), p. 39.

46. See note 9 above.

THE BRITISH ENLIGHTENMENT: THE SOCIOLOGY OF VIRTUE

1. "SOCIAL AFFECTIONS" AND RELIGIOUS DISPOSITIONS

1. David Hume, *The History of England: From the Invasion of Julius Caesar to the Revolution in 1688* (4 vols., Philadelphia, 1828 [1st ed., 1754–62]), IV, 434. Some commentators on Adam Smith find in his work a Newtonian mode of analysis. One claims that Smith "self-consciously" set out to apply Newtonian principles by the use of mechanical analogies and metaphors (Alan Macfarlane, *The Riddle of the Modern World: Of Liberty, Wealth and Equality* [New York, 2000], p. 82; see also Ian Simpson Ross, *The Life of Adam Smith* [Oxford, 1995], p. 179). Yet there is only one passing reference to Newton in the *Theory of Moral Sentiments* (on the initial public neglect of him), and none in *Wealth of Nations.*

2. See A. R. Humphreys, *The Augustan World: Society, Thought, and Letters in Eighteenth-Century England* (New York, 1963), p. 207.

3. On the aesthetic influence of Newton, see the elegant and powerful little book by Marjorie Hope Nicolson, *Newton Demands the Muse: Newton's* Opticks *and the Eighteenth-Century Poets* (Hamden, Conn., 1963 [1st ed., 1946]).

4. John Locke, *An Essay Concerning Human Understanding* (Chicago, 1952 [1st ed., 1690]), pp. 95, 103, 105 (bk. I, chs. 1 and 2); p. 176 (bk. II, ch. 20).

5. Lawrence E. Klein suggests that Shaftesbury's personal relationship with Locke accounts for the "emotional intensity" of his search for his own "philosophical identity" and thus his attack on the Lockean principles (*Shaftesbury and the Culture of Politeness: Moral Discourse and Cultural Politics in Early Eighteenth-Century England* [Cambridge, 1994], p. 15).

6. Anthony Ashley Cooper, third Earl of Shaftesbury, *Characteristics of Men, Manners, Opinions, Times* (3 vols., Indianapolis, 2001 [1711; reprint of 6th ed., 1737–38]), II, 27 (bk. I, pt. 3, sect. 2); p. 18 (bk. I, pt. 2, sect. 3, and passim). "Moral sense" appears only once in the text of the essay (p. 27), but it is clearly meant to be synonymous with "the sense of right and wrong," which appears repeatedly. In the 1714 edition, "moral sense" also appears in the marginal notations and in the index. (Here, and throughout this book, I have modernized the capitalization, punctuation, and spelling of these eighteenth-century writers. To retain the original is distracting and, in the case of the capitalization of common nouns, deceptive because it gives an unintended emphasis to the words.)

7. Ibid., p. 80 (bk. II, pt. 2, sect. 1); p. 25 (bk. I, pt. 3, sect. 1).

8. Ibid., p. 45 (bk. II, pt. 1, sect. 1); p. 57 (bk. II, pt. 1, sect. 1).

9. Ibid., p. 14 (bk. I, pt. 2, sect. 2).

10. Ibid., p. 16 (bk. I, pt. 2, sect. 2).

11. Ibid., p. 100 (bk. II, pt. 2, sect. 3). On "common nature," see pp. 45–46 (bk. II, pt. 1, sect. 1).

12. Other historians dispute this interpretation of the relation of Locke and the moral philosophers. Frank Balog, for example, argues for the "pivotal position of Locke" in the Scottish Enlightenment. He quotes the first English work on the subject, James McCosh's *Scottish Philosophy from Hutchinson to Hamilton* (1875): "The Scottish metaphysicians largely imbibed the spirit of Locke, all of them speak of him with profound respect; and they never differ from him without expressing a regret or offering an apology." But Balog admits that the Scottish philosophers differed with Locke on "one fundamental issue, the nature of conscience and morality"—for moral philosophers, a fundamental issue, indeed. And he cites Hume as criticizing Locke for being "unhistorical and subversive"(Balog, "The Scottish Enlightenment and the Liberal Political Tradition," in *Confronting the Constitution,* ed. Allan Bloom [Washington, D.C., 1990], pp. 193, 207, 205).

13. Quoted in Klein, *Shaftesbury and the Culture of Politeness,* p. 65.

14. One editor of the *Fable* says that Mandeville had not read Shaftesbury when he published the first edition of the book in 1714 (*The Fable of the Bees,* ed. Philip Harth [London, 1970 (reprint of 1723 ed.)], p. 32). But the book has so many echoes of Shaftesbury—in reverse—that this seems improbable. It is unlikely that Mandeville would have failed to read a book published three years earlier which was so much discussed and praised. The editor also suggests that the *Fable* may be understood as a satire, "an outstanding ornament of the greatest age of English satire" (p. 43). But this is to take the book far less seriously than contemporaries did.

15. Ibid., pp. 67, 75.

16. Ibid., pp. 158, 165, 264.

17. Ibid., p. 329.

18. Ibid., p. 370.

19. Adam Smith, *The Theory of Moral Sentiments,* ed. D. D. Raphael and A. L. Macfie (Oxford, 1976 [reprint of 6th ed., 1790]), pp. 306, 308 (pt. VII, sect. 2, ch. 4). Many years later, Gibbon commended William Law for attacking "the licentious doctrine" that private vices are public benefits (see Harth, introduction to the *Fable,* p. 14).

20. See Locke's *Some Thoughts Concerning Education* (1693), especially the discussion of why children should be taught not to be cruel to animals.

21. *The Life, Unpublished Letters and Philosophical Regimen of Anthony, Earl of Shaftesbury,* ed. Benjamin Rand (London, 1900), p. 158.

22. Francis Hutcheson, *An Inquiry Concerning the Original of Our Ideas of Virtue or Moral Good* (2nd ed., 1726), reprinted in *British Moralists,* ed. L. A. Selby-Bigge (Oxford, 1897), I, 107.

23. Ibid., p. 118. See also Hutcheson, *A Short Introduction to Moral Philosophy in Three Books* (5th ed., Philadelphia, 1788 [1st ed., 1747]), pp. 12–13, 21–22. The theme reappears in his *Observations on the Fable of the Bees* (1726) and in *An Essay on the Nature and Conduct of the Passions and Affections, with Illustrations on the Moral Sense* (1728).

24. *The Correspondence of Jeremy Bentham,* ed. Timothy L. S. Sprigge (London, 1968), I, 134n., and II, 99 (letter to John Forster, April–May 1778); Smith, *Moral Sentiments,* p. 321 (pt. VII, sect. 3, ch. 3).

25. Hutcheson, *Inquiry,* pp. 86, 93, 140–43; *Short Introduction,* pp. 9, 12.

26. Hutcheson, *Inquiry,* p. 156.

27. Hutcheson, *A System of Moral Philosophy* (London, 1755), I, 69–70.

28. Joseph Butler, *Fifteen Sermons Preached at the Rolls Chapel* (London, 1970 [1st ed., 1726]), p. 86 (sermon 5); p. 101 (sermon 6).

29. Ibid., pp. 19–20 (sermon 1). See also sermon 11.

30. Thomas Reid, *Essays on the Active Powers of Man* (1788) in *The Scottish Moralists: On Human Nature and Society,* ed. Louis Schneider (Chicago, 1967), p. 105.

31. Adam Ferguson, *Principles of Moral and Political Science* (1792), in Schneider, ed., *Scottish Moralists,* p. 88.

32. David Hume, *A Treatise of Human Nature,* ed. Ernest C. Mossner (Baltimore, 1969 [1st ed., 1739–40]), p. 632 (bk. III, pt. III, sect. 1); p. 522 (bk. III, pt. I, ch. 2); p. 652 (bk. III, pt. III, ch. 3).

33. Ibid., p. 507 (bk. III, pt. 1, sect. 1); p. 522 (bk. III, pt. 1, sect. 2).

34. Ibid., p. 668 (bk. III, pt. 3, sect. 6); p. 635 (bk. III, pt. 3, sect. 1).

35. Ibid., pp. 626–27 (bk. III, pt. 3, ch. 1).

36. David Hume, *An Enquiry Concerning the Principles of Morals* (LaSalle, Ill., 1938 [reprint of 1777 ed.; 1st ed., 1751]), pp. 138–43 (appendix II, "Of Self-Love").

37. Ibid., pp. 67, 109.

38. Smith, *Moral Sentiments,* p. 9 (pt. I, sect. 1, ch. 1). Smith used the words "pity," "compassion," and "sympathy" almost interchangeably, although he did at one point distinguish sympathy from the others (p. 10).

39. Ibid., p. 25 (pt. I, sect. 1, ch. 5).

40. Ibid., pp. 113–14 (pt. III, ch. 2).

41. Ibid., p. 62 (pt. I, sect. 3, ch. 3).

42. Smith's distinction between "positive" and "negative" virtues was

similar to Hume's distinction between "natural" and "artificial" virtues—ethics and justice. These are not quite how the terms are used in some recent commentaries, where "virtue" is said to characterize the discourse of the civic humanists and "justice" that of Smith and Hume. See, for example, the essays by Ivan Hont and Michael Ignatieff and by J. G. A. Pocock in *Wealth and Virtue: The Shaping of Political Economy in the Scottish Enlightenment,* ed. Hont and Ignatieff (Cambridge, 1983). For the concept of "civic humanism," see J. G. A. Pocock, *The Machiavellian Moment: Florentine Political Thought and the Atlantic Republican Tradition* (Princeton, 1975).

43. Smith, *Moral Sentiments,* pp. 81–82 (pt. II, sect. 2, ch. 1).

44. Ibid., p. 317 (pt. VII, sect. 3, ch. 1).

45. Ibid., p. 320 (pt. VII, sect. 3, ch. 2). It is interesting that in a brief survey of moral philosophy from the ancients to the moderns, Smith mentions Locke only once, contrasting Locke's view of "reflection" with Hutcheson's "moral sense," to the advantage of Hutcheson, p. 322 (pt. VII, sect. 3, ch. 3). There is only one other passing reference to Locke in the entire book (p. 241).

46. James Gleick, *Isaac Newton* (New York, 2003), p. 108.

47. Ibid., p. 104.

48. Shaftesbury, "A Letter Concerning Enthusiasm" (1708), in *Characteristics,* I, 21, 26.

49. B. W. Young, "'Scepticism in Excess': Gibbon and Eighteenth-Century Christianity," *The Historical Journal* (1998), p. 181 (citing essay by John Toland published in 1720). Leslie Stephen quotes this witticism, applying it to Hume, in his *History of English Thought in the Eighteenth Century* (New York, 1962 [1st ed., 1876]), I, 289.

50. David Hume, "Of Superstition and Enthusiasm," in Schneider, ed., *Scottish Moralists,* pp. 173–77.

51. *The Autobiographies of Edward Gibbon,* ed. John Murray (London, 1896), p. 127. (This is an edition of the six sketches left by Gibbon as the raw material for his memoirs. It varies somewhat from the *Autobiography of Edward Gibbon,* edited by his friend and executor, Lord Sheffield, and published in 1796; cf. note 72 below.)

52. Ernest Campbell Mossner, *The Life of Hume* (London, 1954), p. 485, quoting a letter by James Macdonald, June 6, 1764.

53. Will R. Jordan, "Religion in the Public Square: A Reconsideration of David Hume and Religious Establishment," *Review of Politics* (Fall 2002), p. 693.

54. Hume, *History of England,* III, 134–35.

55. Mossner, *Life of Hume,* pp. 239–40. See also Jordan, "Religion in the Public Square"; Ingrid A. Merikoski, "A Different Kind of Enlightenment," *Religion and Liberty* (November–December 2001); and Ingrid A. Merikoski, "The Challenge of Material Progress: The Scottish Enlightenment and Christian Stoicism," *Journal of the Historical Society* (Winter 2002).

56. Mossner, *Life of Hume,* p. 110.

57. Joseph Butler, *The Analogy of Religion, Natural and Revealed, to the Constitution and Course of Nature* (London, 1900 [1st ed., 1736]), p. 5.

58. Butler, *Sermons,* p. 109 (sermon 11).

59. Hutcheson, *Inquiry,* pp. 176–77 (sect. 7, XIII).

60. Hutcheson, *A System of Moral Philosophy* (New York, 1968 [reprint of 1755 ed.]), p. 313 (vol. II, bk. 3, ch. 9).

61. Smith, *Moral Sentiments,* p. 19 (letter to Alexander Wedderburn, Aug. 14, 1776, quoted in the editor's introduction). Some commentators have seen a diminution of religiosity in some of the changes in the several editions of this work, e.g., pp. 91–92 (pt. II, sect. 2, ch. 3); pp. 383–87 (appendix II). I think too much has been made of these revisions.

62. Ibid., pp. 163, 166 (pt. III, ch. 5).

63. Ibid., pp. 169–70.

64. Ibid., p. 164.

65. Ibid., p. 214 (pt. VI, sect. 1).

66. Ian Simpson Ross, *The Life of Adam Smith* (Oxford, 1995), pp. 339–40.

67. Donald Winch, *Riches and Poverty: An Intellectual History of Political Economy in Britain, 1750–1834* (Cambridge, 1996), p. 168 n. 4.

68. Adam Smith, *An Inquiry into the Nature and Causes of the Wealth of Nations,* ed. Edwin Cannan (New York, 1937 [1st ed., 1776]), pp. 740–46.

69. Voltaire, *Letters Concerning the English Nation* (New York, 1974), p. 35 (letter 6); *The Federalist: A Commentary on the Constitution of the United States,* ed. Robert Scigliano (New York, 2001), p. 61 (*Federalist* 10).

70. Smith, *Wealth of Nations,* p. 746.

71. Ibid., pp. 746–47.

72. *Autobiography of Edward Gibbon* (1796), ed. Lord Sheffield (Oxford, World's Classics, 1950), p. 181 (letter from Hume to Gibbon, March 18, 1776).

73. Edward Gibbon, *The Decline and Fall of the Roman Empire* (Chicago, 1952 [1st ed., 1776–88]), pp. 190–91, 205–6.

74. Ibid., p. 233.

75. Gibbon, *Autobiography,* pp. 180, 185.

76. Ross, *Life of Smith,* p. 285.

77. The subject has been a matter of much controversy. An excellent account is that by Young, "'Scepticism in Excess,'" pp. 179–99.

78. Gibbon, *Decline and Fall,* p. 179.

79. Shaftesbury, "A Letter Concerning Enthusiasm," in *Characteristics,* I, 34.

80. See above, p. 40.

81. J. G. A. Pocock, *Barbarism and Religion* (Cambridge, 1999), I, 151. Pocock describes Gibbon's response to d'Alembert's *Discours Préliminaire,* in 1761, as "instantly hostile" (p. 139). But there Gibbon's quarrel was not with d'Alembert's religious views but with his denigration of "erudition."(See also Pocock, pp. 67 and passim.)

82. Young, "'Scepticism in Excess,'" p. 199.

83. Gibbon, *Decline and Fall,* p. 634.

84. H. R. Trevor-Roper, "The Religious Origins of the Enlightenment," in his *The Crisis of the Seventeenth Century: Religion, the Reformation and Social Change* (New York, 1968), pp. 193–236 (esp. p. 203).

85. J. G. A. Pocock, "Post-Puritan England and the Problem of the Enlightenment," in *Culture and Politics: From Puritanism to the Enlightenment,* ed. Perez Zagorin (Berkeley, 1980), pp. 103, 106. See also J. G. A. Pocock, "Gibbon and the Primitive Church," in *History, Religion and Culture: British Intellectual History, 1750–1950,* ed. Stefan Collini, Richard Whatmore, and Brian Young (Cambridge, 2000), pp. 59–60.

86. Roy Porter, "The Enlightenment in England," in *The Enlightenment in National Context,* ed. Roy Porter and Mikulas Teich (Cambridge, 1981), p. 6.

87. J. C. D. Clark, *English Society, 1688–1832: Ideology, Social Structure, and Political Practice During the Ancien Régime* (Cambridge, 1985).

88. Baron de Montesquieu, *The Spirit of the Laws,* trans. Thomas Nugent (New York, 1949 [1st French ed., 1750]), p. 321 (vol. I, bk. 20, sect. 7).

89. *Memoir, Letters, and Remains of Alexis de Tocqueville* (London, 1861), II, 397 (letter to M. de Corcelle, July 2, 1857).

2. POLITICAL ECONOMY AND MORAL SENTIMENTS

1. On this "problem," see, for example, Richard Teichgraeber III, "Rethinking *Das Adam Smith Problem,*" *Journal of British Studies* (Spring 1981); Teichgraeber, "Adam Smith and Tradition: *Wealth of Nations* Before Malthus," in his *Economy, Polity, and Society: British Intellectual History, 1750–1950* (Cambridge, 2000); and the introduction to Smith, *The The-*

ory of Moral Sentiments, ed. D. D. Raphael and A. L. Macfie (Oxford, 1976 [reprint of 6th ed., 1790]), pp. 20–25 and passim. The literature on Smith has always been vast, but it has taken on a new character since the centenary celebrations of the *Wealth of Nations.* Much of it derives from the concept of "civic humanism" as developed by J. G. A. Pocock in *The Machiavellian Moment: Florentine Political Thought and the Atlantic Republican Tradition* (Princeton, 1975). For Smith's relation to that tradition (and his departure from it), as reflected in the *Wealth of Nations* as well as the *Theory of Moral Sentiments,* see the essays by Istvan Hont and Michael Ignatieff, Nicholas Phillipson, and Donald Winch in *Wealth and Virtue: The Shaping of Political Economy in the Scottish Enlightenment* (Cambridge, 1983), and the essay by John Dwyer in *Adam Smith Reviewed,* ed. Peter Jones and Andrew S. Skinner (Edinburgh, 1992).

2. Dugald Stewart, *Biographical Memoir of Adam Smith* (New York, 1966 [1st ed., 1793]), pp. 67–68.

3. Ibid., p. 52.

4. Ibid., p. 87 (note G).

5. John Ruskin, *Fors Clavigera: Letters to the Workmen and Labourers of Great Britain,* in *Works,* ed. E. T. Cook and Alexander Wedderburn (London, 1907 [1st ed., 1871–84]), XXVIII, 516, 764.

6. E. P. Thompson, "The Moral Economy of the English Crowd in the Eighteenth Century," *Past and Present* (1971), pp. 89–90.

7. Joseph Schumpeter, *History of Economic Analysis,* ed. Elizabeth Boody Schumpeter (New York, 1974 [1st ed., 1954]), pp. 141, 182, 185.

8. Adam Smith, *An Inquiry into the Nature and Causes of the Wealth of Nations,* ed. Edwin Cannan (New York, 1937 [1st ed., 1776]), p. 250.

9. Ibid., p. 98.

10. Ibid., pp. 128, 460–61, 463, 577, 609.

11. Ibid., p. 14.

12. Ibid., p. 651.

13. Ibid., p. 14.

14. Smith, *Theory of Moral Sentiments,* pp. 184–85 n. 7. The editors point out that Smith had used the expression still earlier in his essay "The History of Astronomy," where he said that the ancients did not see the "invisible hand of Jupiter" in such natural agencies as fire, water, or gravity. See also A. L. Macfie, "The Invisible Hand of Jupiter," *Journal of the History of Ideas* (1971), pp. 595–99.

15. *Wealth of Nations,* p. 423. (This is the only use of the phrase in this book.)

16. Ibid., p. 11.

17. Ibid., pp. 78–79.

18. Arthur Young, *The Farmer's Tour Through the East of England* (London, 1771), IV, 361.

19. Arthur Young, *A Six Months' Tour Through the North of England* (London, 1770), I, 196.

20. *Wealth of Nations,* p. 81.

21. Ibid., p. 141.

22. Ibid., p. 683; see also pp. 777, 821.

23. Ibid., p. 11.

24. Robert Heilbroner attributes to Smith something like the Malthusian theory. So far from positing a progressive, expanding economy, Heilbroner maintains, Smith foresaw an eventual decline and decay. See Heilbroner, "The Paradox of Progress: Decline and Decay in the *Wealth of Nations," Journal of the History of Ideas* (1973), p. 243, reprinted in *Essays on Adam Smith,* ed. Andrew S. Skinner and Thomas Wilson (Oxford, 1975). See also the reply by E. G. West, "Adam Smith and Alienation: Wealth Increases, Men Decay?" in *Essays on Adam Smith.* (In his earlier work, *The Worldly Philosophers* [New York, 1953], Heilbroner had presented the conventional "optimistic" Smith.) Alan Macfarlane, in *The Riddle of the Modern World: Of Liberty, Wealth and Equality* (London, 2000), describes Smith's view as "short-term optimism and long-term pessimism" (p. 145).

25. *Wealth of Nations,* pp. 734–35. Similar remarks about the "inconveniences . . . arising from a commercial spirit" (i.e., the division of labor) appear in Smith's *Lectures on Jurisprudence,* ed. R. L. Meek, D. D. Raphael, and P. G. Stein (Oxford, 1978), pp. 539–41 ("Report of 1766"). Smith was working on the *Wealth of Nations* at this time, so it is not surprising to find much the same sentiments expressed here.

26. *Wealth of Nations,* p. 3.

27. Ibid., p. 735.

28. Ibid., p. 737.

29. Karl Marx, *Capital: A Critique of Political Economy* (New York, 1936 [1st German ed., 1867]), p. 398 (pt. IV, sect. 5).

30. Ibid., pp. 528–29, 534 (pt. IV, sect. 9).

31. Karl Marx and Friedrich Engels, *The Communist Manifesto,* ed. Samuel H. Beer (New York, 1955 [1st German ed., 1848]), pp. 28, 32.

32. Hannah Arendt, *The Human Condition* (Chicago, 1958), pp. 101 ff.

33. At one other point, Smith compared the industrial worker with the agricultural laborer, to the advantage of the latter—the agricultural laborer having to perform many tasks in the course of the day, unlike the factory worker, who was confined to one. Here, too, the context is inter-

esting, for the paragraph appeared in the course of his criticism of manufacturers and tradesmen who found it easy to "combine together" to further their own interests against those of the public (and of the workers), whereas farmers were too dispersed to engage in such practices (*Wealth of Nations,* p. 127).

34. See above, p. 59.

35. *Wealth of Nations,* pp. 324–25, 326.

36. Joseph Cropsey, *Polity and Economy: An Interpretation of the Principles of Adam Smith* (The Hague, 1957), p. 95. See also Cropsey, "Adam Smith," in *History of Political Philosophy,* ed. Leo Strauss and Joseph Cropsey (Chicago, 1987 [1st ed., 1963]).

37. *Wealth of Nations,* p. 385.

38. Ibid., pp. 248–49.

39. Ibid., pp. 121–22.

40. Ibid., p. 13.

41. Ibid., pp. 15–16.

42. David Hume, "Of the Original Contract," in Hume, *Political Essays* (Indianapolis, 1953 [1st ed., 1741–42]), p. 44.

43. John Locke, *An Essay Concerning Human Understanding* (Chicago, 1952 [1st ed., 1690]), p. 390.

44. John Morley, *Diderot and the Encyclopaedists* (New York, 1978), p. 338.

3. EDMUND BURKE'S ENLIGHTENMENT

1. Isaiah Berlin, *Against the Current: Essays in the History of Ideas* (Princeton, 2001 [1st ed., 1955]), pp. 13–14. Berlin was not entirely consistent. In his essay on the Counter-Enlightenment, he described Burke's idea of an organic society as having "strongly conservative and, indeed, reactionary implications." Elsewhere he placed Burke in a chain of anti-Enlightenment thinkers including Hamann, Fichte, de Maistre, and Bonald, culminating in the Fascist writers of World War II. Yet in still another essay, he located Burke's roots in Richard Hooker, Montesquieu, and Hume, who have good liberal and Enlightenment credentials (pp. 151, 185, 250, 344). I have come across only one anthology on the Enlightenment (*The Enlightenment,* ed. David Williams [Cambridge, 1999]) that includes an excerpt from *Reflections on the Revolution in France.* Burke's *The Sublime and Beautiful* (1757) is occasionally excerpted or mentioned respectfully, almost invariably attributed to the young Burke in contrast to the Burke of the *Reflections.*

2. J. G. A. Pocock, *Barbarism and Religion,* Vol. I: *The Enlightenment of*

Edward Gibbon, 1737–1764 (Cambridge, 1999), p. 7. See also p. 109: "It is important to understand that Burke spoke as a philosopher of Enlightenment, not of Counter-Enlightenment."

3. Conor Cruise O'Brien, *The Great Melody: A Thematic Biography and Commented Anthology of Edmund Burke* (Chicago, 1992), pp. 608, 595 n. 1. The appendix has extracts from O'Brien's review of Berlin's *The Crooked Timber of Humanity* (1991) and an exchange of letters with Berlin on the subject of Burke (pp. 605–18). Jerry Z. Muller, in *The Mind and the Market: Capitalism in Modern European Thought* (New York, 2002), implicitly places Burke within the Enlightenment (pp. 104–38).

4. *Autobiography of Edward Gibbon* (1796), ed. Lord Sheffield (Oxford, World's Classics, 1950), p. 216.

5. Gertrude Himmelfarb, *The Idea of Poverty: England in the Early Industrial Age* (New York, 1983), p. 66. The quotation first appeared in a biography of Burke by Robert Bisset in 1800.

6. Burke, "Letter to a Noble Lord" (1796), in *The Works of Edmund Burke* (London, 1909), V, 124. Although one editor has Smith consulting Burke and paying "great deference" to him while he was writing the *Wealth of Nations,* they did not, in fact, meet until 1777, and their only communication before that, in 1775, was on a trivial matter. See Rothschild, *Economic Sentiments,* pp. 275–76 nn. 77 and 81.

7. Burke, "Speech . . . on the Economical Reformation of the Civil and Other Establishments" (Feb. 11, 1780), in *Works,* II, 109–10.

8. Burke, *Thoughts and Details on Scarcity,* in *Works,* V, 83–109. (The pamphlet was written and circulated in 1795 but published only posthumously.) See also *Letters on a Regicide Peace* (third letter, 1797), in *Works,* V, 321–22. In my *Idea of Poverty* (pp. 61–73), I overemphasized, I now believe, the differences between Burke and Smith. I said that Smith opposed the law of settlement but not the Poor Laws themselves, whereas Burke rejected the very principle of the Poor Laws. In this essay, however, Burke was discussing not the Poor Laws as such but the regulation and supplementation of wages. On this issue the two were in substantial agreement.

9. Donald Winch alludes to this "Problem" (a *"mésalliance,"* he calls it) in *Riches and Poverty: An Intellectual History of Political Economy in Britain, 1750–1834* (Cambridge, 1996), pp. 128 and passim. Winch himself does not think that the inconsistencies, either in Smith or in Burke, are significant. Nor does he think that the differences between Smith and Burke are great: "Those who stress the connections between Smith and Burke are on safer ground than those who wish to emphasize the 'liberal,' radical, or pro-revolutionary affiliations of some of Smith's English and French admirers" (p. 175). A more ingenious resolution of this "problem" is that

of C. B. Macpherson, who regards Burke as essentially laissez-fairist. If he posed as a "traditionalist," it was because by his time "the capitalist order *had in fact been* the traditional order in England for a whole century" (italics in original). And when Burke attacked the French Revolution, it was because he did not realize that it was a "bourgeois revolution" (Macpherson, *Burke* [New York, 1980], pp. 51 ff.).

10. Burke, *Reflections on the Revolution in France* (New York, 1961 [1st ed., 1790]), pp. 92, 89.

11. Ibid., p. 93.

12. Burke, *A Philosophical Inquiry into the Origin of Our Ideas of the Sublime and Beautiful,* in *Works,* I, 52.

13. Ibid., 52, 56.

14. Burke, *Reflections,* pp. 93–94, 70.

15. Burke, *A Vindication of Natural Society: or, a View of the Miseries and Evils Arising to Mankind from Every Species of Artificial Society,* in *Works,* I, 3–5.

16. Burke, *The Sublime and Beautiful,* in *Works,* I, 127.

17. Ibid., 79.

18. Burke, review of *The Theory of Moral Sentiments* in the *Annual Register* (1759), in *On Moral Sentiments: Contemporary Responses to Adam Smith,* ed. John Reeder (Bristol, 1997), p. 52.

19. Burke, *Thoughts on the Cause of the Present Discontents* (April 1770), in *Works,* I, 351, 354. In private letters, Burke doubted whether Wilkes was a man of prudence or principles. See J. C. D. Clark, "Edmund Burke's *Reflections on the Revolution in America* (1777); or, How Did the American Revolution Relate to the French?" in *Faith, Reason, and Economics: Essays in Honour of Anthony Waterman,* ed. Derek Hum (Winnipeg, Canada, 2003), pp. 36 and 45 n. 95.

20. Burke, *Thoughts on the Cause of the Present Discontents,* in *Works,* I, 368–69.

21. Ibid., 310.

22. Burke, "Speech on Mr. Fox's East India Bill" (1783), in *Works,* II, 176.

23. Ibid., 195, 226.

24. John Morley, *Burke* (London, 1904), p. 134. Burke's attention was first drawn to India many years earlier by the disastrous financial speculations of his brothers in East India stock. But his subsequent concern with this issue went well beyond that personal episode (he himself had no stake in those failed investments), and his actual views of the Indian situation were very different from those of his brothers. On this last point, see Stanley Ayling, *Edmund Burke: His Life and Opinions* (New York, 1988), pp. 167–68.

25. A very different interpretation of Burke on the American Revolution appears in the essay by J. C. D. Clark (see note 19 above). In an ingenious (and, of course, fictitious) "Reflections on the Revolution in America," Clark has Burke applying to America the principles he enunciated in connection with France. Clark minimizes Burke's interest in America and criticizes him for not realizing that the American Revolution was as profoundly revolutionary as the French. My own view is the conventional one, that the American Revolution was fundamentally, qualitatively different from the French, and that Burke recognized it as such.

26. Burke, "Observations on a Late Publication Entitled 'The Present State of the Nation'" (February 1769), in *Works,* I, 277, 280.

27. Burke, "Speech on Moving his Resolutions for Conciliation with the Colonies" (March 22, 1775), in *Works,* I, 456, 462.

28. Ibid., 464–69.

29. Adam Smith, *An Inquiry into the Nature and Causes of the Wealth of Nations,* ed. Edwin Cannan (New York, 1937 [1st ed., 1776]), pp. 586–87.

30. Winch, *Riches and Poverty,* pp. 142–43.

31. Burke, "Letter to the Sheriffs of Bristol on the Affairs of America" (April 3, 1777), in *Works,* II, 30–31 (italics in original).

32. Burke, "Speech on Conciliation," in *Works,* I, 466. Roy Porter says that Burke "jeered" at the "dissidence of dissent" (Porter, *The Creation of the Modern World: The Untold Story of the British Enlightenment* [New York, 2000], p. 480). I think this is a misinterpretation of this passage.

33. *Letters of Edmund Burke: A Selection,* ed. Harold J. Laski (Oxford, 1922), p. 195 (letter to William Burgh, Feb. 9, 1775).

34. Burke, *Reflections,* p. 266.

35. Burke, "Speech on Conciliation," in *Works,* I, 456.

36. Burke, *Reflections,* p. 19.

37. Samuel Taylor Coleridge, *Biographia Literaria* (London, 1939 [1st ed., 1817]), p. 97.

38. Burke, *Reflections,* pp. 15, 28, 39.

39. Ibid., pp. 36, 44–45.

40. Ibid., pp. 43, 47, 50.

41. Ibid., p. 62. See Harvey Mansfield, *Statesmanship and Party Government: A Study of Burke and Bolingbroke* (Chicago, 1965), pp. 201 ff.

42. Burke, *Reflections,* p. 100.

43. Ibid., p. 174.

44. Ibid., p. 104.

45. Ibid., p. 115.

46. Ibid., p. 105.

47. I have been one of those who made this charge, and have since rebutted it. See the two essays on Burke in my *Victorian Minds* (New York, 1968), pp. 4–31.

48. Burke, *Reflections,* p. 106.

49. Ibid., p. 110.

50. Ibid., p. 89.

51. Ibid.

52. Ibid., p. 90.

53. Ibid.

54. Thomas Paine, *The Rights of Man* (New York, Dolphin ed., 1961 [1st ed., 1791–92]), p. 288.

55. Burke, *Reflections,* p. 92; Conor Cruise O'Brien, ed., *Reflections on the Revolution in France* (London, 1968), pp. 173, 385 n. 66.

56. Burke, *Reflections,* p. 68.

57. Ibid., pp. 50–51.

58. Burke, *Letters on a Regicide Peace* (1796), in *Works,* V, 210–11.

59. Burke, *Reflections,* pp. 93, 95.

60. J. G. A. Pocock, ed., *Reflections on the Revolution in France* (Indianapolis, 1987), p. xxxvii. Elsewhere Pocock places Burke in the Enlightenment tradition. Here he makes of him a counsel and prophet for our times. In yet another book, however, Pocock describes Burke's *Letters on a Regicide Peace* as "that wild jeremiad of a mind at the end of its tether" (*Virtue, Commerce, and History: Essays on Political Thought and History, Chiefly in the Eighteenth Century* [Cambridge, 1985], p. 205).

4. RADICAL DISSENTERS

1. Richard Price, *A Review of the Principal Questions and Difficulties in Morals* (1757); Joseph Priestley, *Examination of Scottish Philosophy* (1774).

2. See Elie Halévy, *The Growth of Philosophical Radicalism,* trans. Mary Morris (Clifton, N.J., 1972 [1st French ed., 1901–4]), pp. 153, 178, 251.

3. Roy Porter applies this term to Price and William Frend (an actuarian) (*The Creation of the Modern World: The Untold Story of the British Enlightenment* [New York, 2000], p. 208).

4. Edmund Burke, *A Vindication of Natural Society* (1756), in *The Works of Edmund Burke* (London, 1909), I, 3.

5. J. C. D. Clark makes a large point of this in his *English Society, 1688–1832: Ideology, Social Structure and Political Practice During the Ancien Régime* (Cambridge, 1985), pp. 277 ff.

6. Clark stresses the Arian aspect of Price's thought (ibid., p. 330); Donald Winch the Lockean aspect. See Winch, *Riches and Poverty: An*

Intellectual History of Political Economy in Britain, 1750–1834 (Cambridge, 1996), pp. 145–46.

7. Joseph Priestley, *An Essay on the First Principles of Government and on the Nature of Political, Civil, and Religious Liberty* (1768) and *The Present State of Liberty in Great Britain and Her Colonies* (1768), in *Political Writings*, ed. Peter N. Miller (Cambridge, 1993), pp. 32, 134, and passim.

8. Burke, "Letter to the Sheriffs of Bristol" (1777), in *Works*, II, 29–30. (Donald Winch calls attention to this passage in *Riches and Poverty*, pp. 145–46.)

9. Richard Price, "A Discourse on the Love of Our Country," in *The Debate on the French Revolution, 1789–1800,* ed. Alfred Cobban (London, 1950), pp. 63–64. It is odd that Burke should have quoted a previous paragraph of the peroration, but not this final incendiary passage. See *Reflections on the Revolution in France* (New York, Dolphin ed., 1961), p. 78.

10. Smith, *The Theory of Moral Sentiments,* ed. D. D. Raphael and A. L. Macfie (Oxford, 1976 [reprint of 6th ed., 1790]), p. 318 (pt. VII, sect. 3, ch. 2); p. 229 (pt. VI, sect. 3, ch. 2).

11. Ibid., p. 229 n. 2.

12. Quoted by Isaac Kramnick, *The Rage of Edmund Burke: Portrait of an Ambivalent Conservative* (New York, 1977), p. 14.

13. Priestley, *Essay on the First Principles of Government* (1768), in *Political Writings,* p. 51.

14. Thomas Paine, *Common Sense* (New York, 1992 [reprint of 1791 ed.]), p. 5.

15. Ibid.

16. Paine, *The Rights of Man* (New York, Dolphin ed., 1961 [1st ed., 1791–92]), p. 400. (This edition, like many others, gives the title, incorrectly, as *The Rights of Man*. The common article was added to an edition in 1817, eight years after Paine's death.)

17. Ibid., p. 433.

18. Smith, *An Inquiry into the Nature and Causes of the Wealth of Nations,* ed. Edwin Cannan (New York, 1937 [1st ed., 1776]), pp. 669, 681.

19. Paine, *Rights of Man,* pp. 418, 429, 315.

20. Ibid., p. 304.

21. Ibid., pp. 400–401.

22. Ibid., p. 448.

23. Ibid., p. 480.

24. Ibid., p. 482.

25. On the "welfare state," see, for example, Eric Foner, *Tom Paine and Revolutionary America* (New York, 1976), p. 218, and Francis Canavan, "The Burke-Paine Controversy," *Political Science Reviewer* (1976), p. 403;

on "social security," Henry Collins, introduction to Paine, *Rights of Man* (London, Penguin ed., 1969), p. 37; and on "social democracy," S. Maccoby, *English Radicalism, 1786–1832* (London, 1955), p. 53. E. P. Thompson hails *Rights of Man* as the "foundation-text of the English working-class movement," setting "a course towards the social legislation of the twentieth century" (*The Making of the English Working Class* [New York, 1964], pp. 90, 94).

26. Collins, introduction to Penguin ed. of *Rights of Man,* p. 43. Collins concedes that Paine never crossed that threshold, but this implies that any redistribution scheme approaches the "threshold of socialism." On *Rights of Man* compared with *Agrarian Justice Opposed to Agrarian Law and to Agrarian Monopoly* (1797), see Gertrude Himmelfarb, *The Idea of Poverty: England in the Early Industrial Age* (New York, 1983), pp. 86–99.

27. Paine, *Age of Reason: Being an Investigation of True and Fabulous Theology* (New York, 1975 [1st ed., 1794–95]), pp. 5–6.

28. For a serious discussion of the millenarian views of Price and Priestley, see Jack Fruchtman, Jr., *The Apocalyptic Politics of Richard Price and Joseph Priestley: A Study in Late Eighteenth-Century English Republican Messianism* (Philadelphia, 1983), and Iaian McCalman, "New Jerusalems: Prophecy, Dissent and Radical Culture in England, 1786–1830," in *Enlightenment and Religion: Rational Dissent in Eighteenth-Century Britain,* ed. Knud Haakonssen (Cambridge, 1996). Henry F. May, *The Enlightenment in America* (Oxford, 1976), recognizes the millenarianism of Price and Priestley but does not dwell on it in any detail.

29. Cited by Alan Tapper, "Priestley on Politics, Progress and Moral Theology," in Haakonssen, ed., *Enlightenment and Religion,* p. 272.

30. See Fruchtman, *Apocalyptic Politics,* p. 1.

31. Ibid., p. 35.

32. See Clark, *English Society, 1688–1832,* pp. 333, 335.

33. Ibid., p. 335.

34. Porter, *Creation of the Modern World,* p. 414.

35. Fruchtman, *Apocalyptic Politics,* p. 42.

36. William Godwin, *An Enquiry Concerning Political Justice, and Its Influence on General Virtue and Happiness* (London, 1793), I, 237. (In the second edition, *General Virtue* in the title was changed to *Morals.*)

37. Halévy spoke of Godwin as a disciple of Smith, quoting passages suggesting that he shared Smith's view of the "identity of interests" (*Philosophic Radicalism,* pp. 209–12). Yet Godwin rejected the very idea of interests.

38. Godwin, *Enquiry Concerning Political Justice,* II, 846–47.

39. Ibid., I, 163.

40. Ibid., 83.

41. Ibid., II, 862–71.

42. Ibid., I, 1–2.

43. Ibid., II, 870–72.

44. Ibid.

45. Ibid., I, 43.

46. Ibid. (3rd ed., 1798), II, 510.

47. Joan B. Landes, *Women and the Public Sphere in the Age of the French Revolution* (Ithaca, N.Y., 1988), p. 149.

48. Mary Wollstonecraft, *A Vindication of the Rights of Men* and *A Vindication of the Rights of Woman,* ed. Sylvana Tomaselli (Cambridge, 1995), p. xxvi.

49. Quoted in Peter H. Marshall, *William Godwin* (New Haven, 1984), p. 324.

50. Ibid., p. 359.

51. Condorcet, *Sketch for a Historical Picture of the Progress of the Human Mind,* trans. J. Barraclough (New York, 1955), pp. 188–89.

52. C. Kegan Paul, *William Godwin: His Friends and Contemporaries* (London, 1876), I, 80.

53. Price, *Review of the Principal Questions in Morals* (New York, 1974 [reprint of 3rd ed.]), p. 121.

54. Godwin, *Political Justice* (1st ed.), II, 738–39; (3rd ed.), II, 366–69.

55. See M. G. Jones, *The Charity School Movement: A Study of Eighteenth-Century Puritanism in Action* (Cambridge, 1938), p. 3. See chapter 6 below on philanthropy).

5. METHODISM: "A SOCIAL RELIGION"

1. Most writers on the Enlightenment simply ignore the Methodists. Frank E. Manuel, for example, in *The Eighteenth Century Confronts the Gods* (New York, 1959), makes no mention of them—as if they were not doing just that, confronting the gods (or rather, God). Other writers explicitly write them out of the Enlightenment. See, for example, Roy Porter, *The Creation of the Modern World* (New York, 2000), pp. 128, 224–25, 409, and J. G. A. Pocock, "Conservative Enlightenment and Democratic Revolutions: The American and French Cases in British Perspective," in *Government in Opposition* (1989).

2. Quoted in Stuart Andrews, *Methodism and Society* (London, 1970), p. 64. Today, the label "Methodist" is often applied to those who left the Church of England after John Wesley's death, as distinct from the Evan-

gelicals who remained in the church. In fact, the word was used of the Wesleyans from the beginning—indeed, from before the beginning—to describe the religious society in Oxford frequented by the Wesley brothers and George Whitefield several years before the revival itself.

3. Leslie Stephen, *History of English Thought* (New York, 1962 [1st ed., 1876]), II, 361, 364.

4. W. E. H. Lecky, *History of the Rise and Influence of the Spirit of Rationalism in Europe* (London, 1946 [1st ed., 1865]), p. 3; Lecky, *A History of England in the Eighteenth Century* (New York, 1891), II, 687.

5. Elie Halévy, *The Birth of Methodism in England,* ed. and trans. by Bernard Semmel (Chicago, 1971 [French ed., 1906]), p. 51. Semmel points out that Halévy did not claim that this theory was original with him. He certainly knew of Hippolyte Taine's *History of English Literature,* published in 1874, which propounded a similar thesis (Taine was a friend of the family), and of W. E. H. Lecky's *History of England in the Eighteenth Century,* published a few years later. (See Semmel, introduction to *Birth of Methodism,* pp. 12–18.)

6. J. H. Plumb, *England in the Eighteenth Century* (London, 1950), p. 90. See also A. R. Humphreys: "There are few greater Englishmen than John Wesley, and to compress his achievement into a paragraph is like trying to see the world in a grain of sand and eternity in an hour" (*The Augustan World: Society, Thought, and Letters in Eighteenth-Century England* [New York, 1963 (1st ed., 1954)], p. 145).

7. Plumb, *England in the Eighteenth Century,* pp. 95–96.

8. E. P. Thompson, *The Making of the English Working Class* (New York, 1964), pp. 738, 368 (italics in the original).

9. Ibid., pp. 355, 41, and passim.

10. The Halévy thesis is still being debated. See, for example, Gerald W. Olsen, ed., *Religion and Revolution in Early-Industrial England: The Halévy Thesis and Its Critics* (Lanham, Md., 1990).

11. Bernard Semmel, *The Methodist Revolution* (New York, 1973), pp. 87 and passim. See also Gertrude Himmelfarb, *Victorian Minds* (New York, 1968), pp. 292–99; D. W. Bebbington, *Evangelicalism in Modern Britain: A History from the 1730s to the 1980s* (London, 1989), p. 52; and Frederick Dreyer, "Faith and Experience in the Thought of John Wesley," *American Historical Review* (1983), pp. 29 and passim.

12. Semmel, *Methodist Revolution,* pp. 88–90.

13. Porter, *Creation of the Modern World,* p. 96.

14. Dreyer, "Faith and Experience in the Thought of John Wesley," p. 26. Dreyer sees Wesley's "spiritual sense" as a "theological counterpart" to Hutcheson's "moral sense."

15. J. D. Walsh, "Elie Halévy and the Birth of Methodism," *Transactions of the Royal Historical Society* (1975), pp. 14–15.

16. Robert Wearmouth, *Methodism and the Common People of the Eighteenth Century* (London, 1945), p. 229.

17. M. Dorothy George, *London Life in the Eighteenth Century* (New York, 1965 [1st ed., 1925]), p. 12. See also W. J. Warner, *The Wesleyan Movement in the Industrial Revolution* (London, 1930), p. 163.

18. John Wesley, *Works* (Grand Rapids, Mich., 1872), VI, 126–36.

19. Semmel minimizes this tension, finding Wesley essentially in accord with the "individualistic, entrepreneurial mood of a commercial England." Upon all the critical economic issues, Semmel says, Wesley agreed with Smith (Semmel, *Methodist Revolution,* p. 75).

20. Quoted by Max Weber, *The Protestant Ethic and the Spirit of Capitalism* (Chicago, n.d. [1st ed., 1904–5]), p. 175.

21. Semmel, *Methodist Revolution,* p. 74.

22. Andrews, *Methodism and Society,* p. 37.

23. Wearmouth, *Methodism and the Common People,* pp. 207–8.

24. Semmel, *Methodist Revolution,* pp. 95–96, quoting Wesley, *Thoughts Upon Slavery* (1774) and *Letters* (Feb. 24, 1791).

25. Thompson, *Making of the English Working Class,* pp. 377–78. (The expression "religious terrorism" comes from Lecky.) See also Plumb, *England in the Eighteenth Century,* p. 96.

26. George, *London Life in the Eighteenth Century,* pp. 65–66.

27. Andrews, *Methodism and Society,* p. 53.

28. Ibid., p. 55.

29. James Boswell, *Life of Samuel Johnson, LL.D.* (Chicago, 1952), p. 373 (entry dated 1778).

30. Dreyer, "Faith and Experience," p. 21.

31. Bebbington, *Evangelicalism in Modern Britain,* p. 52 .

32. Semmel, *Methodist Revolution,* p. 90.

33. J. C. D. Clark, *English Society, 1688–1832: Ideology, Social Structure and Political Practice during the Ancien Régime* (Cambridge, 1985), p. 235.

34. Andrews, *Methodism and Society,* p. 46; Semmel, *Methodist Revolution,* p. 56.

35. Quoted in Roy Hattersley, *The Life of John Wesley: A Brand from the Burning* (New York, 2003), p. 207.

36. Andrews, *Methodism and Society,* p. 44.

37. Bebbington, *Evangelicalism in Modern Britain,* p. 26.

38. The term "political theology" is Clark's (*English Society, 1688–1832,* pp. 216ff).

39. Andrews, *Methodism and Society,* p. 52 (Feb. 24, 1791).

40. Semmel, *Methodist Revolution,* p. 193.

41. Adam Smith, *An Inquiry into the Nature and Causes of the Wealth of Nations,* ed. Edwin Cannan (New York, 1937 [1st ed., 1776]), p. 741.

42. Bebbington, *Evangelicalism in Modern Britain,* p. 21. The membership figures are for 1767, the first year such statistics were available. See also Gordon Rupp, *Religion in England, 1688–1791* (Oxford, 1986), pp. 372, 449.

6. "THE AGE OF BENEVOLENCE"

1. M. G. Jones, *The Charity School Movement: A Study of Eighteenth-Century Puritanism in Action* (Cambridge, 1938), p. 3; M. Dorothy George, *England in Transition: Life and Work in the Eighteenth Century* (London, 1931), p. 65. (Hannah More made that statement in 1788.)

2. Bernard Mandeville, *The Fable of the Bees,* ed. Philip Harth (London, 1970 [reprint of 1723 ed.]), p. 329.

3. George, *England in Transition,* pp. 73–74.

4. A. R. Humphreys, *The Augustan World: Society, Thought, and Letters in Eighteenth-Century England* (New York, 1963), p. 201, quoting Fielding, February 1740.

5. William Maitland, *The History of London from Its Foundations by the Romans to the Present Time* (London, 1739), pp. 635, 800.

6. William Maitland, *The History and Survey of London* (London, 1756), II, 764.

7. Alexis de Tocqueville, *Democracy in America,* trans. and ed. Harvey Mansfield and Delba Winthrop (Chicago, 2000 [1st French ed., 1835, 1840]), pp. 183, 489–90.

8. See the lists of societies and institutions in Ford K. Brown, *Father of the Victorians: The Age of Wilberforce* (Cambridge, 1961), pp. 329–34. See also the identification in reference books of so many public figures as "philanthropist."

9. Edmund Burke, "Speech at the Guildhall in Bristol," in *The Works of Edmund Burke* (London, 1911), II, 142.

10. M. Dorothy George, *London Life in the Eighteenth Century* (New York, 1965), p. 26, and appendix, p. 406.

11. Roy Porter, *The Creation of the Modern World: The Untold Story of the British Enlightenment* (New York, 2000), pp. 207–8.

12. Eveline Cruikshanks, *Hogarth's England* (London, 1957), p. 55.

13. Frederick Antal, *Hogarth and His Place in European Art* (New York, 1962), p. 10.

14. Cruikshanks, *Hogarth's England,* p. 58.

15. Antal, *Hogarth and His Place in European Art,* p. 10.

16. Lawrence Stone, *The Family, Sex and Marriage in England, 1500–1800* (New York, 1977), p. 238.

17. Ibid.

18. Ibid. Almost in passing, Stone noted that "conformity to this new ideal positively reinforced the legitimacy of the ruling class." But this disparaging note did not detract from his judgment that "the movement was a genuinely moral one," affecting attitudes toward both animals and human beings.

19. See, for example, G. J. Barker-Benfield, *The Culture of Sensiblity: Sex and Society in Eighteenth-Century Britain* (Chicago, 1992), and John Mullan, *Sentiment and Sociability: The Language of Feeling in the Eighteenth Century* (Oxford, 1988). Barker-Benfield emphasizes the relationship of the culture of sensibility to women, characterizing humanitarian attitudes to animals, for example, as "a kind of surrogate feminism" (p. 236).

20. Barker-Benfield, *The Culture of Sensibility,* p. 69.

21. Anthony Ashley Cooper, third Earl of Shaftesbury, *Characteristics of Men, Manners, Opinions, Times* (Indianapolis, 2002 [reprint of 6th ed., 1737–38; 1st ed., 1711]), I, 84, 88, 91, 121; III, 238–39.

22. Francis Hutcheson, *An Inquiry Concerning Moral Good and Evil,* in *British Moralists,* ed. L. A. Selby-Bigge (Oxford, 1897), I, 148.

23. Adam Smith, *The Theory of Moral Sentiments,* ed. D. D. Raphael and A. L. Macfie (Oxford, 1976 [reprint of 6th ed., 1790]), pp. 9, 185. See also p. 179.

24. Peter Gay, for example, admits Burke into his work on the Enlightenment only on the basis of this book (Gay, *The Enlightenment: An Interpretation* [New York, 1969], pp. 303ff). The book was even more youthful than is generally supposed. Published in 1757, when Burke was twenty-eight, it was written almost ten years earlier, and was the subject of a talk by him before a club he had formed at Trinity College, Dublin.

25. Edmund Burke, *A Philosophical Inquiry into the Origin of Our Ideas of the Sublime and Beautiful* (1757), in *Works,* I, 90.

26. Ibid, pp. 52, 79–80.

27. Quoted in Porter, *Creation of the Modern World,* p. 284.

28. Humphreys, *The Augustan World,* p. 202, quoting Johnson in the *Idler,* May 6, 1758.

29. David Owen, *English Philanthropy, 1660–1960* (Cambridge, Mass., 1965), p. 68. It is curious that this is the only mention of Wesley in Owen's book, in spite of his substantial contributions to the philanthropic movement—and in spite of Owen's sympathetic view of him as one of the "humane and informed observers of the eighteenth-century world."

One other passing reference includes the Wesleyans among those active in the anti-slavery movement (p. 129).

30. Eric Midwinter, *Nineteenth-Century Education* (London, 1970), p. 19. See also Gordon Rupp, *Religion in England, 1688–1791* (Oxford, 1986), pp. 300ff.

31. Thomas A. Horne, *The Social Thought of Bernard Mandeville: Virtue and Commerce in Early Eighteenth-Century England* (New York, 1978), p. 16.

32. Mandeville, *Fable of the Bees,* pp. 276–78, 295.

33. Smith, *Theory of Moral Sentiments,* p. 308. (See chapter 1 on moral philosophy, p. 31).

34. Thomas Walter Laqueur, *Religion and Respectability: Sunday Schools and Working-Class Culture, 1780–1850* (New Haven, 1976), p. xi.

35. Ibid., p. 35.

36. Ibid., p. 130. Laqueur attributes the book to Sir Thomas Eden (p. 97), but this is evidently a typo.

37. Ibid., pp. xi, 9.

38. David G. Green, *Reinventing Civil Society: The Rediscovery of Welfare Without Politics* (London, 1993), pp. 30ff.

39. Smith, *Theory of Moral Sentiments,* p. 231 (pt. VI, sect. 3, ch. 2).

40. James Boswell, *The Life of Samuel Johnson, LL.D.* (Chicago, 1952 [*Encyclopedia Britannica* ed.]), p. 182.

41. Ibid., p. 363.

42. See above, p. 117.

43. Elie Halévy, *The Birth of Methodism in England,* trans. Bernard Semmel (Chicago, 1971 [French ed., 1906]), p. 66. See also p. 37: "They [the Methodists] regenerated the Church of England. . . . They even had an effect on free thinkers, who subsequently refrained from criticizing Christian doctrine in order to devote themselves to political economy and philanthropy. Utilitarians and evangelicals agreed to work together for commercial freedom, the abolition of slavery, and the reform of criminal law and prison organization."

44. Owen, *English Philanthropy, 1660–1960,* p. 93.

45. Dorothy Marshall, *Dr. Johnson's London* (London, 1926), p. 227; George Rudé, *The Crowd in History: A Study of Popular Disturbances in France and England, 1730–1848* (New York, 1964), p. 37.

46. Owen, *English Philanthropy, 1660–1960,* p. 15.

47. See, for example, Gordon Rupp: "Their motives ranged from local patriotism and self-advertisement to human pity and Christian conviction" (*Religion in England, 1688–1791,* p. 311). Or Dorothy Marshall: "The benevolence of eighteenth-century London was not the less gen-

uine because it expressed itself in language that strikes a discordant note to modern ears" (*Dr. Johnson's London,* p. 283).

48. Porter, *Creation of the Modern World,* p. 19.

49. Diderot, "*Encyclopedia,*" in Denis Diderot, *Rameau's Nephew and Other Works,* trans. and ed. Jacques Barzun and Ralph H. Bowen (New York, 1956), p. 304.

THE FRENCH ENLIGHTENMENT: THE IDEOLOGY OF REASON

1. Alexis de Tocqueville, *The Old Regime and the French Revolution,* trans. Stuart Gilbert (New York, 1955 [1st French ed., 1856]), pp. 145–46. This statement has been disputed by, for example, Peter Gay, *Voltaire's Politics: The Poet as Realist* (Princeton, 1959), pp. 7–10, and by Keith Baker, *Inventing the French Revolution: Essays on French Political Culture in the Eighteenth Century* (Cambridge, 1990), pp. 20–21 and passim. Some of the *philosophes*—Montesquieu, Mably, Voltaire, Turgot, Helvétius— did engage in public affairs as magistrates, tax farmers, or on occasional diplomatic missions. Except for Turgot, however, they had only transient and peripheral relationships to political affairs. On this issue, see also Norman Hampson, "The Enlightenment in France," in *The Enlightenment in National Context,* ed. Roy Porter and Mikulas Teich (Cambridge, 1981), pp. 45–46.

2. Jean le Rond d'Alembert, "Preliminary Discourse," in *Denis Diderot's The Encyclopedia: Selections,* ed. and trans. Stephen J. Gendzier (New York, 1967), p. 12. (I have used published translations of the articles from the *Encyclopédie* when available and satisfactory. Citations to the *Encyclopédie* itself are my own translations. It is awkward to use multiple sources, but the alternative, to cite only the original, would deprive the reader of accessible translations.)

3. Diderot, "Encyclopedia," in Denis Diderot, *Rameau's Nephew and Other Works,* trans. and ed. Jacques Barzun and Ralph H. Bowen (New York, 1956), p. 291.

4. *The Federalist: A Commentary on the Constitution of the United States,* ed. Robert Scigliano (New York, 2000), p. 561 (*Federalist* 85).

5. John Lough, "Reflections on Enlightenment and *Lumières,*" *British Journal of Eighteenth-Century Studies* (Spring 1985), p. 13.

6. Diderot, "Encyclopedia," in *Rameau's Nephew,* pp. 312–13.

7. Diderot, "*Philosophe,*" in *Encyclopédie, ou dictionnaire raisonné des sciences, des arts et des métiers* (Paris, 1751–52), XII, 510.

8. Ibid., p. 509.

9. Tocqueville, *The Old Regime and the French Revolution,* p. 6. According to Tocqueville, the church was attacked "less as a religious faith than as a political institution." I think the evidence points to an animus against religion itself as the rival and enemy of reason.

10. Diderot, *"Raison,"* in *Encyclopédie,* XIII, 773–74.

11. Peter Gay, *The Enlightenment: An Interpretation,* Vol. I: *The Rise of Modern Paganism* (New York, 1966), p. 391.

12. Ibid. While documenting this "obsession," Gay sympathetically comments: "And so Voltaire assailed intolerance in the name of tolerance, cruelty in the name of kindness, superstition in the name of science, revealed religion in the name of rational worship, a cruel God in the name of a beneficent God" (p. 392).

13. Diderot, "Encyclopedia," in *Rameau's Nephew,* p. 304. In the preface to *The Spirit of the Laws,* Montesquieu wrote: "It is not a matter of indifference that the minds of the people be enlightened" (*The Spirit of the Laws,* trans. Thomas Nugent, ed. Franz Neumann [New York, 1949], I, lxviii). But it is not clear what he meant here by either "the people" or "enlightened."

14. *"Multitude,"* in *Encyclopédie,* X, 860.

15. See John Morley, *Diderot and the Encyclopaedists* (New York, 1978), p. 338. Diderot's last work, *Réfutation d'Helvétius,* written about 1773, was published posthumously.

16. Gay, *The Enlightenment,* Vol. II: *The Science of Freedom* (New York, 1969), p. 521.

17. Maurice Cranston, *Philosophers and Pamphleteers: Political Theorists of the Enlightenment* (Oxford, 1986), p. 44. Gay, *Voltaire's Politics* (p. 265), quotes part of this but says Voltaire has been misinterpreted.

18. Voltaire, "Atheism," in his *Philosophical Dictionary* (New York, 1943), pp. 34, 43.

19. Ronald I. Boss, "The Development of Social Religion: A Contradiction of French Free Thought," *Journal of the History of Ideas* (October–December 1973), p. 583, quoting Voltaire, *Histoire de Jenni.*

20. Ibid., p. 577.

21. See above, p. 154.

22. See, for example, Peter Gay, *The Party of Humanity: Essays in the French Enlightenment* (New York, 1964), pp. 103–8, and *Voltaire's Politics,* where the subject is relegated to an appendix (pp. 351–54). In Gay's two-volume *Enlightenment,* it is mentioned only in a note (II, 38 n. 7).

23. Arthur Hertzberg, *The French Enlightenment and the Jews* (New York, 1968), p. 303, quoting Voltaire's *Essai sur les moeurs.*

24. Ibid., pp. 300–301 and passim. See also Adam Sutcliffe, *Judaism and*

Enlightenment (Cambridge, 2003). On anti-Semitism in the Revolution, see Shanti Marie Singham, "Betwixt Cattle and Men: Jews, Blacks, and Women, and the Declaration of the Rights of Man," in Singham's *The French Idea of Freedom: The Old Regime and the Declaration of the Rights of 1789* (Stanford, Calif., 1994), pp. 114–53.

25. Edmund Burke, *Reflections on the Revolution in France* (New York, Dolphin ed., 1961 [1st ed., 1790]), pp. 60–61, 67, 97–98.

26. David Hume, *The History of England from the Invasion of Julius Caesar to the Revolution in 1688* (4 vols., Philadelphia, 1828), I, 377.

27. John Lough concludes, from his comprehensive study of the French Enlightenment, that "the search for the views of the *philosophes* on the future government of France brings very little reward" (*The Philosophes and Post-Revolutionary France* [Oxford, 1982], p. 42).

28. Diderot, "Political Authority," in *Encyclopedia,* ed. Gendzier, p. 185.

29. Montesquieu, *Spirit of the Laws,* p. 293 (bk. XIX, sect. 4).

30. *A Critical Dictionary of the French Revolution,* ed. François Furet and Mona Ozouf, trans. Arthur Goldhammer (Cambridge, Mass., 1989), p. 729.

31. Isaiah Berlin, *Against the Current: Essays in the History of Ideas,* ed. Henry Hardy (Princeton, 2001), p. 145.

32. Rousseau, *Emile* (1762), trans. Allan Bloom (New York, 1979), p. 458.

33. Robert Anchor, *The Enlightenment Tradition* (New York, 1967), p. 49; Berlin, *Against the Current,* p. 145.

34. Gay, *Voltaire's Politics,* pp. 29, 185.

35. Montesquieu, *Spirit of the Laws,* p. xxvii.

36. Gay, *Voltaire's Politics,* p. 147.

37. Geoffrey Bruun, *The Enlightened Despots* (2nd ed., New York, 1967), p. 38.

38. Gay, *Voltaire's Politics,* p. 177, quoting Voltaire's *Commentary on the Spirit of the Laws.*

39. Leonard Krieger, *An Essay on the Theory of Enlightened Despotism* (Chicago, 1975), p. 86.

40. Lough, *The* Philosophes *and Post-Revolutionary France,* pp. 16–17.

41. Saint-Lambert, "Legislator," in *Encyclopedia,* ed. Gendzier, p. 160.

42. Krieger, *Essay on the Theory of Enlightened Despotism,* p. 42.

43. Ibid., p. 99 n. 43.

44. Isaiah Berlin, "The Art of Being Ruled," *Times Literary Supplement,* Feb. 15, 2002, p. 15.

45. Quoted in Bruun, *Enlightened Despots,* p. 32.

46. Ibid., p. 36.

47. Emma Rothschild, *Economic Sentiments:Adam Smith, Condorcet, and the Enlightenment* (Cambridge, Mass., 2001), p. 54.

48. Walter Bagehot, "Adam Smith as a Person," *Collected Works,* ed. Norman St John-Stevas (Cambridge, Mass, 1968), III, 104.

49. Diderot, *"Droit Naturel,"* in *Encyclopédie,* V, 116.

50. Ibid.

51. Gay, *The Enlightenment,* II, 435.

52. Montesquieu, *Spirit of the Laws,* I, 183 ff. (bk XII).

53. See pp. 167–68 above.

54. *"Misère,"* in *Encyclopédie,* X, 575.

55. D'Holbach, *Universal Morality,* in *The Age of Enlightenment,* ed. Lester G. Crocker (New York, 1969), pp. 66–68.

56. Lamettrie, "Discourse on Happiness," ibid., p. 145.

57. Alan Charles Kors, *D'Holbach's Coterie: An Enlightenment in Paris* (Princeton, 1976), p. 323, quoting Helvétius's *De l'esprit.*

58. Gay, *Voltaire's Politics,* pp. 221–22. (On Diderot's remark to Voltaire, see p. 155 above.) Gay says that although Voltaire's views on the *canaille* moderated in the course of time, he never lost his "distrust of the masses" and continued to identify "the masses with passion, the educated classes with reason" (p. 226).

59. *"Compassion,"* in *Encyclopédie,* III, 760–61.

60. *"Bienfaisance,"* ibid., II, 888.

61. Allan Bloom gives Rousseau's idea of compassion a prominent place in the introduction to his translation of *Emile,* pp. 17–18. See also Hannah Arendt, *On Revolution* (New York, 1963), pp. 54 and passim; Judith N. Shklar, "Jean-Jacques Rousseau and Equality," *Daedalus* (Summer 1978), p. 13; and Clifford Orwin, "Compassion," *American Scholar* (Summer 1980), p. 319. Orwin, in a paper delivered at the 1977 meeting of the American Political Science Association, said that Smith was indebted for the idea of compassion to Rousseau's *Discourse on Inequality* (1755), which he reviewed in July 1755, three years before *The Theory of Moral Sentiments* was published. By the same token, one could argue that Rousseau's *Emile* was indebted to Smith's *Theory of Moral Sentiments,* published three years earlier. More significant than the issue of priority is the fact that compassion (or "sympathy," as Smith more often called it) plays a much larger role in *The Theory of Moral Sentiments* than in either the *Discourse* or *Emile.*

62. Rousseau, *The First and Second Discourses* (1755), trans. Victor Gourevitch (New York, 1986), pp. 162, 184–85. See also Rousseau's note, p. 226.

63. Donald Winch, *Riches and Poverty: An Intellectual History of Political*

Economy in Britain, 1750–1834 (Cambridge, 1996), p. 67. Winch observes that Smith was one of the first to notice the fundamental affinities between Rousseau and Mandeville, so that Smith's refutation of Mandeville in *The Theory of Moral Sentiments* was also a refutation of Rousseau (p. 60). Joseph Cropsey, on the other hand, emphasizes the similarity of the *Discourse* and *The Theory of Moral Sentiments* ("Adam Smith and Political Philosophy," in *Essays on Adam Smith,* ed. Andrew S. Skinner and Thomas Wilson [Oxford, 1975], p. 136 n. 4).

64. Rousseau, *Emile,* p. 235n.

65. Ibid., p. 250.

66. Ibid., p. 253.

67. Ibid., pp. 40, 52.

68. Rousseau, *Julie, ou La Nouvelle Héloïse,* in *Oeuvres complètes de Jean-Jacques Rousseau* (Paris, Pléiade ed., 1959), II, 567 (letter 3).

69. Rousseau, "Political Economy," in *Encyclopedia,* ed. Gendzier, p. 195.

70. Rousseau, "Considerations on the Government of Poland" (1772) in *Age of Enlightenment,* ed. Crocker, p. 242.

71. "*Ecole,*" in *Encyclopédie,* V, 303.

72. "*Education,*" ibid., V, 397.

73. "Legislator," in *Encyclopedia,* ed. Gendzier, pp. 161–62.

74. Lough, *The Philosophes and Post-Revolutionary France,* p. 250.

75. Gay, *Voltaire's Politics,* pp. 221–22.

76. Diderot, "Observations on the Instruction of the Empress of Russia to the Deputies for the Making of the Laws," in Diderot, *Political Writings,* ed. John Hope Mason and Robert Wokler (Cambridge, 1992), p. 141. Diderot began to write the "Observations" after his return from Russia in 1774 and worked on it for several years after that. After his death in 1784, it was sent to Catherine, together with other material from his library. It was first published in 1920.

77. See p. 154 above.

78. Daniel Roche, *France in the Enlightenment,* trans. Arthur Goldhammer (Cambridge, Mass., 1998), p. 432.

79. Ibid., p. 428. The figures were higher in the North of France than in the South, and considerably higher in Paris (pp. 428, 659). Another estimate has literacy rising from 25 percent in 1686–90 to 40–45 percent in 1786–90 (Carlo M. Cipolla, *Literacy and Development in the West* [London, 1969], p. 62). Neither of these figures supports Simon Schama's extraordinary statement that "literacy rates in late eighteenth-century France were much higher than in the late twentieth-century United States" (*Citizens: A Chronicle of the French Revolution* [New York, 1989],

p. 180). Today, of course, literacy is no longer defined as merely signing one's name.

80. Alan Charles Kors, "Just and Arbitrary Authority in Enlightenment Thought," in *Modern Enlightenment and the Rule of Reason,* ed. John C. McCarthy (Washington, D.C., 1998), p. 25.

81. Diderot, *"Indigent,"* in *Encyclopédie,* VIII, 676.

82. See Alexis de Tocqueville, *Memoir on Pauperism,* trans. Seymour Drescher, ed. Gertrude Himmelfarb (Chicago, 1997).

83. Turgot, *"Fondations,"* in *Encyclopédie,* VII, 75.

84. Diderot, *"Hôpital,"* ibid., VIII, 294.

85. Jaucourt, *"Mendiant,"* ibid., X, 331.

86. Jaucourt, *"Le Peuple,"* ibid., XII, 476.

87. Lough, *The* Philosophes *and Post-Revolutionary France,* p. 127.

88. Montesquieu, *The Spirit of the Laws,* II, 25–26. The beginning of this passage, but not the later sentences, is quoted by Norman Hampson, *Will and Circumstance: Montesquieu, Rousseau and the French Revolution* (Norman, Okla., 1983), p. 22.

89. Jaucourt, *"Philantropie,"* in *Encyclopédie,* XII, 504.

90. Bruun, *Enlightened Despots,* p. 102.

91. For the Encyclopedists during the Revolution, see the monumental work by Frank A. Kafker, *The Encyclopedists as a Group: A Collective Biography of the Authors of the* Encyclopédie (Oxford, 1996), and, with Serena L. Kafker, *The Encyclopedists as Individuals: A Biographical Dictionary of the Authors of the* Encyclopédie (Oxford, 1988). See also Kors, *D'Holbach's Coterie.*

92. See, for example, Alan Forrest, *The French Revolution and the Poor* (New York, 1981), pp. 169 ff. Some historians have made much of these measures, describing them as forerunners of the welfare state, but even they admit that they failed. See, for example, George Rudé, *Robespierre: Portrait of a Revolutionary Democrat* (New York, 1975), p. 140, and Colin Jones, *Charity and* Bienfaisance: *The Treatment of the Poor in the Montpelier Region, 1740–1815* (Cambridge, 1982), pp. 8, 159 ff., 184 ff.

93. Emmanuel Sieyès, *Qu'est-ce que le tiers état?* (New York, 1979 [1st French ed., 1789]), p. 10.

94. François Furet, "Rousseau and the French Revolution," in *The Legacy of Rousseau,* ed. Clifford Orwin and Nathan Tarcov (Chicago, 1997), p. 181. See also James Miller, *Rousseau: Dreamer of Democracy* (New Haven, 1984), pp. 132 ff.

95. Hampson, "The Enlightenment in France," in Porter and Teich, eds., *Enlightenment in National Context,* p. 49.

96. Robespierre, *Lettres à ses commettans* (Paris, 1792), II, 55; Ernest

Hamel, *Histoire de Robespierre* (Paris, 1865), I, 427–28; F. A. Aulard, ed., *La Société des Jacobins* (Paris, 1891), V, 254.

97. Rousseau, "Political Economy," in *Encyclopedia,* ed. Gendzier, p. 191.

98. Rousseau, *The Social Contract,* trans. G. D. H. Cole (Chicago, Great Books ed., 1952), p. 439 (bk. IV, ch. 8).

99. Ibid., p. 400 (bk. II, ch. 7).

100. *Réimpression de l'ancien Moniteur* (Paris, 1858), XVII, 135 (session of July 13, 1793); ibid., XVI, 748 (session of June 25, 1793).

101. Tocqueville, *The Old Regime,* pp. 12–13, 156.

102. Mona Ozouf, "Regeneration," in *A Critical Dictionary of the French Revolution,* ed. Furet and Ozouf, p. 781. "Regeneration" is also described as the aim of education (p. 785). Another article in the same volume, "Enlightenment" by Bronislaw Baczko, ascribes to the Enlightenment in general the idea of "national regeneration": the belief that institutions and men are "endlessly malleable," and that the "transformative potential" of politics is unlimited (pp. 664, 661).

103. Hannah Arendt, *On Revolution* (New York, 1963), pp. 54–55, 66, 69–70.

104. Maurice Cranston, *The Solitary Self: Jean-Jacques Rousseau in Exile and Adversity* (Chicago, 1997), p. 189.

THE AMERICAN ENLIGHTENMENT: THE POLITICS OF LIBERTY

1. *The American Enlightenment: The Shaping of the American Experiment and a Free Society,* ed. Adrienne Koch (New York, 1965), p. 191 (John Adams to Count Sarsfield, Feb. 3, 1786). For Adams, that vision was sharpened by contrast with Britain where he was then serving as ambassador.

2. Isaiah Berlin, "Two Concepts of Liberty," in *Four Essays on Liberty* (Oxford, 1969). Hannah Arendt, for whom the "social question" was the defining issue in the French Revolution, distinguished between political "liberation" and social "freedom." But she then blurred the distinction by speaking of "political freedom" (*On Revolution* [New York, 1963], p. 22). Geoffrey Nunberg restated this distinction in "Freedom vs. Liberty: More Than Just Another Word for Nothing Left to Lose," *New York Times,* March 23, 2003, p. 6.

3. Gordon S. Wood, *The Creation of the American Republic, 1776–1787* (Chapel Hill, 1969), pp. 11–13. For the indebtedness of the new country to the old, in terms of institutions and traditions rather than ideas, see, for

example, David Grayson Allen, *In English Ways: The Movement of Societies and the Transferral of English Local Law and Customs to Massachusetts Bay in the Seventeenth Century* (Chapel Hill, 1981), and David Hackett Fischer, *Albion's Seed: Four British Folkways in America* (Oxford, 1989).

4. *The Federalist: A Commentary on the Constitution of the United States,* ed. Robert Scigliano (New York, 2000), p. 48. In focusing on the theme of corruption, the colonists were echoing the complaints of the "Countrymen" or "Commonwealthmen" in England, who, in the late seventeenth and early eighteenth centuries had brought the same charges against Parliament and the king's ministers.

5. Thomas Paine, *Common Sense* (New York, 1992 [reprint of 1791 ed.]), p. 58; *The Rights of Man* (New York, Dolphin ed., 1961 [1st ed., 1791–92]), p. 420 (pt. II, ch. 4).

6. Henry Steele Commager, *The Empire of Reason: How Europe Imagined and America Realized the Enlightenment* (New York, 1977), p. 182.

7. *The Political Writings of John Adams,* ed. George W. Carey (Washington, D.C., 2000), p. 701 (letter to H. Niles, Feb. 13, 1816).

8. John Adams, to the abbé de Mably, 1782, in appendix to *A Defence of the Constitutions of Government of the United States of America,* in *The Works of John Adams* (Boston, 1851), V, 495. See also Alexis de Tocqueville, *Democracy in America,* trans. and ed. Harvey C. Mansfield and Delba Winthrop (Chicago, 2000 [1st French ed., 1835, 1840]), pp. 53 ff. (vol. I, pt. 1, chs. 4–5).

9. Bernard Bailyn, *To Begin the World Anew: The Genius and Ambiguities of the American Founders* (New York, 2003), pp. ix and passim.

10. *Federalist* 6, p. 27.

11. Thomas Jefferson, *Writings,* ed. Merrill D. Peterson (New York, 1984), p. 911 (letter to William S. Smith, Nov. 13, 1787).

12. Ibid., pp. 889–90 (letter to Abigail Adams, Feb. 22, 1787).

13. Ibid., pp. 959–64 (letter to Madison, Sept. 6, 1789).

14. Marvin Meyers, *The Mind of the Founder: Sources of the Political Thought of James Madison* (Hanover, Mass., 1981), pp. 176–79.

15. *Federalist* 49, p. 323. Madison's quotation of this provision differed from the version in the *Notes on the State of Virginia.* As cited in *The Federalist,* repeal required a convention called by two thirds of the members of any two of the three branches of government. In the *Notes,* the power of repeal was vested in the electorate in two thirds of the counties in the state. (See Jefferson, *Writings,* p. 343.)

16. Paine, *Rights of Man,* pp. 277–78, 304 (italics in original).

17. *Political Writings of John Adams,* pp. 665, 668 (Oct. 18, 1790).

18. Montesquieu, *The Spirit of the Laws,* trans. Thomas Nugent (New

York, 1949 [1st French ed., 1750]), p. 34 (bk. IV, sect. 5). On Montesquieu as an American classic, see Paul Merrill Spurlin, *The French Enlightenment in America: Essays on the Times of the Founding Fathers* (Athens, Ga., 1984), pp. 89 ff.

19. Quoted in Herbert J. Storing, *What the Anti-Federalists Were For* (Chicago, 1981), p. 73 (a reprint of Storing's introduction to Vol. I of *The Complete Anti-Federalist* [Chicago, 1978]). For the idea of "classical virtue" as the Anti-Federalists understood it, see Wood, *Creation of the American Republic.* Wood somewhat modifies his thesis in the preface to the 1998 edition.

20. Jefferson, *Writings,* p. 290 (*Notes on Virginia,* query 19).

21. *Federalist* 84, p. 549.

22. On the Lockean interpretation, see, for example, Thomas L. Pangle, *The Spirit of Modern Republicanism: The Moral Vision of the American Founders and the Philosophy of Locke* (Chicago, 1988); Michael P. Zuckert, *The Natural Rights Republic: Studies in the Foundation of the American Political Tradition* (Notre Dame, Ind., 1996); and T. H. Breen, "The Lockean Moment: The Language of Rights on the Eve of the American Revolution," lecture delivered at Oxford University, May 15, 2001. On the Scottish interpretation, see Garry Wills, *Inventing America: Jefferson's Declaration of Independence* (New York, 1978), and Garry Wills, *Explaining America: The Federalist* (New York, 1981).

23. Jefferson, *Writings,* p. 874 (letter to Maria Cosway, Oct. 12, 1786).

24. Ibid., pp. 901–2 (letter to Peter Carr, Aug. 10, 1787). See Henry May, *The Enlightenment in America* (Oxford, 1976), p. 296, for letter to Adams, Oct. 14, 1815.

25. *Federalist* 12, p. 70. The role of commerce and capitalism in the thinking of the Founders has been a subject of much debate. In *Capitalism and a New Social Order: The Republican Vision of the 1790s* (New York, 1984), Joyce Appleby maintains that the Jeffersonian Republicans in that period were favorably disposed to capitalism. This is disputed by Stanley Elkins and Eric McKittrick, *The Age of Federalism: The Early American Republic, 1788–1800* (Oxford, 1993), pp. 109–13 and p. 760 n. 31. See also Peter McNamara, *Political Economy and Statesmanship: Smith, Hamilton, and the Foundation of the Commercial Republic* (Dekalb, Ill., 1998), and *How Capitalistic Is the Constitution?*, ed. Robert A. Goldwin and William A. Schambra (Washington, D.C., 1982).

26. *Federalist* 51, p. 331.

27. *Federalist* 10, p. 61.

28. Richard Hofstadter, *The American Political Tradition and the Men Who Made It* (New York, 1948), p. 3 (quotation from Horace White).

29. David Hume, "Idea of a Perfect Commonwealth," in *David Hume's Political Essays,* ed. Charles W. Hendel (Indianapolis, 1953), p. 157.

30. *Federalist* 9, p. 50.

31. *Political Writings of John Adams,* p. 652 (letter to Abigail Adams, July 1, 1776).

32. Wood, *Creation of the American Republic* (1998 ed.), p. 124 (Samuel Adams letter to John Langdon, Aug. 7, 1777).

33. Ibid. (Rush to John Adams, Aug. 8, 1777).

34. *Federalist* 55, p. 359.

35. *Federalist* 10, p. 59.

36. *The Debates in the Several State Conventions, on the Adoption of the Federal Constitution,* ed. Jonathan Elliot (Philadelphia, 1907), III, 536–37.

37. Michael Novak, *On Two Wings: Humble Faith and Common Sense at the American Founding* (San Francisco, 2002), p. 34, quoting Rush, "Of the Mode of Education Proper to a Republic," 1798.

38. The document with the handwritten correction is in the Library of Congress.

39. Richard D. Brown, "The Idea of an Informed Citizenry in the Early Republic," in his *Devising Liberty: Preserving and Creating Freedom in the New American Republic* (Stanford, Calif., 1995), p. 160.

40. *Memoir, Letters, and Remains of Alexis de Tocqueville* (London, 1861), I, 359 (letter to M. de Kergorlay, n.d.).

41. Tocqueville, *Democracy in America,* pp. 282, 278 (vol. I, pt. 1, ch. 9). He made the point even more sharply in the letter to M. de Kergorlay: "I believe that, as a general principle, political freedom rather increases than diminishes religious feeling. There is a greater family likeness than is supposed between the two passions" (*Memoir,* I, 360).

42. Mark A. Noll, *America's God: From Jonathan Edwards to Abraham Lincoln* (Oxford, 2002), pp. 161 ff. A subtitle in Noll's chapter on evangelicalism gives ca. 1790 as the date for the reemergence of evangelicalism as a vital force (p. 161), but in the text that date is sometimes moved up to the mid-1780s (e.g., pp. 179, 181). On the relation between evangelicalism and the Revolution, see also J. C. D. Clark, *The Language of Liberty, 1660–1832: Political Discourse and Social Dynamics in the Anglo-American World* (Cambridge, 1994), pp. 336 and passim. (American "evangelism," in the theological and spiritual sense, appears here with a lowercase "e," as distinct from British "Evangelism," capitalized, which denoted a specific sect within the Church of England.)

43. Noll, *America's God,* p. 162.

44. Roger Finke and Rodney Stark, *The Churching of America, 1776–1990* (New Brunswick, N.J., 1994), p. 30.

45. James H. Hutson, *Religion and the Founding of the American Republic* (Washington, D.C., 1998), p. 32.

46. Noll, *America's God,* p. 64.

47. Hutson, *Religion and the Founding of the American Republic,* pp. 32–33.

48. Nathan O. Hatch, *The Sacred Cause of Liberty: Republican Thought and the Millennium in Revolutionary New England* (New Haven, 1977), pp. 2–3; see also p. 17. In another book, *The Democratization of American Christianity* (New Haven, 1989), Hatch associates the democratization of Christianity with the "Christianization" of American society. That book deals with a later period, the early nineteenth century, where the term "democratization" is appropriate. Henry May properly warns against identifying the eighteenth-century Enlightenment with democracy (*The Enlightenment in America,* pp. 361–62). It was republicanism, not democracy, that was at issue in America.

49. Martin E. Marty, *Religion, Awakening and Revolution* (Wilmington, N.C., 1977), p. 130.

50. Tocqueville, *Democracy in America,* p. 278 (vol. I, pt. 2, ch. 9).

51. Hutson, *Religion and the Founding of the American Republic,* pp. 91–93.

52. Jefferson, *Writings,* pp. 285, 289 (*Notes on the State of Virginia,* queries 17, 18).

53. Hutson, *Religion and the Founding of the American Republic,* p. 96, citing a Ms in the Library of Congress by the Rev. Ethan Allen.

54. Tocqueville, *Democracy in America,* pp. 43–44 (vol. I, pt. 1, ch. 2).

55. Ibid., p. 280 (vol. I, pt. 2, ch. 9).

56. Ibid., p. 282.

57. Ibid., p. 280.

58. Ibid., pp. 519–20 (vol. II, pt. 2, ch. 15).

59. George Washington, *Writings* (New York, Library of America ed., 1997), p. 971.

60. Vincent Phillip Munoz, "George Washington on Religious Liberty," *Review of Politics* (Winter 2003).

61. *Works of John Adams,* IX, 229 (letter to Officers of the 1st Regiment, Oct. 11, 1798).

62. *Political Writings of John Adams,* p. 663 (letter to Richard Price, Apr. 19, 1790, acknowledging receipt of the sermon that inspired Burke's *Reflections*).

63. William Cabell Bruce, *Ben Franklin Self-Revealed* (New York, 1917), p. 90.

64. Hatch, *Sacred Cause of Liberty,* pp. 2–3.

65. *The Autobiography of Benjamin Franklin* (New York, 1995 [reprint of 1886 ed.]), pp. 133–35.

66. Quoted in Walter Isaacson, *Benjamin Franklin: An American Life* (New York, 2003), p. 451 (speech, June 28, 1787).

67. May points out this curious situation, "a coincidence very unlikely ever to be repeated in American politics" (*The Enlightenment in America,* p. 278).

68. Ibid., p. 137.

69. *Works of John Adams,* X, 53 (July 13, 1813).

70. Spurlin, *The French Enlightenment in America,* p. 115.

71. See above, p. 44n.

72. J. Hector St. John de Crèvecoeur, *Letters from an American Farmer and Sketches of Eighteenth-Century America,* ed. Albert E. Stone (London, 1986 [1st ed. 1782]), p. 240. (This passage appears in the *Sketches,* a dozen essays omitted from the *Letters* as originally published, and first printed by Yale University Press in 1925.)

73. Jefferson, *Writings,* p. 259 (*Notes on the State of Virginia,* query 14).

74. Ralph Lerner, *The Thinking Revolutionary: Principle and Practice in the New Republic* (Ithaca, N.Y., 1987), p. 65.

75. *Jefferson's Letters,* ed. Willson Whitman (Eau Claire, Wis., n.d.), p. 32 (letter to Mrs. Trist, Aug. 18, 1785). Five years later, Jefferson spoke of a republic of 30 million.

76. Daniel J. Boorstin, *The Americans: The Colonial Experience* (Norwalk, Conn., 1987 [1st ed. 1958]), p. 79.

77. Jefferson, *Writings,* pp. 1312–13 (letter to Alexander von Humboldt, Dec. 6, 1813).

78. Washington, *Writings,* p. 788 (Message to Congress, Oct. 25, 1791). Tocqueville loosely rendered this passage: "We are more enlightened and more powerful than the Indian nations; it is to our honor to treat them with goodness and even with generosity" (*Democracy in America,* p. 320 [vol. I, pt. 2, ch. 10]). The editors of Tocqueville's work note the difference between his quotation and Washington's actual statement.

79. Washington, *Writings,* p. 956 (Address to Cherokee Nation, Aug. 29, 1796).

80. Jefferson, *Writings,* pp. 1115–16 (letter to Benjamin Hawkins, Feb. 18, 1803).

81. Quoted by Lerner, *The Thinking Revolutionary,* p. 150.

82. Dee E. Andrews, *The Methodists and Revolutionary America, 1760–1800: The Shaping of an Evangelical Culture* (Princeton, 2000), pp. 125, 130.

83. Bernard Bailyn, *The Ideological Origins of the American Revolution* (rev. ed., Cambridge, Mass., 1992), p. 236.

84. Washington, *Writings,* p. 973.

85. *Federalist* 54, p. 349; *Federalist* 42, p. 268.

86. *American Enlightenment,* ed. Koch, p. 568 (Hamilton to Jay, March 14, 1779).

87. Jefferson, *Writings,* p. 264 (*Notes on Virginia,* query 14). Blacks, Jefferson said, were much the inferior of Indians; the latter had artistic and verbal abilities he had never encountered in a black.

88. Ibid., p. 44 (*Autobiography*).

89. *American Enlightenment,* ed. Koch, pp. 458–60 (Madison to Robert J. Evans, June 15, 1819).

90. Herbert J. Storing, "Slavery and the Moral Foundations of the American Republic," in *The Moral Foundations of the American Republic,* ed. Robert H. Horwitz (2nd ed., Charlottesville, Va., 1979), p. 225. Storing goes on to argue that the liberty proclaimed in the Declaration was itself equivocal, because it presupposed the Lockean right of self-preservation which was equated with self-interest, thus creating a conflict between the right (or liberty) of the slave and that of his master.

91. *Federalist* 38, p. 236. See also *Federalist* 85, p. 561.

EPILOGUE

1. Bernard Bailyn, *To Begin the World Anew: The Genius and Ambiguities of the American Founders* (New York, 2003), p. 104. See also pp. 126–30.

2. Alexis de Tocqueville, *Democracy in America,* trans. and ed. Harvey C. Mansfield and Delba Winthrop (Chicago, 2000 [1st French ed., 1835, 1840]), p. 363 (vol. I, pt. 2, ch. 10).

3. Ibid., p. 395.

4. For a discussion of Malthus in relation both to Smith and to his successors, see Gertrude Himmelfarb, *The Idea of Poverty: England in the Early Industrial Age* (New York, 1983), pp. 100 ff.

5. Joseph A. Schumpeter, *History of Economic Analysis,* ed. Elizabeth Boody Schumpeter (New York, 1954), p. 835.

6. Gertrude Himmelfarb, *Poverty and Compassion: The Moral Imagination of the Late Victorians* (New York, 1991), p. 309.

7. Tocqueville, *Democracy in America,* pp. 502–3 (vol. II, pt. 2, ch. 8).

8. Peter Gay, *The Party of Humanity: Essays in the French Enlightenment* (New York, 1964), p. 130.

INDEX

Adams, Abigail, 195
Adams, John, 191, 193, 198, 200, 202, 210–11, 215–16, 218
Adams, Samuel, 198, 202–3
Addison, Joseph, 10, 13, 140
Alembert, Jean le Rond d', 11, 17–18, 155, 159–60, 166*n*, 182, 216; *see also* French Enlightenment
American Academy of Arts and Sciences, 215–16
American Constitution, 20–1, 151, 193–205, 207–12, 222–6
American Enlightenment, 10–11, 18–21, 80–2, 191–226, 227–9, 232–4
  and education, 204, 218
  and Indians, 219–21, 223
  and liberty, 19–21, 80–2, 159, 191–3, 198, 217, 225, 233–5
  and the poor, 217–19
  and religion, 204–17
  and science, 212–15
  and slavery, 219, 221–6
  and virtue, 198–204
American Philosophical Society, 215–16

American Revolution, 7–8, 19, 193–8, 227–8
  and Burke, 79–82, 84–5, 91–2, 96
  and French Revolution, 21, 85, 207
  and Smith, 81
Anglicans, *see* Church of England
Anti-Federalists, 20, 194, 198–203, 217
anti-Semitism, *see* Jews
Antoninus, 152
Arendt, Hannah, 8, 65, 186, 234
Arianism, 95
Arminianism, 50, 120, 126, 129

Bacon, Francis, 5, 125
Bagehot, Walter, 166
Bailyn, Bernard, 194, 227*n*
Barrington, John Shute, 32*n*
Beccaria, Cesare Bonesana, Marchese di, 32*n*
Bentham, Jeremy, 32, 93–4*n*
Berkeley, George, 15, 31
Berlin, Isaiah, 71, 165, 191–2*n*
Bernard, Thomas, 134
Blackstone, Sir William, 192

www.vintage-books.co.uk